THE
COMPLEET MOLESWORTH

7/12

THE COMPLEET MOLESWORTH

Geoffrey Willans
and
Ronald Searle

PAVILION
MICHAEL JOSEPH

First published in paperback in 1985
by Pavilion Books Limited
196 Shaftesbury Avenue, London WC2H 8JL
in association with Michael Joseph Limited
44 Bedford Square, London WC1B 3DP

Willans, Geoffrey
The compleet Molesworth.
I. Title   II. Searle, Ronald
823'.914 J   PZ7

Printed and bound in Great Britain by
Biddles Limited, Guildford, Surrey

ISBN 1 85145 001 7

Foreword

nigel molesworth, molesworth 2, grimes the headmaster, fotherington-tomas (like e e cummings they only look right in lower case) and the other inmates of st custards entered my life in the mid-fifties and have never left it. An early edition of *The Compleet Molesworth* is one of the most valued books on my shelves and I am still rather ashamed that I did not take it to Roy Plomley's desert island when I was the castaway on *Desert Island Discs*. (It was on my short list of four, but in the end lost out to the *Complete Works of Lewis Carroll*, as did *The Conquest of Space* by Chesley Bonnestal and Willy Ley, and *Wisden 1954*.)

I was at my own prep school when the molesworth memoirs appeared and in the perfect position to appreciate nigel's struggle against everything that life could fling at him. His problems were mine; there was (there still is) a rice 2, and so many of his philosophical gems so meticulously recorded by Geoffrey Willans and so wonderfully illustrated by Ronald Searle summed up my own situation and outlook precisely. nigel always got right to the heart of the matter, whether his topic was some tiny detail of skool life (e.g. his note by note assessment of the skool piano), or whether he turned his world-weary gaze onto a broader canvas, revealing metaphysical powers which justify his inclusion in anybody's list of leading twentieth century philosophers.

molesworth discovered at a tender age that life was a deck-chair, hard to assemble into a coherent, useful or permanent shape, and even if assembled, liable to collapse without notice at any moment. While lesser mortals grappled desperately with their deck-chairs, nigel molesworth's wise answer to the struggle was to stand aside and watch. Other observers of a set-up such as st custard's saw nothing more than rows of identical and unattractive students presided over by a group of identical and uninspiring masters – this scenario itself one to be found in every educational institution in the British Isles; molesworth saw behind superficial uniformity, comprehended the many and essential differences between one ink-stained inmate and the next, perceived that the authoritarian façade of the staff was an attempt to conceal a rag-bag of human frailities. He was equally astute about his family in the hols.

In short, nigel saw the futility of life. Yet, like Dorothy Parker, he felt 'you might as well live'. He was no iconoclast, he played the game, or at least had no wish to change the rules. Destroy one deck-chair and another will fall off the back of a lorry to take its place. Re-reading his thoughts in 1984 one realises that Orwell was not the only writer from the century's middle decades whose words still have a pungent relevance today. And molesworth never hid behind the shelter of a pseudonym.

Where is nigel today? Like many achievers, he did his greatest work in his youth. Few in this position recognise this fact and plough on repeating themselves with less and less impact (e.g. Sir Peter Hall, Bernard Levin, the Sex Pistols). molesworth knew that he had said all he needed to say by the end of the fifties. His life since then has been private, not to say recluse. I have a feeling he might have entered the Church where his study of human nature and the decline of civilisation could proceed unmolested by the insanities of the daily grind. It may be that he will emerge one day to stun another generation with fresh wit and wisdom, but the re-publication of his collected masterpieces renders this pleasing prospect even more unlikely and indeed unnecessary. Besides, his work, with its emphasis on private education and minimal interest in women's activities or ethnic minorities, would certainly be regarded in progressive circles today as elitist, sexist and racist. (When molesworth does turn his attention to women as in his 'Guide To Gurls' he daringly emphasises the difference between the sexes.) There are also dangerous acknowledgements of the theses that all men are not equal and that violence is endemic in human nature. What is the point of giving your all only to be banned by the GLC?

This re-publication may therefore not find itself on the library shelves of the councils who are the most enthusiastic censors of works that oppose their own narrow point of view, but we at Pavilion Books are undaunted! We feel that the genius of molesworth, Willans and Searle will find a vast new audience come what may, mainly because it is wildly funny.

Tim Rice

Molesworthography

In 1951, about the time I had decided to abandon drawing St Trinian's, D.B. Wyndham Lewis – always ready to stick his neck out – suggested that we should collaborate on a St Trinian's romance. His *alter ego* 'Timothy Shy' would write a story if I would agree to do the pictures. I decided to have this last fling and made the drawings, which confirmed to me that I was sick to death of the subject.

The Terror of St Trinian's appeared in October 1952. By Christmas it had sold around 45,000 copies and Max Parrish, its publisher, urged us to follow up the success at once with a sequel. Wyndham Lewis was keen, but not me, and I refused.

To cheer up a despondent Max, I rashly promised that he should have a better best-seller for the following Christmas. The promise was kept.

Shortly before my meeting with Max Parrish, a journalist friend, Geoffrey Willans, then working with the BBC European Service, had asked whether I could help him put together – and even find a publisher for – a book about schoolboys (Groan). Geoffrey had written an occasional series for *Punch* in the forties, based on his experiences as a school teacher. It was written through the myopic eyes of one Nigel Moleworth, later known as 'the curse of St Custards'.

What Geoffrey had given me to read I finally got round to reading and (surprise) I thought it madly funny. With Max Parrish in mind we set about shaping the idea into a book and I took the result to Max. He wasn't exactly overwhelmed, but finally agreed to take it on for an advance of £300 between Geoffrey and myself, provided I would illustrate the text as 'profusely' as I had the St Trinian's book.

In less time than it takes to produce a baby, *Down With Skool* appeared, and between October and Christmas 1953, had sold 53,848 copies. The saga of The Curse of St Custards was away.

Before Geoffrey died of a heart attack in August 1958, at the ludicrously young age of 47, an anthology – *The Compleet Molesworth* – was already in proof, comprising by then three best-selling volumes and most of a fourth to come the following year – *Back in the Jug Agane*.

Like *The Compleet Molesworth*, *Back in the Jug Agane* was published after Geoffrey's death. Molesworth joined St Trinian's on the Elysian playing fields and that was the end of school(girl or boy) drawings for me.

Sad that Geoffrey is not around to see the phoenix arise after a quarter of a century of hibernation ect ect chiz moan drone. But whilst he lingers up there in Universt Space (hello clouds hello sky) Nigel is his worthy spokesperson AS YOU WILL SEE. Nowe read on . . .

Ronald Searle

Contents

DOWN WITH SKOOL!

CONTENTS (CONTINUED)

HOW TO BE TOPP

CONTENTS (CONTINUED)

WHIZZ FOR ATOMMS

CONTENTS (CONTINUED)

BACK IN THE JUG AGANE

DOWN WITH SKOOL!

'O.K. Come In.'

This is me e.g. nigel molesworth the curse of st custard's which is the skool i am at. It is uterly wet and weedy as i shall (i hope) make clear but of course that is the same with all skools.

e.g. they are nothing but kanes, lat. french, geog. hist. algy, geom, headmasters, skool dogs, skool sossages, my bro molesworth 2 and MASTERS everywhere.

The only good things about skool are the BOYS wizz who are noble brave fearless etc. although you hav various swots, bulies, cissies, milksops greedy guts and oiks with whom i am forced to mingle hem-hem.

In fact any skool is a bit of a shambles
AS YOU WILL SEE.

ST CUSTARD'S:

this is st custard's our skool taken with my brownie but i made a bit of a bish and didn't get it all in. Anyway what i hav got in is probably quite enuff. That is the front door in front but you can't get in since the boys nailed it up you hav to go in somewhere behind which fortunately you can't see as it is most unsavoury. On the right is the fire escape which props up the skool i think or the skool props it up i am not sure. It is good to get out by at night but if there is a fire it is quicker to use that drane pipe. It is still quicker to jump out but in my case they might take the blanket away chiz.*

* a chiz is a swiz or swindle as any fule kno.

BY THE CAMERA CLUB

A few unhappy snaps from the Molesworth album

This is the east wing. St custard's hav a very interesting history if you are interested in hist which few boys are. It was built by a madman in 1836 and he made a few improvements before he was put in the bin e.g. the observatory to study worms, the fortifications to pot at game-keepers and that round thing which hav no use at all.

it is a wonder this one didn't bust the cammera it is peason, he is my grate frend which means we tuough each other up continually. Acktually he not bad tho we argue a lot saying am not am not am not am etc until we are called on to tuough up a few junior ticks.

This is gillibrand on the high diving board and we all sa go it go it. His pater is a general so he is not very brany you can't expect it n.b. he came down off the diving board after this he said he could do it any time pappy but did not feel like it toda chiz.

grabber who is head of the skool captane of everything and winer of the mrs joyful prize for rafia work. His pater is very rich and hav a super rolls enuff said. He is bigger than me so i must be careful

Our skool dog thinking. He is planning to dash across the pitch and pinch the cricket ball then bite the umpire in the leg which was super. He is not bad but he scored a gole against us in one match.

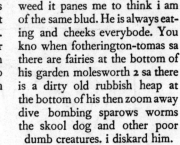

fotherington-tomas. As you see he is skipping like a girlie he is uterly wet and a sissy. He reads chaterbox chiz and we suspeckt that he kepes dollies at home. Anyway his favourite charakter is little lord fauntleroy and when i sa he hav a face like a tomato he repli i forgive you molesworth for those uncouth words.

Gosh chiz this is molesworth 2 my bro he is uterly wet and a weed it panes me to think i am of the same blud. He is always eating and cheeks everybode. You kno when fotherington-tomas sa there are fairies at the bottom of his garden molesworth 2 sa there is a dirty old rubbish heap at the bottom of his then zoom away dive bombing sparows worms the skool dog and other poor dumb creatures. i diskard him.

Of course there are a grate number of other weeds and wets about the place but i hope this will give you some idea of st custards's which with all the other skools will explane why britain is what it is toda. There is nothing more to add about st custard's except that it smell of chalk latin books skool ink foopball boots and birdseed. Now read on.

1

HEAD BEAKS AT BAY

FROM BEAK TO TAIL

Headmasters are always very ferce and keep thousands of KANES chiz moan drone. With these they hound and persecute all boys who are super like sir galahad.

Headmasters are always very proud of their skools and think they are the best in the world in britain in space or at any rate better than the nearest one in the districk. They sa 'Ah ahem to tell the truth the boys are ahem ahem not er quite in fact just not the *type* we want.' A fine thing to sa with me around i must sa.

Second to swots headmasters like boys who are good at foopball and shoot goals then they can shout 'Pile in caruthers strate for goal' or other weedy things from the touchline.

Personally i am not good at foopball i just concentrate on hacking everbode. Headmaster yell at me he sa MARK YOUR MAN MOLESWORTH ONE what does he think i am the arsenal chiz. Acktually fotherington-tomas is worse than me he is goalie and spend his time skipping about he sa Hullo clouds hullo sky hullo sun etc when huge centre forward bearing down on him and SHOT whistles past his nose. When all the team sa you should hav stoped it fotherington-tomas he repli 'I simply don't care a row of buttons whether it was a goal or not nature alone is beattful.'

i do not think he will catch the selectors eye.

Every headmaster hav a study or sitting room with easy chair for boys to bend over in fact it is not so much the kaning we object to it is the smell of the cushions and all that fluff down there. Peason sa he once found 2/6 in the lining but i expect that was a woper he always tells them.

Otherwise there is a bookshelf to stare at when geting pi-jaw about why you are being kaned. We hav Comentary on bible (six vols) gone with the wind, Ruff's guide to the turf and Rider of Murder Range confiscated three years ago which headmasters wife thort was wonderful.

Once i try wizard wheeze to put a curl inside trousis then it will break the kane.

Tiptoe shuffle shuffle zoom down on fotherington-tomas and shave his curly locks. While he blub i stuff the locks inside my trousis.

Go to study. Kane descend whack gosh oo gosh oo gosh and hares fly out like H-bomb xplosion. Kane undamaged so it is not such a wizard wheeze after all but Headmaster gets a piece of his wife's mind (making mess after maids hav been in). So BOYS triumphant agane WIZZ.

Kane descend whack gosh oo gosh oo gosh.

Kanes I Have Known
by N. Molesworth

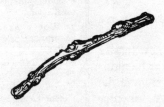

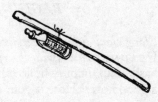

1. 'Old Faithful'. Whippy, no ferrule, 'palm-tree' ends. Can be thrown for dogs to fetch in the holidays.

2. The 'Nonpliant' or 'Rigid' with silencer attachment to drown victims cries.

3. 'Creaker' or split-seam. For use by 'hurt-me-more-than-it-hurts-you' kaners.

4. The first weapon he can lay hands on.

5. The 'Caber', Scotch-type for senior boys.

6. The hair-fine specialists kane for marksmen. Fitted with telescopic sights and range finder.

TWO SHORT SPEECHES FOR HEADMASTERS

TOGETHER WITH THE MOLESWORTH CRIB TO REEL THORTS

1 *BEGINNING OF TERM*

Clang clang bell All sour-faced boys xsembl in skool hall.

HEADMASTER: (*with cheerful smile*) hullo basil hullo timothy hullo john did you hav a good hols?[1] How is your dear mother?[2]

(*to all more cheerful than ever*)

We hav twelve weeks ahead of us and i want you to cram[3] as much aktivity into them as you can in work and pla. This term we hav a new head of the skool grabber ma.[4] (*Claps noone join in*) You all kno the vertues we prize most loyalty and good influence.[5]

We expect grate things at foopball this term. grabber ma[6] is captain. We shall be a young side but do not forget david and goliath (*hearty larff*) a good little 'un is better than a good big 'un (*fits of larffter*) a terrier can worry a st bernard. (*he is going to die it is not good for him to larff so much*)[7]

But perhaps grabber ma does not agree with that?[8]

I should like to introduce a new master who hav joined us in place of mr blenkinsop who left sudenly.[9] i feel sure he will fill the place ocupied by his predecessor.[10] . . .

etc etc until the bell ring for coco.

CRIB TO REEL THORTS

(*N. molesworth knos all*)

1. So they are back agane the little beasts.

2. As if i cared give me young mrs filips every time.

3. All they will cram is my food and tuck.

4. His father a millionaire enuff said.

5. Hem-hem hav to sa that sort of thing you kno.

6. Make him head of anything for the usual amount.

7. Wot a ham performance i'm giving.

8. He'd better or else.

9. who would hav thort it he semed so nice.

10. not too fathefully i sincerely hope.

16

A headmaster's study with layout of the runways

ANOTHER SPEECH

2. *PRIZE-GIVING AT THE SKOOL SPORTS*

HEADMASTER: (*tucking M.C.C. tie over his clean dicky*) i should like to say how much my wife and i appreciate the grand turn-out of parents.[1]

i am sory *all* the boys could not win a race but it is the sporting spirit which counts most.[2] i am happy to be able to tell you from matron that gillibrand 2 who fell on his nose in the sack race is not severely hurt.[3]

Each year it is my privilege to introduce the charming lade who give away the criket bats balls spoons cups etc.[4] 3 years ago it was the Duchess of Dabley, the following year Lady Hogtale, last year we were honoured by Royalty, and *this* year i am delited to sa a few words about another charming lade, as young as she is attractive – mrs grabber.[5]

(*Headmaster beams and claps loud cheers and yells.*)

It is all the grater pleasure as grabber ma hav won all the races and is victor ludorum.[6] mrs grabber herself i think you will all agree showed where her sons talent came from in the parents potato race.[7]

Therefore i welcome mrs grabber and thank her for performing this task.[8]

CRIB TO THORTS

1. They hav eaten 29000 mackaroons and 5034 eclares. Wot do they think i am U.N.R.A.?

2. Only coshing from behind alowed in the obstacle race.

3. Pity.

4. Lucky i got 'em back from the pornbroker hemhem.

5. If that isn't good for a few thousand in the endowment fund i don't kno wot will.

6. For the ushual pament. They call me nero always fiddling.

7. How long can I go on with this?

8. Deep breath. Now for it.

(*A courtly bow, vast cheers, for she's a joly good felow etc mrs grabber rises and begins speech:* 'Cor strike a lite i never made a speech in me life. . . .')

A GAUL marching into Italy.

MORE CHIZZES ABOUT HEADMASTERS

It is a funy thing but headmasters are always very keen on conferences comittees etc when they discuss how to educate boys chiz tho it does not seme to make much diference we are all IGNORANT cheers cheers cheers and do not kno the pluperfect of moneo i am glad to sa.

Another funy thing is that conferences always on same day as oxford and cambridge, test match wimbledon, rugby international or something of that sort. Coincidence? Anyway skool much more peaceful masters slepe in the sunshine boys stretch benethe tropic palms skool dog bites everbode when headmasters away so boo and snubs.

Headmasters all work v. hard. (See plan below)

TIMETABLE OF DAY

0700.	Jump out of bed singing cheerful songs chase the matron round the dorms pull sheets off masters beds rout out all boys to wash basins freeze freeze.
0710.	Chase out all boys who hav climbed back into bed.
0730.	Drive boys matron and masters into brekfast. eat wot the good lord hav provided as if truly thankful.
0736.	Greet wife with luving kiss.
0736.00001.	Stop greeting wife wipe moustache and eat more hadock.
0900.	Drive boys and masters into class. Lock them in. Take latin class qui quaue quod stoke boiler peel potatoes more latin quibus quibus quibus rush out to garden to pick sprouts mend punkture and answer leters.

1000.   Break. Milk buns boys for the kane.

1015.   Drive in boys and masters agane lay table clean
             silver feed hens teach 3A more latin. Romans
             v benevenuti. Treble chance pool forum
             packed.

1300.   lunch stew and prunes. eat with relish.

1330.   eat secret lunch smoked salmon duck green
             peas strubres and cream.

1430.   Flay boys and masters from changing room to
             foopball field. coach boys remove corpses blow
             up foopball mend net. Demonstrate how to
             head ball. Fall stunned. Wake up in time to
             beat boys and masters back to change.

1600.   More latin. Benevenuti playing at home sla
             romans with spears and arows from ditches and
             ramparts. Wizz! About time romans got some
             new players put Caesar on the transfer list
             Aurelius inside-right and Remus into gole.

1800   Tea bred and scrape.

1830.   Eat second tea meringues eclairs honey and
             sossages. Flog boys to bed. Chase matron
             round dorm. Lock masters in cells.

1930.   *BEER!*

2000.   Frugal super haunch of venison or rosted ox
             folowed by soup partridge wine jely and trifle.
             Push stale bred into masters cells. Prowl round
             dorm and kane raggers. Confiskate dormy
             feast and eat same.

2100.   Latin corections with left hand xxxxxxx
             xxxxxx do pools with the other xxoooo
             xxxxxx.

2200.   Snore.

A Few Headmasters

Mr Wesson thinks it's the ball-cock, Mrs Gordon thinks it's the shuttle pan. But *I* think it's you boys in fact I'm sure of it.

Come *on*, St. Custards.

That one, Postlethwaite, would have bowled Bradman.

Unless the culprit owns up the whole school will dig the vegetable garden.

This is *not* going to hurt me as much as it hurts you.

Procul procul o este profani.

He's holding up the whole side is Dick 2.

Your psycho-analyst may say one thing, Blatworthy, but I say another. And my treatment is *free*.

Mens Sana in Corpore Sano.

Facile Princeps.

Usque ad Nauseam.

Virtus in Arduis.

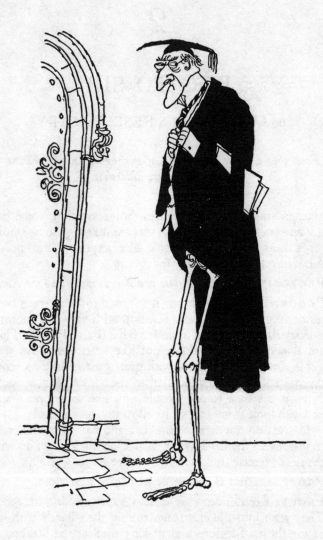

No reference is intended to any master alive or half-dead.

2

BOO TO SIR

or ARE MASTERS NESESSESSARY?

(Four theorems by permission of pythagoras now apearing at garison theatre aldershot.)

Masters are all shapes and sizes. Some are thin, some hav got an enormous pot on them some smoke cigs some smoke pipes poo gosh which ponk like anything and nearly ALL hav a *face like a squashed tomato.*

PROPOSITION: *All Masters are Weeds and Love the Kane.*

PROOF: The job of masters is suposed to be to teach boys lessons e.g. geog lat fr. div hist bot. arith algy and geom.

Aktually most of them prefer BEER and PUBS. They are always late for brekfast not like keen alert boys who goble force poridge cereal with grate gusto and look scorn on masters pale yelow faces when they see a skool sossage. Then is the time to ask Would you like some cream sir? or Gosh look at my egg sir its all runny. (Manners.)

Masters do not care for brekfast and hav to be driven in to lessons by the headmaster chiz. They then sa get on with the next exercise and go to sleep snore snore. Q.E.D.

PROPOSITION: *Warning. Some Masters are Keen.*

PROOF: Keen masters are usually super weeds with specs. They rush into the classroom rubing their hands with joy at the thort of lessons and make a dash at the blakboard. They sit on pins needles rat traps hedghogs etc without jumping chiz they are so enthusiastick that all should learn.

Then is the time to ask Would you like some cream sir? or Gosh
look at my egg sir its all runny.

Keen masters get on with the job at once they sa: 'Latin
ex. forty-four a. Caesar where were we molesworth?' i do
not repli as am removing toffe paper under desk. Master
then sa: 'Where were we smith tomas matson one gillibrand
two myers jonson jones' until he go through class. Of course
noone kno as Caesar is uterly wet and a weed.

The thing about keen masters is that they are never discouraged. When you look at smith tomas matson one
gillibrand two myers jonson and jones you could think they
would put a gat or germ gun to their heads. But they do not
chiz and all boys DRINK AT THE TREE OF
KNOLWEDGE hem-hem i do not think. Q.E.D.

PROPOSITION: *Masters Are Swankpots.*

PROOF: Wise boys like me use FLATERY with masters from time to time e.g. When a master hav a new pair of shoes which is not often heaven knos molesworth 2 always sa About time too then run away.

My method is this i sa Oosir goshsir pleezesir what a super tie sir. The master repli Do you think so molesworth. You may stop your deten and pla foopball after all. WIZZ! SUPER!

Masters can often be tempted by this way to talk about wot they did in the war.

Masters hav always been brave in the war and it is a wonder they hav not all got the VC for capturing hitler holding the bridge etc. In fact if all the masters did wot they sa they did its a wonder we did not win the war in 1940.

Still it is not bad aktually as during a bit of parsing or drawing a map of Spane you can just look up and sa.

'Did you hav a tomy gun during the war sir?'

'Get on with your map molesworth one.'

'No but did you sir really?'

'As a mater of fact i did molesworth.'

'gosh sir did you shoot many germans sir.'

'Get on with your map, boy.'

'No sir but did you?'

'Altho it hav nothing to do with the lesson i got 9 thousand with one burst once . . . etc.'

The master will then go on for twenty minutes telling the class how he won the war etc just like pop who was only in a weedy ack-ack brigade near chiselhurst with a lot of soppy Ats and mum sa never hit an aeroplane in his life.

Occasionally master's story is ruined by ass like gillibrand whose pater is Major general sir gustave godolfin gillibrand who ask: 'When you led your men forward in the hale of fire sir was that not tacktically unsound in view of the enfillade fire from numbers two and three German patrols.'

Or perhaps molesworth 2 zoom by he is pretending to be a meteor jet and he sa Able baker calling i bet a million trillion pounds sir never saw a german at all. Able Baker out. He then go ah-ah-ah-ah-ah with machine guns and sixteen chickens and skool dog bite the dust he is a weed. Q.E.D.

PROPOSITION: *Masters Are Sloppy And Like Gurls*.

PROOF: Masters not only like BEER some hav fotos of Gurls hem-hem like sabrina in their rooms. In fact instead of thinking of NOTHING which is wot most masters do they look more dopey than ever they are in luv. That is all very well they hav got to hav something in their lives besides Caesar pythagoras and other weeds but i ask you wot could any GURL see in a master? Especially one like sabrina? Q.E.D.

They hav got to hav something in their lives besides Caesar pythagoras and other weeds.

Know the Enemy
or Masters at a Glance

I cannot keep order.

The boys all look on me as a friend.

I am hoping to get a job in the colonial service somewhere.

I am keen on the latest developments in education.

I advise you strongly
not to start ragging *me*.

You may think I'm soft but I'm
hard, damned hard.

Mr Chips? No such character
ever existed.

And when I asked him the
supine stem of confiteor the fool
didn't know.

I may not know much but I am
jolly good at football.

No. The spirit of tolerance,
you fool.

The crested grebes are mating!

I am still hoping for a job in
the colonial service somewhere.

I was sent by the agency at the last minute before the term began.

A joke's a joke chaps but don't go too far.

I have been here thirty years. I have always said that and do not
intend to change now.

Of course the fellow doesn't realize he's a typical schoolmaster.

3

A TOUR OF THE CAGES

or MASTERS ONE BY ONE

1. ENGLISH MASTERS

English masters hav long hair red ties and weeds like wordsworth throw them into exstatsies.

They teach english e.g. migod you didn't ort to write a sentence like that molesworth. For prep they always set an essay if they can think of one. In the good old days it was always something like:

> What i did in the hols.
> A country ramble.
> A day at a railway station.

Now english masters are ADVANCED chiz and kno all about t.s. eliot cristopfer fry auden etc. etc and they read them so beatifully they make fotherington-tomas blub he is a sissy, and not worth a d. For essays english masters give us weedy things like –

> A trip in a space ship.
> my favourite machine gun.
> what to do with masters.

you see wot i mean in the old days you knew where you were but now they are trying to read your inmost thorts heaven help them. Anyway you hav to write them so as ushual boys are ground benethe palsied heel of mummers. (auden.)

When english masters canot think of an essay they set
ten lines of Peotry.

PEOTRY

Peotry is sissy stuff that rhymes. Weedy people say la and
fie and swoon when they see a bunch of daffodils. Aktually
there is only one piece of peotry in the english language.

The Brook

     i come from haunts of coot and hern
     i make a sudden sally
     and-er-hem-er-hem-the fern
     to bicker down a valley.

that is the lot tho the Charge of the light brigade and the
loss of the royal george are nearly peotry too. Even advanced
english masters set THE BROOK they sa it is quaint
dated gejeune etc but really they are all in leag with parents
who can all recite it. And *do* if given half a chance.

Even gillibrand's pater General sir gustave godolfin
gillibrand sa THE BROOK is tip-top and commend it
to his men before going into batle insted of RUM. Not
a bad wheeze aktually but i would hav an english master
in front instead of a piper. In all the bulets, wams, bonks and
xplosions no english master would escape his fate.

Sometimes we hav to recite which is girly in the extreme
and there is no chance to read famous CRIB which you
copied out in prep.

when i recite it is something like this:

     Tomow and tomow and tomow
     Um ah um ah
     Tomow and tomow and tomow
     Um – ah creeps creeps in the last syll—
     No!
     Tomowandtomowandtomow

A ROMAN marching into Gaul.

Creeps in this um um
Out!
OUT!
brief candle
Yes i kno sir half a mo sir
Yes
fie
O fie!
Um um tis an unweeded syllable an un—
No!
Tomowandtomowandtomow etc. . . .

In other words quite frankly i just don't kno it.
Also quite frankly
I COULDN'T CARE LESS
What use will *that* be to me in the new atomic age?
Occasionally english masters chide me for this point of view o molesworth one you must learn the value of spiritual things until i spray them with 200 rounds from my backterial gun. i then plant the british flag in the masters inkwell and declare a whole holiday for the skool. boo to shakespeare.
So much for english masters.

LITERRARY CORNER

A book for the hols. '*Rob Roy*' *by Charles Dickens.*
(*Grabber & Grabber 6s.*)

To judge from the first page which i hapned to see by mistake this is something about a small boy who had to climb chimneys. Acktually i would hav thort this was quite super as you get black but this one seemed to be rather sorry for himself. On page 5 there is a pressed leaf and on page 77 some orange juice i spilt while the book was acting as part of a fort. There seemed to be something about some water babies or something soppy but i don't really kno. i supose he must hav climbed the chimney to rob roy but this is only a guess.

o molesworth one you must learn the value of spiritual things.

2. *LATIN MASTERS*

Latin masters teach lat. which is different from eng. geom algy fr and others becos it is first period after break. (imagine puting lat. of all things after coco and buns they ort to give us indigestion tablets which FIZZ like mum hav with a hangover)

If you wake up for long enuff you find that everything in lat. hapned a long time ago. Latin masters therefore are always old and bent with age. You can hear there footsteps a long way off thump thump shuffle shuffle and can put all sweets bludgeons dagers, coshes swords white mice cheese marbles or whatever is hapning to engage your fancy back inside the desk.

Latin master finally make grate heave and toter towards desk you would think it was mount everest. Will he make it? Effort! He sits in the chair panting.

THE LESSON WILL COMENCE

Open hillard and botting turn to ex ia section 2 sentence 6.

If latin masters are slo starters, once they get a latin ex. they go like a jet rocket, in fact you would think they were runing in the darby like hard ridden only faster chiz.

They sa: 'The gauls – galli – subject – go on molesworth oppugnant – what does oppugnant mean – they are attacking fossas. Ditches. What did you say molesworth? Why on earth atack a ditch? Keep your mind on the sentence. The gauls are atacking the ditches. What? *I am quite unable to inform you molesworth for what purpose the Gauls wished to attack the ditches*. The latin is correct. That sufices.'

We proceed. sagittis. What's sagittis molesworth what case come along boy – sagitta sagitta sagittam first declension – *with* arows by with or from arows. What is that? molesworth for the last time your opinion that it is soppy to atack a ditch does not interest me. Or what you personally would do with an arow. nor do i kno where the bows are. Likewise the question of whether there was buckets of blud is immaterial. The gauls are atacking the ditches with arows – telisque – telisque, molesworth? ...

Aktually the trick is to look dopey and then the latin master will do all the translation himself.

Latin prose is difrent. It is either about a weed called Cotta who is always beating the Belgians or about Romulus

and Remus who are a couple of babies who founded the city of Rome chiz if only they had abstained there would be no lat and no one could sa hunc hanc hoc without being put in a sty with the skool pig and rightly too. Anyway latin masters would be out of a job if there was no latin so they keep it going.

All latin masters hav one joke.

> *Caesar adsum jam forte*
> or
> caesar had some jam for tea.

n.b. a good roare of larffter will cut the leson by two minits six seconds or half a gender rhyme a ab absque coram de palam clam cum ex and e etc. wot rot eh i mean to say?

3. *FRENCH MASTERS*

Acording to ancient tradition no fr. master can keep order.

Whenever a french master apere in the doorway it is a signal for hale of ink pots rubers chalk and stink bombs poo gosh. The fr. master then loose his temper and sa:

> *mon diue canaille allez-hoop*
> or
> my god they're at it agane

n.b. if the fr master is english this amount of french is ushually beyond him. he sa:

> turn it up 2B now now turn it up
> (*tournez-le dessus maintenant*)

Acktually fr. masters seldom get a chance to sa anything either in eng. or fr. But sometimes the boys are exorsted with raging and glad of the rest so the fr. master speaks. He speaks then of M. Dubois who is uterly wet.

M. Dubois is tall, thin and weedy: he wears a bowler hat and is very respectable. Sometimes he is in the kitchen with Mme Dubois. Sometimes he is taking Rose Amelie Fifi and the little dog Tou Tou for a promenade in the gardens of the luxembourg. Sometimes he is in the garden and sometimes he is smoking a pipe in his study. In fact, the felow never does a stroke of work. In the afternoons he is back in the gardens of the Luxermbourg pointing out plants and pigeons. He eats his dinner and goes to bed.

After M. Dubois comes Armand (lesson 5 du dela des).

Armand is a small boy who wear a striped shirt and a round sissy straw hat like a girly. One day Armand is eating his breakfast when his father sa Toda we go for our holidays au bord de la mer. Armand is thrilled he sa O Papa are there flowers by the seaside you can tell the sort he is. in any case there must hav been something wrong if they only told him he was going to dieppe in the morning.

Armand sa: 'May I take my buket and spade, Papa?'

'Yes,' said Papa, 'and your windmill.' (You see?)

'How shall we go to the station, Papa?'

'Yes I must hire a cab. On arriving at the station i shall pay the driver then i go to the guichet and buy our tickets. The porter will take our bagage to the compartment. In the compartment are two ladies, three dirty old men and a postman who is smoking a pipe.'

'Are there boats on the sea?' asks Armand so you can see that i think Papa is only taking him to dieppe in order to drown him.

There is also another character called papa rat. He is always eating cheese. He loves cheese. Mama rat loves cheese too. They hav ten little rats who love cheese. In fact, the whole business is unspeakably sordid.

a signal for hale of ink pots rubers chalk and stink bombs.

Finally there is loptimisme and pessimisme which is pierre et jean who spend all day looking out of a window. Jean looks out of the careau bleu and sa helas il pleut the day est sombre. Pierre looks out of the careau jaune and sa Houp la le solay brillent. Aktually they are both wrong as according to the pikture in my book there is a thick fog due to rubbing out rude saings with bungy.

All fr. masters hav a joke too if they manage to shout it loud enuff.

> Je suis i am a pot of jam
> tu es thou art a clot etc.

n.b. with a fr. master this roar of larffter can be xtended safely for as long as five minits or more. This can be xtended when peason hav his famous fit of hystericks when he put fruit salts in his mouth and fome as he fall writhing to the ground WIZZ. The whole form then help him to matron leaving the fr. master with fotherington-tomas papa rat M Dubois, Armand and PEACE reigns agane.

4. *MATHS MASTERS*

$$\frac{a \times b\ (c-d)}{d \times c\ (b-a)} \times \frac{pq+rs}{xg-nbg}$$

The above is what maths masters thrive on and explanes why they are so very stern strict and fearsome. noone in a class ever stirs as a maths master approche you can hear a pin drop and no wonder when you think of the above sum which is enuff to silence anebode.

The only way with a maths master is to hav a very worried xpression. Stare at the book intently with a deep frown as if furious that you cannot see the answer. at the same time scratch the head with the end of the pen. After 5 minits it is not safe to do nothing any longer. Brush away all the objects which hav fallen out of the hair and put up hand.

SCENES IN THE LIFE OF

PYTHAGORAS

useful for conversations at luncheon with maths masters

'Sir?' (*whisper*)

'Please sir?' (*louder*)

'Yes, molesworth?' sa maths master. (*Thinks: it is that uter worm agane chiz*)

'Sir i don't quite *see* this.'

nb it is esential to sa you don't quite '*see*' sum as this means you are only temporarily bafled by unruly equation and not that you don't kno the fanetest about any of it. [*Dialog continue:*]

'What do you not see molesworth?' sa maths master (*Thinks: a worthy dolt who is making an honest efort*)

'number six sir i can't make it out sir.'

'What can you not make out molesworth?'

'number six sir.'

'it is all very simple molesworth if you had been paing atention to what i was saing at the beginning of the lesson. Go back to your desk and *think*.'

This gets a boy nowhere but it show he is KEEN which is important with maths masters.

The Discovery of the Rhomboid.

Maths masters do not like neck of any kind and canot stand the casual approach.

HOW NOT TO APPROACH A MATHS MASTER

'Sir?'
'Sir sir please?'
'Sir sir please sir?'
'Sir sir please sir sir please?'
'Yes molesworth?'
'I simply haven't the fogiest about number six sir.'
'Indeed, molesworth?'
'It's just a jumble of letters sir i mean i kno i couldn't care less whether i get it right or not but what sort of an ass sir can hav written this book.'

(*Maths master give below of rage and tear across room with dividers. He hurl me three times round head and then out of the window.*)

Maths masters do not stop at arith and algy they include

Pythagoras puzzled by one of my theorems.

geom and to do this they hav a huge wooden compass with chalk in the end for the blakboard. The chalk make a friteful noise which set our delicate nerves jangling my dear but this is better than doing the acktual geom itself.

Pythagoras as a mater of fact is at the root of all geom. Insted of growing grapes figs dates and other produce of greece Pythagoras aplied himself to triangles and learned some astounding things about them which hav been inflicted on boys ever since.

Whenever he found a new thing about a triangle Pythagoras who had no shame jumped out of his bath and shouted 'Q.E.D.' through the streets of athens its a wonder they never locked him up.

To do geom you hav to make a lot of things equal to each other when you can see perfectly well that they don't. This agane is due to Pythagoras and it formed much of his conversation at brekfast.

A few lazy parrallelograms basking on Mount Olympus Pythagoras stalking them.

PYTHAGORAS (*helping himself to porridge*): Hmm. I see the sum of the squares on AB and BC = the square on AC.

WIFE: Dear dear.

PYTHAGORAS: I'm not surprised, not surprised at all. I've been saying that would come for years.

WIFE: Yes dear.

PYTHAGORAS: Now they'll hav to *do* something about it. More tea please. There's another thing – the day is coming when they're going to have to face the fact that a strate line if infinitely protracted goes on for ever.

WIFE: Quite so.

PYTHAGORAS: Now take the angle a, for xsample.

(*His wife sudenly loses control and thro the porridge at him. Enter Euclid: another weed and the 2 bores go off together*)

All this taken into consideration it is no wonder that no cunning wheezes or super dodges can be plaed on maths masters. You just hav to sufer so boo to fractions long div short div decimals.

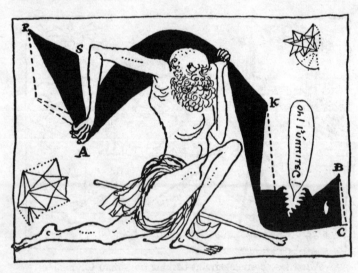

A battle of giants. Pythagoras bends the angle A.

5. SINGING MASTERS

Singing masters are frequently fr. maths lat or geog masters. This is becos when they first come up to the headmaster and sa 'Any odd jobs going? Chop your wood,' the head sa, 'Yes, you could take 2B in div. geog. handiwork and carpenty but only if you pla the organ and take singing as well.' Singing master then touch his cap. 'Give you a bit of a jingle,' he sa and take out a mouth organ at which headmaster flee into the woods.

Singing master then sit on stool of skool piano as if he could pla it with ring of worms and cads round him. fotherington-tomas hand round books full of minims crotchets etc which hav been made into beetles by boys mischievous fingers dear dear wot will they be up to next. Master than sa Number 56 hearts of oak class sing mightily and windows burst all over the skool.

As singing masters stray into the job so to speak you get all sorts and there is no real telling. i mean we had one you kno the one with the super sports car *urum-urum-urum-uraaaaaa* who used to sa O.K. hep cats snap into the boogie. which was super but the trouble with singing is headmasters hear it they can't help it. That master was soon in his sports car headed for town *urum-urum-urum-uraaaa* etc which was hard cheddar really.

On the other hand there are ones who sa lets hav a opera i mean to sa with our mob. Not that he didn't get a few weeds on his side and wot with fotherington-tomas as lieutenant pinkerton and molesworth 2 as tanhauser you couldn't hear yourself rag chiz.

Personaly it is not the noise i object to in music it is the words. i could not care less if i find the minstrel boy in the ranks of death the sooner the better he is uterly wet and unable to lift his fathers sword. On the other hand you can always put goldfish in the piano or something so if music be the food of luv pla on etc. fortissimo.

Table of Grips and Tortures for Masters

The plain blip for numskulls.

Side hair tweak exquisitely painful.

Single-hair extraction for non-attenders.

The cork in the storm for violent temperaments.

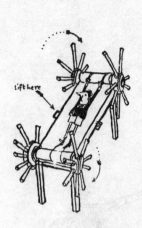

Portable rack for maths masters
(with thumbscrew attachment).

The headshave with ruler.

The Cumberland creep from behind with silver pencil.

The simple open furnace.

Aktually masters are not bad really and you hav got to hav them. They are absolutely like weeds becos when one goes another always aperes. (Som in fact are quite d. you might almost think they were human but on the whole i keep on with my batle cry DOWN WITH THE USHERS. LET HONEST SKOOLBOYS PREVAIL MASTERS UNFAIR TO MOLESWORTH.)

4

LESSONS

AND HOW TO AVOID THEM

1. *BOTANY*

Hurra for the botany walk!

Now boys get into croc. Tinies in front seniors at the rear. Off for the woods and keep your eyes skinned. Ha-ha – what do we see at once but a little robin! There is no need to burst into tears fotherington-tomas swete tho he be. Nor to buzz a brick at it, molesworth 2.

Pause at the zebra look left look right. Strate into the vicar's bicycle. That's all right we were none of us hurt and i canot believe that the vicar *really* said that grabber.

Ho for the woods agane!

Tread softly softly tippy toes. There is a bunny sprinting to its warren. And there a rook – one of the most fasscinating of the crow family. Keep that leaf for your pressings book, plunkett 2. You can see *what*, molesworth? A man-eating tiger? It hav a horible face with beedy eyes and weedy whiskers? i am sure you are mistaken. Ah, it was only the matron. Good afternoon, mato!

Now scater for specimens and when i blo the whistle scamper back to the fairy ring.

Peep!

Now

Wot hav we?

A dead bird, peason? i don't think that would find its place in the nature museum it is so very dead. A beetle a green spangle a brace of frogs. A worm, molesworth? Ha-ha. I see a resemblance. A fern frond, fotherington-tomas. I shall kepe it and wear it on my hat.

To me all and let us be very silent. Wot do we hear? Gillibrand bloing his nose? No, molesworth the corncrake. CHIRUK–QUARK–HONK–HONK–CHIRUK–QUARK. The corncrake is a clever felow he is a ventriloquist and can thro his voice. Did you sa he could thro it in the dustbin as far as you are concerned, peason? That is not nice. 'Who were you out with Friday, baby?' Wot boy said that? The corncrake, molesworth? I saw your lips move i shall report you on return.

Fall into croc agane. Tinies in front. Back thro the woods. Out into the road and cross by the zebra look left look right. Cross! Ah, the vicar's bicycle agane. What a coincidence! He *did* sa that word, grabber? Which word? Oh.

Ho and away agane all!

This is the sort of chiz that miss pringle indulges herself in with a botany walk. all boys are browned off and could not care less if a bee place its long nose into a flower and suck honey etc. or if anebode place their long nose anywhere in the world in space. The same goes for brite eyed creatures watching us from their lairs. No wonder when they see our skool they all run away. i would do the same if i was a stoat.

HOW TO AVOID BOTANY

Suply yourself with a paket of cigs. When in woods ask permission to seek for a nest. Zoom away and climb a tree with peason or some other chump. Smoke a couple restfully. When ready return to fairy ring with three twigs and some straw then burst into tears a teeny ringtale ever so sweet hav been singing. Really botany make you sick – and if you smoke those cigs more so.

Boo to birds beasts crows trees grass flowers also cristopfer robin and wind in the wilows. Charge at the tinies and mow them down.

Fragrant Leaves from
My Botany Book

A Glurk Trolling.

A Blue-nosed Chuck Brooding.

A Lesser Titwort Avoiding a Worm.

A Mongolian Thick Surprised (Rear View.)

2. *HISTORY*

History started badly and hav been geting steadily worse. It is like racing really when peason and i have a modest fluter thro the under gardener. All the favourites go down.

Harold beaten at Hastings.

Richard the Lion-Hart couldn't beat Saladin who was black as your hat.

Bruce victorious at Banockburn tho Scotish pack heavily outweighted.

Cavaliers beaten by the roundheads.

Finally beaten by the Yanks who thro all our tea into Boston harbour dressed like red indians that was the absolute end.

History began with a lot of barons who opresed everbode. Then they became respectable and agreed king john was going too far. Thou mayest hav the body they cried so he signed magna carta in xchange. When king john had got the body he didn't kno what to do with it of course. He ort to hav put a gun in its hand and make it appere like suicide chiz like in the detective stories.

Everything went on and people like Prince Rupert zoom about on their chargers at mach 1 or close to speed of sound. Mcanwhile they discovered books and lots of people learned to read. This is nothing to boste about aktually as even molesworth 2 can read, but they thort it was wonderful and it all led to skools chiz chiz chiz.

It also led to KNOLEDGE.

> A SERF: We are not hapy in our lot.
> AN APRENTICE: Nor in our lot either.

This meant the Rise of the People and the People hav gone on rising ever since like yeast until you kno where they are now hapy and prosperus you ask them when the television programme is over.

And if you ask all those who hav gone before i am not sure whether they would agree that it is worth it. But it is too late now.

HOW TO AVOID HISTORY

Noone hav ever found a way of avoiding history it is upon us and around us all. The only thing when you look at the cuning vilaninous faces in our class you wonder if history may not soon be worse than ever.

Sometimes you can get out of a hist. lesson by SEMING ILL. Pinch some flour from the kitchen if molesworth 2 hav not eaten it and rub well into face. After ten minits hold the brow and groan. The hist. master stops in the middle of agincourt:

'Thou semest pale, molesworth 1. Is ort the mater? Come, youth, impart wot ails thee.'

(*Note:* Hist. masters always talk like ivanhoe, blak arow etc.)

'No really sir i am quite alright.'

'Zounds it semeth thou hast the plague, good skolar.'

'Nay, sirrah.'

(You talk like that too it is catching)

'But tis most remarkable i trow. Hi ye to matronnes room for a phial of phisick.'

'Nay nay sir no witches brew from yon crone shall ever pass my lips.'

'But thy eye is bright with fever thou shakest with palsy and would seme to hav the ague. Tis surely the king's evil.'

'Does that put you off foopball. It is a chiz.'

Note: the real chiz about this method of avoiding history is that if the hist master go on long enuff you begin to believe that death is really upon you. You hav something wrong with your heart which hav stoped beating: your jaw is stuck open and you canot close it also you are going blind. On the whole it is beter to put up with the hist. lesson and draw beetles on the blotch quietly or dab criket.

Untold History

How sir molesworth stormed the castle of sir sirloin de peason in Picardy. (The original is preserved in the fly leaf of his latin dictionary.)

How sir molesworth led the apprentices from the City stormed the skool and claped the headmaster in the Tower.

3. SCIENCE

Old fashioned skolars i.e. Tom Brown jan ridd 5th form at st dominicks etc. used to regard science as a joke. They called it stinks ha-ha which semed v. funy to them. They mixed lots of acids and powders in test tubes and the worse it smelt the more sucessful the lesson.

Progress is striking. Let us review some of the achievements of our science group. Here are some projects on which we are working. Forward the young elizabethans this is wot orange juice hav done for the world.

IN THE PLANNING STAGE

Long term. The peason-molesworth space ship to reach the moon in twenty years. By the time we are twenty we may hav worked out how to get back. Or will civilisation abandon us? Space ship is made out of a tin bath so we can keep clean when we get there.

Advanced stage: The plunket radio-controlled germ beamed to atack all masters.

The molesworth 2 thermometer with thermostatic control. Registers normal with matron and then pops up to 102.

The jet bowling attachments for criketers. Fits on arm and delivers ball at mach 8. Swerve off-break and googly atachment extra.

Quick-firing chalk gun for violent masters. Telescopic sights.

Electronick brane in difrent sizes. Does latin sentences tots up sums Greek, French German speaking up to C. entrance standard. Answers everything and bafles masters.

All these are just wizard wheezes at the moment but all boys are plotting hard except molesworth 2 he is inventing the wheel as he feel in science nothing should be accepted he is uterly wet and couldn't hurt a flea.

Meanwhile new society of robot ant boys are pressing headmaster for better equipment. Why not a proton syncrotron to accelerate protons beyond 10 mil eh? We must make haste sloly sa headmaster.

All the same once we hav the syncrotron we shall all be a google eyed ant society. At the moment we hav the google eyes at any rate which is something especially peason. When we arive in our helicopters we shall take over the skool and feed all with cream. FREE THE SLAVES. WE LOOK TO THE DAY.

HOW TO AVOID SCIENCE

A good way in a science lesson is to wait until some old-fashioned poison like sulphurick acid etc. turns up. As per ushual science master, who not forward-looking, sa: No boy is to touch the contents of the tube.

Make up tube which look the same and place alongside acid. Master begins lesson drone drone drone. Sudenly you spring to feet with grate cry: 'Sir Sir I can't stand it any longer!'

Drink coloured water and collapse to be carried out as if dead. n.b. if you make a mistake with this one you are still carried out as if dead and you *are*.

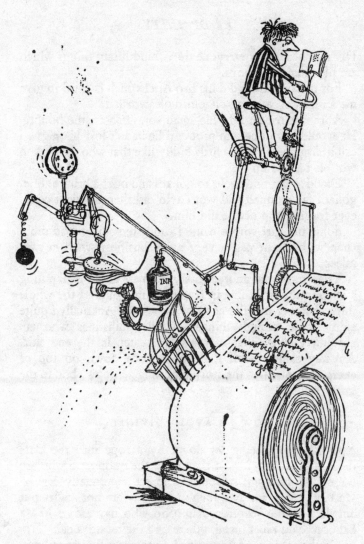

The Molesworth-Peason Lines Machine. Runs off
a hundred in one minit. (patnt pnding.)

4. *DIVINITY*

Div is super becos everyone do v. bludthirsty things which are pleasing to all boys.

For instance Cain did his bro Abel which is enuff to give me an idea occasionally about molesworth 2.

Abraham tried to do his small son isaac on the bonfire. He would hav done him proper if he hadn't lost his nerve i call it disgraceful with a little kiddy like that who didn't kno wot his pa was up to.

David sa yar boo sucks to goliath and buzz a brick at him. goliath fall stunned and wot david did then no giant could ever forgive him i.e. he did him.

Some old girl whose name i canot remember also did a chap with a tent peg a very nasty business when he was asleep.

Then there was another nasty business about Saul puting a chap in the front line in fact as mum would sa the whole thing is rather like the news of the world. Acktually i quite enjoy these tuough things but the philistines who are absolutely super chaps always get beaten in the end chiz. Anyway samson pull the whole place down on top of everbode just when the story is getting xciting so boo to the infant samuel.

HOW TO AVOID DIVINITY

You could try being let down by a rope into the class dressed as an angel. You then sa to the master Lo who are these cherubim and seraphim who are continually crying. He repli Form 3B. You then sa Lo they are not angles but angels with the xception of peason who hav a face like a baboon. You must dismiss them and the master oba.

On the other hand he may sa Lo molesworth do 200 lines. It is quite a good wheeze but probably would not work.

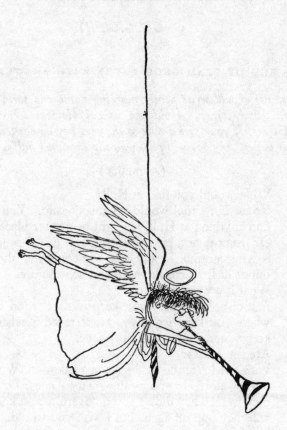

You could try being let down into the class dressed as an angel.

5. *GEOGRAPHY*

END OF TERM GEOG PAPER WITH ANSWERS

Students should write neatly marking name and form in the right hand corner. Avoid the ushual blotches like atomic xplosions. If you write a note to the next boy do not tear it off your paper. Any boy will pass who slip examiner half a crown.

(40 minits.)

Q. What would you find at Hull?

A. Noone but a fool would ask this question. You might find anything at Hull. It might be a razor blade or an ear trumpet or a pair of bag-pipes it just depends wot is lying around. In any case you could find the same things in Ipswich. Be more precise in future.

Q. What is a watershed?

A. A toolshed is where you keep tools a wood shed is where you keep wood . . . a watershed is where you keep water. Don't waste my time.

Q. Are the Andes?

A. I ask you! Are the Andes? wot a question. Wot does it mean clot? Do you mean *were* the Andes? Of course they were. They didn't pop up overnite you kno. Nor will they pop off agane but i wish you would.

Q. in Africa?

A. i am waiting. the lunatick bin is second turning on the right. they will be waiting for you. In africa indeed! n.b. if the words 'in Africa' belong to 'Are the Andes' i neither kno nor care.

Q. Where would you expect to find india ruber?

A. You never kno with a bungy it might be at the bottom of the inkwell or it might hav been cut into little bits for pellets. It might be all mixed up with tooffe pen-knife string stamps skoolboys diary french coins etc in one of my pockets. If it is any use to you fotherington-tomas hav a beatiful pink bungy in that hole in his pencil box.

Q. From what tree do you get quinine?

A. You don't get quinine from a tree you ass. You get it from matron on fridays. You wouldn't call matron a tree. An old stick perhaps ha-ha-ha-ha that is a good one. Next question.

Q. What are the positions occupied by the sun when it is most remote from the equator and how many are there in a year and on what dates? Does the sun appear to remain stationary on reaching these points? Is the sun vertical over the earth's surface N. of the tropic of Cancer or South of the tropic of Capricorn? What is an ecliptic?

A. A man who sufers from eclipsy.

Q. What is manioc?

A. Now you're asking. But who else whould hav asked all these stupid q's eh?

HOW TO AVOID GEOGRAPHY

i should think that if you answer a paper like that you might stand a good chance of never doing a geography lesson aganc at least not in that skool. it might be better down a coal mine at least you get wages which you don't at skool. You could try and see.

6. *GENERAL KNOWLEDGE*

General knowledge is all the stuff that is not covered by latin geog algy geom fr. div. hist. etc. This is a lot for a boy to stuff in his head especially if he could not care less whether mountain goats are found in turkey. The less i kno about mountain goats the better and the same go for the height of the nelson column.

Lots of general knoledge these days is called current events about the state of the world just to cheer you up between latin and maths. gran you kno gran who was a lade porter and made munitions during the war hav been flying everywhere. She hav been to friends in South Africa and New York and Singapore and now talking of zooming to rome for lunch in a comet. Pop sa you can't expect the world to be peaceful with her about and the whole Mess is due to her.

Aktually the Mess is due to the rusians who are roters. The points i wish to make about the world are contained in the molesworth newsletter.

(*a*) the rusians are roters.

(*b*) americans are swankpots.

(*c*) the french are slack.

(*d*) the germans are unspeakable.

(*e*) the rest are as bad if not worse than the above.

(*f*) the british are brave super and noble cheers cheers cheers.

The only way for Peace is for all of them to dive into the sea and end it all. This will leave the whole place to the mountain goats who inhabit turkey and they may make a beter job of it.

HOW TO AVOID GENERAL KNOWLEDGE

Ask the master whether he hav passed security check as integrated personality in global struggle against communism. Add Are you sir and hav you ever been a member of communist party then run like the wind.

A Gaul and a Roman passing each other in the Alps.

How to Succeed with Masters

What is x + y + a − b, sir?

Gosh sir what a tie.

They're down there, sir.

But you told me to report to you and sa the whole of the Charge of the Light Brigade, sir.

Well kicked sir!

Look what we've got in here, sir.

You should hear what my pater
says about you, sir.

I suppose you can't *afford* a car.

Flight of the Ink Dart

I   II

V   VI

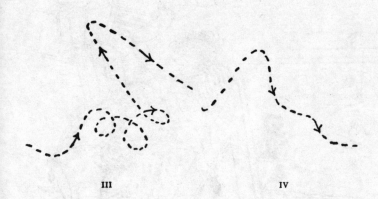

III   IV

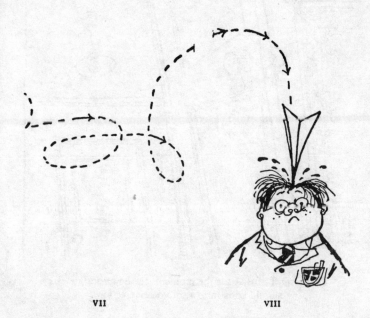

VII   VIII

That's enuff of that for the moment. In the meantime *this*
should constitute a provocative action.

5

IN LOCO PARENTIS

*(For whom we are about to deceive
may the Lord make us truly thankful)*

Boys ushually hav 2 parents. These parents are very like their dear children chiz chiz which shows that you can look like peason or grabber or molesworth 2 and still get on in the world.

For some reason all these parents are anxious about their dear little chicks and think they are the only boy in the skool chiz wot a fate you'd have to make up a class of masters. All mums think we are so delicate we are going to pass out any moment its a wonder they don't come down to the skool with a bunch of lilies for the funeral.

Families often hav 2 grans on the strength borne for critical duties and for making remarks i.e. wot a curious smell skools hav in a v. loud voice.

You can tell the two grans apart becos one gran do not aprove of your mater and your mater's mama thinks your pater is selfish thriftless vague lazy undependable untidy neglectful poor dilatory unreliable shiftless conceited helpless and an uter wet who is not worthy of your mater's hand.

Grans are quite d. to boys however becos they think poor little wretches blub blub none of it is their fault with a pater and/or mater like that.

It seems strange that all the tuough boys around with faces like wild baboons started life as babes in prams chiz chiz chiz. i mean you kno wot weeds babes are they lie about and gurgle and all the lades sa icky pritty and other uterly wet things.

75

Being a baby is alright but soon all the boys who hav been wearing peticoats chiz chiz chiz begin to get bigger. they start zooming about like jet fighters climb drane pipes squirt water pistols make aple pie beds set booby traps leave tools about the garden refuse to be polite to visiting aunts run on the flower beds make space rockets out of pop's golf bag and many other japes and pranks.

It is at this time that parents look thortfully at their dear chicks and sa

IT IS TIME WE SENT NIGEL TO SKOOL.

CHIZ!

Parents then search for a skool and dream of the day when the bath will not be full of plastic tugs speedboats queen marys etc. They look on the map until they find a place that is millions and trillions of miles away from home, and send for a prospectus.

The prospectus take a bit of time to arive owing to grate pressure of business on headmaster during term time (boat race, golf matches, University sports and international ruger). Finally headmaster enclose prospectus which was printed in 1914 and a bit dusty.

If headmasters were honest a prospectus would be a book which sa how many kanes he hav, contane a warning about the skool dog and the amount of prunes and rice served during the term. Acktually it sa the skool is simply super just like claridges hotel chiz in fact when your pater see the fees he sa he could do three months in a suite at claridges more cheaply but this is just biterness. the noble boy must point out that if parents are to fob off dreadful offspring who climb drane pipes squirt water pistols etc no one is going to take him xcept for a fat price so boo and snubs to kruschev and the whole world.

✱

An Ideal Setting

st custards is splendidly situated in bracing downland country yet
within easy reach of the town with main line railway station. A brook
with clear sparkling water babbles by. It is a haunt for feathered folk
who flock into the extensive grounds. The house is modern and
nearby is the famous girls college. The air is tempered with sea
breezes. An ideal setting for a seat of learning.

A Corner of the Playing Fields

Games are a recognised part of the curriculum and matches are played
with neighbouring skools. The sporting spirit is fostered as part of
the skool tradition.

A Peep into Matron's Room

Special attention is paid to health and all boys are under the supervision of a qualified matron who has at her disposal the full resources of the sick room.

Academic

The classical standards of st custards have long been established. Boys are prepared for scholarship examinations. The school is recognised.

Boys are encouraged to develop their individual characters and
expand their personalities.

The Football Team

Played 8. Won 0. Drawn 0. Lost 8.

VISITING THE SKOOL

The day the parents come means much acktivity at the skool.

All rude drawings and propaganda down with the warmongers meeting at dalston friday are wiped off blakboards. Skool dog is muzled boys wash their necks and the bath is cleaned.

Next masters are let out of their cells in new suits mashers ties etc. and are forced by the headmaster to toe party line.

"Hav you been guilty of imperialist dogma in break by pinching a boys cup of coco?"

"I hav."

"Hav you practised sabotage against the skool piano by cutting wires so that low C sounds plunk?"

"I hav."

"Do you admit this led to subversive singing of D'ye Ken John Plunk in his plunk so gay?"

"I do."

"Do you further admit to placing 3 tin ash trays on the top of the said piano?"

"I do."

"So that class sing D'ye tinkle plunk John plunk tinkle in his tinkle tinkle zing?"

"They did."

"Were you also a tool of wall street by interfering with the metronome while Musick mistress was singing 'Trees' at the skool concert?"

"I was."

"Did you express the view that even if the Musick mistress was a tree you would not like her planted in your garden?"

"Yes."

"Who invented the first railway engine?"

"Stalin."

"Did you pawn the boxing cup to buy beer?"

"I did."

"Hav Form 3A fallen below output target on Latin sentences?"

"They hav."

"Are you guilty of everything?"

"Very guilty indeed."

The masters are then sent off to their classes looking keen and brisk.

The bell is then rung for big skool and all xemble. Carpets are put down and all smoking forbidden old masters are hung on the walls n.b. rembrandt etc not the deaf master and all is ready. Headmaster sa:

"Do you love the old skool?"

"Yes."

(*it isn't bad sometimes acktually*)

"Do you love the staff?"

"Yes."

"Do you love the skool dog?"

"Yes."

"Wot do you think of the skool food?"

(*A pause*)

"Scrumptous, especially the smoked salmon."

"Will you all sing the skool song."

"Hurra hurra hurra."

"SKOOL-A, *SKOOL*" etc.

After this the boys are manacled to desks and all who die of boredom during french and other lessons are carried out and concealed. Matron is propped up in her chair by wooden stake and skool gardener wakened from deep sleep in onion bed.

The stage is set. *CAVE!* They're coming.

*

6

HOW TO TORTURE
PARENTS

1. *SKOOL PLAYS DISPLAYS BUN FIGHTS AND JAMBOREES*

Once a boy hav been sent to a skool the die is cast. all the
same every so often parents wake up and wonder how their
little dear is doing. It is then that the headmaster hav to
organise a pla or something which prove to parents that their
sons are worth their salt and can learn a lot of tricks if
pressed like dogs or even seals.

Imagine the scene. i am in 2B just flying a few darts or
guided misiles when molesworth 2 sa Hav you heard the
latest you are in the skool pla and must wear silk tights chiz
chiz chiz. i pause only to tuough him up and zoom off to
learn i am to be prince charming curses i shall never live this
down.

Acktually not bad as i learn part in big skool after prep
and think i am rather super.

La m'dear are you a fairy? Can so pritty a creature be
sitting in rags by the fire? I invite you to sup with me etc etc.

As i am saing this amid hale of inkpots darts rags and yells
molesworth 2 come up and sa wot are you doing molesworth
1 go on tell me o you might. I am touched by his evident
faith and recite the words but he sa if you ask me prince
charming is a naughty old man and zoom away. O for peace
and solitude to practise my art hem-hem.

When the day of the pla comes all the parents are driven into skool hall and locked in so none can escape. Prince charming zoom upon the stage and pla begin:

PRINCE CHARMING: 'pon my soul it is indeed a pritty wench. Who art thou?

CINDERELLA: I am Cinderella.

PRINCE CHARMING: Thou art not thou art peason with a lot of rouge lipstick and a straw wig and thou lookest like the wrath of god.

CINDERELLA (*dimpling*): And thou molesworth 1 thou canst not call thyself prince charming when thou hast a face like a mad baboon.

PRINCE CHARMING: I will tuough you up for that my pritty maid.

CINDERELLA: Yar boo sucks thou art much too girly in thy white silk tights that are made from i kno not wot. Thou couldst not tuough up a flea ha-ha-hee.

PRINCE CHARMING (*with a low bow*): Wilt thou with me to the ball my sweet one?

CINDERELLA: I hav seen you dancing strip the wilow in our dancing class and i kno you are like 1000 elephants o measly weed. Get thee gone or i will heave the pumpkin at thee.

PRINCE CHARMING: And i will place the fairy mice down thy unwashed neck.

(*He boweth low and his silk britches bursteth.*)

Aktually parents could not stand this kind of strong meat so we must give them the old soft soap as per ushual and sa the printed words. They then look softly at their dear ones and the paters all dream of the bar at the golf club. One day they will come to see the pla and get the horid truth.

CINDERELLA ON THE RUN. A PRINCE CHARMING WHO STUMBLE UPON A GANG-STERS MOLL. See n. molesworth as a PRINCE in search of an IDEAL. CERTIFICATE 'X'.

2. *COUNTRY DANCING*

Another form of torture for parents is the displa of country dancing on ye sham vilage green. The skool gardener is awakened from another sleep in the onion bed and skool piano wheeled from big skool revealing wizard patch of dust marbles dead beetles conkers and skeletons of boys who hav crept away to die. Piano is then carted to the green by 99 boys on ancient wheelbarrow and decorated with laurel leafs as if that could make the old grid sound any beter.

Boys then all dress up in weedy costumes with all sorts of bells everywhere and parents take their seats. miss pringle take seat at skool piano and strike huge opning chord.

WAM WAM BONK ZUNK PLUNK
(*dancers enter*)

ALL: Dilly dilly dilly dilly O
    With a rilly dilly, strawberry, o.
(*pointing toes*)

    Rilly-me Dilly me.
(*jangling a bell on the end of the nose*)

EBENEZER: Rilly-dilly jingle. Rilly-dilly jingle.
EPHRAIM: With a raspberry o.
ALL: Rilly-dilly raspberry rilly-dilly raspberry o.

Piano then goes WAM PLUNK BISH BASH ZUNK while all boys dance like mad bells jangle dogs yap babes cry squadron of heavy bombers fly overhead rane fall molesworth 2 get strangled in the mayploe man call for the telephone bill and gardener canot sleep in the onion bed.

Piano then finish RUNK DUNK RILLY ME REE etc and burst into flames. miss pringle fante and confusion reigns with super charge of mad morris dancers. In fact the only man who can really enjoy all this is the deaf master who sa he hav always liked hiathwatha and look as if he will sing onaway awake beloved for 2 pins.

Of course there are other organised forms of torture for parents recitation of loss of the royal george latin pla duet (n. molesworth and p. peason Spring song. Mendleson) chorus from mikado cristopher robin carol concerts and not least molesworth 2 who pla mightily his famous piece fairy bells which nothing hav ever been known to stop.

Any case there is only one thing for parents to sa when they recover their speech they must sa it was *much beter than last year*. Wot last year must hav been like then is a lot more than i can imagine.

3. *ASSEMBLY OF THE WIZZO SPACE SHIP*

Bung the box containing the model over to your pater and watch his face as he reads the instructions.

HOW TO ASSEMBLE IN 5 MINITS

Your box will contane the folowing parts:

> 1 cormthruster
> 1 envelop
> 6 Wizzo crabbing pins
> 4 Wizzo girders
> 10 special grabs
> 1 computator with vertical helicons

Provide yourself with Wizzo screwdriver and tube of Wizzo concrete paste (from all dealers). Get a metal drill a spirit level and welding set from your toolbox.

Gum the flap (a) to the cormthruster (c) bending towards the Wizzo girders (d) and inserting the crabbing pins. Be careful that the crabbing pins do not touch the special grabs. Iron the envelop (f) and blow it up until it is the size of a foopball and quickly insert Wizzo girders. Pierce the envelop with a Wizzo skewer (from all dealers) and carefully ease the computator into the envelop securing with the grabs. When the computator is in place adjust the helicons by marrying the cormthruster to grabs and crabbing pins.

A GAUL returning to Gaul.

Your Wizzo Space Ship is now ready for flying.

And your pater after three hours is ready for suicide n.b. as a kindly thort provide a Wizzo sledge hamer for smashing the whole thing to relieve your paters feelings. You will find he sticks to it with the Wizzo concrete paste which is super.

4. *READING ALOUD*

It hapens very often that parents think they are worred about the progress a boy is making. they do not realise that all boys are numskulls with o branes which is not surprising when you look at the parents really the whole thing goes on and on and there is no stoping it it is a vicious circle.

Some parents try to teach lat arith etc. in the hols but either they don't kno enuff or they loose their tempers and get into a terific bate. Other parents try to give culture etc and this is always disastrous.

PARENT: now nigel we hav a quiet half hour before bed i will read you the Hapy prince it is a very beatiful story indeed and will bring tears to your eyes.

SKOLAR: O.K. Super smashing and good show.

PARENT: (*in low voice full of emotion*) high above the city on a tall column stood the statue of the Hapy prince nigel will you stop looking out of the window.

SKOLAR: There's a canbera bomber going past. Look zoom wizz ee-auouw.

PARENT: Boys will be boys i supose i will start agane. High above the city on a tall col—

SKOLAR: It's coming back eeeeeeeee-au-oooooooo.

PARENT: (*with patience*) Column stood the statue of the Hapy prince. He was gilded all over with thin leaves of fine gold.

SKOLAR: Machine guns eh-uh-uh-uh-uh-uh-uh.

PARENT: You kno old chap this is an absolutely tip-top tale but it is no use my reading if you are going to shoot down the enemy like that. Please listen.

SKOLAR: I *am* listning.

PARENT: Where was i for eyes he had two bright sapphires and a large——

SKOLAR: How long would it take to fly to the moon?

PARENT: What hav that to do with this beatiful tale of the Hapy prince?

SKOLAR: Absolutely o with some of the planets you would be 823 before you got there.

PARENT: (*sticking to it*) he is as beatiful as a weathercock remarked one of the town councillors hav you got a handkerchief nigel as this tale gets sad later on a swallow strips the prince of all his gold.

SKOLAR: Did he sell it. O gosh.

PARENT: Why do you sa o gosh. The tale is beatiful becos of the loveliness of the prose it may help you to hav a beter charakter nigel. It may——

(but SKOLAR is not listening he is throing chalk at a black beetle on the window. PARENT chucks the book at him in a collossal rage and stumps off to hav a drink.)

Parent stumps off to hav a drink.

Parents at a Glance

I always think character is more
important than brains.

But we *always* give him gin!

I've brought him some chocs, a
comic, an air gun, a pound of
Turkish Delight and can he come
home next Wednesday?

When I was a boy we got
six of the best every day. Made
me what I am.

And what's behind this wee door?

No darling Schopenhauer did not *quite* mean that.

I don't care if Mrs Bradbury did run for Britain I'm still going to have a cocktail.

I am sorry about his vest and pants but when he was a little boy he always wore combinations.

I think sometimes parents may wonder whether we
are worth the sacrifices they make for us.

7

SKOOL FOOD

OR THE PIECE OF COD
WHICH PASSETH UNDERSTANDING

1. *ETIQUTTE*

Many boys find themselves quite incapable of making any
rude comments on skool food. This is hardly good maners
hem-hem and i must impress on all cads and bounders who
sa poo gosh when they see a skool sossage to mend their
ways.

When faced with a friteful piece of meat which even the
skool dog would refuse do not screw up the face in any
circs and sa coo ur gosh ghastly. This calls atention to
oneself and makes it more difficult to pinch a beter piece
from the next boy.

Rice PUDINGS and jely in the poket are not a good
mixture with fluff and the ushual nauseating contents. Sometimes you can chiz a bit of pink mange into a hankchief but
it is apt to be a bit hard to manage when bloing the nose.
peason hav tried green peas up the sleeve but no good really
as they all come shooting down again.

We in our skool are proud of our maners which maykth
us the weeds we are and when grabber shoot peas from peashooter at the deaf master we are much shoked i do not
think. Nor do we make lakes of treacle in the poridge or
rivers of gravy through the mashed potatoes perish the
thort.

AT TABLE

Acktually whatever boys may sa about skool food the moment deaf master sa lord make us truly etc. whole skool descend upon food with roar like an H bomb and in 2 minits all hav been swept bare. We then hav time for interval of uplifting conversation

i sa e.g.

i think aldous huxley is rather off form in point counter-point, peason. And he repli i simply couldn't agree with you more rat face but peason is very 4th rate and hav not got beyond buldog drummond. Anyway then the next course come and all boys disappear in a cloud of jely blanch mange plums and aple while treacle tart fly in all directions.

WITHDRAWAL

When the repast is finished the head of the skool or head-master should wait for a moment until the conversation shows some small signs of flagging then rising to his feet he indicates that the meal is at an end and the lades may with-draw.

Acktually if he waited for the conversation to flag he would be sitting there until tea time when it would all begin agane. Wot he does is to bawl Silence at the top of his voice separate three tuoughs who are fiting and the whole skool charge into the coridor except molesworth 2 who is pinching the radio malt.

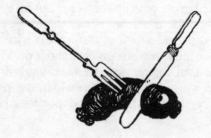

A ROMAN returning to Rome.

2. *A NIGHTMARE*

Everbode kno all there is to kno about prunes but anyway the other day i dreamed about them and this is what hapned.

THE REVOLT OF THE PRUNES

by

n. molesworth.

Once upon a time there was a tribe of savvage prunes who lived in a blak mass in the skool pantry.

The prunes had been brought from the prune country where they lived hapily tuoughing each other up and indulging in cotage industries. Then one day JASPER the huge headmaster with huge and hairy hands from grasping the kane descended upon the prunes and caried them off in his case.

So the prunes lay in the pantry and on Mon tue wed thur and fri the cook came in and chose a few to cook for the boys.

At last a prune more savvage than the rest spoke up.

'There is no future in this,' he said. 'Absolutely none at all.'

'And do you hear what they *sa* about us?' said a sensitive prune.

'The only one who eats us is molesworth 2,' piped up another, 'but he would eat anything.'

A fourth said:

'Imagine being inside molesworth 2 with all those comon lozenges spangles carots radio malt and all the other things he hav pinched.'

This thort was so ghastly that the prunes were silent for 24 hours until the chief prune spoke agane.

'We must rise up,' he sa.

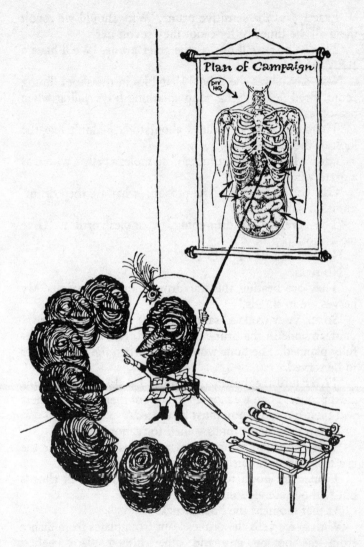

Meanwhile in the prune camp the Revolt had been carefully planned.

'Exactly,' sa the sensitive prune. 'Why should we revolt them all the time? Why canot they revolt *us*?'

'That's what we'll do,' sa the chief prune. 'We'll have a REVOLT.'

Next day it was the ushual shambles in the skool dining room. Bred pelets flying soup splashing boys yeling when peason sa:

'There are a lot of prunes about toda. i don't like the look of them.'

'*i* don't like the taste of them,' sa molesworth 1 who was a grate wit.

'Can you hear drums?' sa peason. 'what are they drumming for sahib?'

'They are always drumming,' sa molesworth 1. 'Give me a chota peg boy.'

He then call BOY BOY BOY.

No repli.

'They are beating the war drums,' quaver peason. 'My nerves are in shreds.'

'So are your trousis,' sa molesworth wittier than ever.

Meanwhile in the prune camp the Revolt had been carefully planned. The hour would strike when the prunes were to be served.

'JASPER the headmaster must be slain first,' sa the chief prune. 'Then we mop up the rest of them. No prisoners will be taken not a boy must be spared.'

So ten thousand prunes waited for action.

'Cuh i sa gosh i mean to say its prunes agane,' came the cry from sixty throats.

'Prunes are good for you,' repli the masters in chorus but without conviction.

At that moment the hour struck.

With fierce yells the prunes leapt from plates from dishes from the boxing cup and other hiding places yeling fiercely.

JASPER the headmaster was the first victim. When

Jasper died horribly.

he saw the prunes he gave a yell of fright his false teeth
shot across the room and lodged in the opposite wall. The
boys noticed no difrence. they thort he was shouting at
molesworth 1 as ushual.

While JASPER died horibly all was calm at molesworth's table.

'the trouble with you peason,' sa molesworth 1, 'is that
the country is geting you. you need furlo.'

'Its the jungle the ceaseless noise the cries of the jackals.'

'if you can hear a jackal in this dining room you'll be
jolly lucky,' sa molesworth.

He larffed a little.

'Perhaps it is we who get on each other's nerves,' sa
peason reflectively. Then he jumped up gasping:

'Look the prunes are marching out of the dining room
door!'

That was what saved the boys.

The chief prune was a regular soldier and the moment the
Revolt broke out he did what all generals do. He burrowed
underground and established his headquarters. He had a lot
of relations and made them all staff prunes.

Then he poured over the map.

'We should strike here,' said the Chief Prune.

'Yes sir,' said the G One prune.

'Yes sir,' said the G Two prune.

'Yes sir,' said the G Three prune.

But unfortunately he hapned to be pointing at the dining
room door so the whole army of prunes marched out of
sight and could not be brought into the batle.

It took the skool half an hour to realize that JASPER
the headmaster was dead murdered by the prunes. Then all
the masters quareled who would wield the kane. At molesworth's table he was recovering from a siesta when the news
was brought.

'Dead?' he said. 'By whom?' (Grammer.)

'The prunes are openly revolting.'

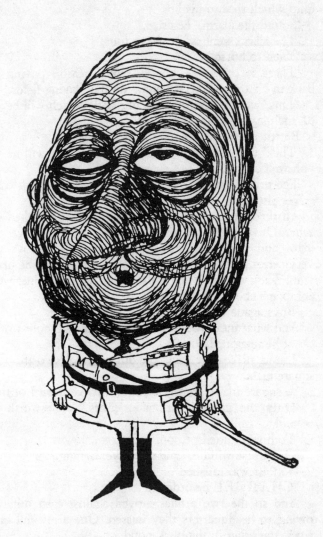

'Yes sir,' said the G One prune.

molesworth by a grate act of heroism choked back the quip which rose to his lips.

'Sound the alarm,' he cried.

'The alarm went off at ten to four.'

'Then to horse.'

'There is only one horse,' replid peason paying him back in his own coin. 'They are on the playing fields.'

'This,' said molesworth, 'is one batle which will be won on the playing fields of eat 'em.'

But there was no responsive larffter.

'This,' sa moleswoth 1, 'is one batle which will be won –oh well carry on.'

The prunes encamped on the onion bed the boys on the criket pitch.

All through the night the oposing forces watched each other. Down in the headquarters both staffs pored over their maps and there was fitful conversation. The boys were very serious. they realized what would hapen if the prunes won. They would be put in the larder and the prunes would complane about them.

'Boys agane toda ugh,' the prunes would sa.

And what they would sa when they tasted molesworth 2 canot be imagined.

'Let us strike here,' said the duke of molesworth. 'Form square men.'

'A square man?' said peason. 'Who ever heard of that?'

'Only the general can make jokes,' molesworth said coldly.

'To horse!' cried peason.

'One horse will do,' said the duke, larffing.

Honour was satisfied.

'CHARGE!' he ordered.

And so the two armies moved against each other but owing to headquarters they missed. One army fell in the river, the other in the duck pond.

The noise in fact was so grate that it woke JASPER

the headmaster who had not been murdered at all but was thinking of latin sentences. With a croak of rage he grasped his kane and rolled out cursing in the name of Beelzebub. He gave six of the best to every boy on sight but i am glad to sa that the prunes were all drowned in the duck pond.

It was a sad loss to JASPER but there was only one thing to do. He sat down and ordered some more.

All drowned in the duck pond.

Curtain Speech

Well that is all there is to kno about skool but it is alright becos the end of the term is in sight cheers cheers cheers. All boys get together with super rags wheezes japes and pranks. Down with the masters no more latin no more french no more sitting on the hard old bench no more earwigs in our stew etc. Pilow fights and feasts in the dorm. Noble boys make bonfires of skool books and toast the staff slowly in the flames Charge at everbode and zoom around.

So the bus arives goodbye to all goodbye to skool pig and skool dog to matron one and all sa hav a good hols we weep with joy. Goodbye headmaster goodbye peason acktually you are joly d. and it is sad to leave. Goodbye to all goodbye.

HOW TO BE TOPP

Cave !

You kno who this is e.g. Me nigel molesworth the curse of st custard's. I can't be a sec becos they hav got me on the run and all the headmasters in britain are after me with their GATS and COSHES ect. I kno what it means when they catch up tho actually headmasters seldom do they are fat and canot run for tooffe.

At the moment I am using the natural history museum as a hideout. My friend peason sa i shall be safe there as they will not tell me from all the newts stoats bats and tiny crawling creatures they hav there chiz.

Anyway there is just time to give my felow suferers the fruits of my xperience. You could becom topp if you want to but most pupils do not. If they use this book they could come half way up or even botom hem-hem. Hist! A noise! If they get me before long this will help to cary on the good work. i confess it was me who pinched the cheese from the matron's mousetrap. Hard cheese on the mouse ha-ha. It was me who—

Blud   Blud

1

BACK TO SKOOL AGANE!

This is wot it is like when we go back on the skool trane. There are lots of new bugs and all there maters blub they hav every reason if they knew what they were going to. For us old lags however it is just another stretch same as any other and no remision for good conduc. We kno what it will be like at the other end Headmaster beaming skool bus ratle off leaving trail of tuck boxes peason smugling in a box of flat 50 cigs fotherington-tomas left in the lugage rack and new bugs stand as if amazed. Skool now smell not only of chalk latin books skool ink foopball boots and birdseed but carbolic soap as well. White jugs stand in rows in the dorms and various weeds are about the place looking unaturaly clean and civilised. Who knows what adventures in work and pla the next term will bring forth. And who cares, eh?

2

HOW TO SUCCEED AS
A NEW BUG

New bugs are wets and weeds their mummies blub when they kiss them goodbye while seniors such as me hem-hem stand grimly by licking their slobering chops. No more dolies or William the bear to cuddle and hug, no more fairy stories at nanny's knee it is all aboard the fairy bus for the dungeons. You hav to hav a bit of patience but once the trane moves out the little victims are YOURS. You put them in the lugage rack with molesworth 2.

Paters at the moment are patting the blubing maters.

'It is all right old gurl,' they sa. 'Skools are not wot they were in my day. Boys are no longer cruel to each other and the masters are frends.'

'But my Eustace hav been taken away. He is only a baby.'

(*You are dead right he is. Fancy sending him to skool with a name like Eustace. They deserve it all.*)

Pater stare at his glass of gin reflectively. It will be peaceful at home now. He can relax at the weekends and if it is a good skool Eustace will soon be strong and brany enuff to bring in the coal. He sa:

'Now in my day it was diferent. When i first went to Grunts they tosted me on a slo fire. Then i ran the gauntlet being flicked with wet towels. Then they stood me aganst the mantelpeace as i am standing now—'

BANG! CRASH!

Mater gives him sharp uper cut folowed by right cross then zoom up to bed leaving pater wondering why women are so unpredictable. Glumly he pours himself another gin.

MEANWHILE AT ST CUSTARDS . . . . . .

Eustace hav been trussed to a chair and a pair of socks are stuffed in his mouth to stifle his desperate cries. 'Now,' sa molesworth the Pukon 'we will submit you to three trillion volts of the nuclear torturer.' . . .

DOWN BELOW IN THE STUDY . . . . . .

Tinkle, tinkle.

Is that the telephone, my dere?

Nothing else go tinkle, tinkle, sweethart, unless it be the photograph of that repulsive old custardian in its brite silver frame. Shall I answer?

Pray do.

Tinkle, tink—

It is mrs togglington to enquire after Eustace. Oh yes he hav setled down very well. He was as quiet and as good as a lamb.

(Thinks: Which one was he?)

Yes, there is no need to wory. He hav no spots his head do not ache his knok knees hav given him no trouble. He is as far as we kno unlikely to develop a disease tonite. He hav changed his socks and cleaned his fangs. I have put him in the charge of a v. reliable boy e.g. dere little nigel molesworth.

Eustace mater ring off very relieved cheers cheers and telephone all the other lades about it. Headmaster and wife continue to make wool rug. Masters shiver in their cells. An owl hoot and Eustace is insensible. St custard's hav begun another term.

TEKNEEK FOR NEW BUGS

HOW NOT TO SUCCEED

New bug is lying back in best chair in the library in portion of the room reserved for prefects. He is eating sweets. Head of the skool enters who hav been chosen for his qualities of leadership devotion to st custard's ect. In other words he is grabber and joly tuough.

GRABBER: You hav a face like a flea and you could not lift a cucumber.

new bug (with a yawn): Tu quoque, oaf. You also hav a face like a flea and could not lift wot the french call a concombre.

GRABBER: Do you kno who you are talking to?

new bug: Can it be stalin?

GRABBER: i am head of the skool captin of games martial of the squash courts custodian of shooting and garter principal of the natural history museum.

new bug: So what? i am not impressed by wot I hav seen around here. The old brigade hav been in too long. There hav got to be changes. The younger generation is knoking at the door hav some buble gum.

GRABBER: Wot's your name?

new bug: the lord cedric furnival crabthorn percy constance charles plunk. (*He blows a balloon in his buble gum cooly*) you may call me pongo.

(*Exit.*)

SUCCESS

In order to sukceed all new bugs should take a vow of silence for 1 year. When a senior pass they should lie down and let him walk over them. They should ofer swetes saing go on take the whole bag. They must clean shoes and think

of pleasing others. They should not shout molesworth is a
grate big wet then run away to matron.

Aktualy you canot ever get new bugs to behave like that
and the best thing is to avoid them If you get put in charge
of them it is like a film of sno white all in technicolour or 3D
or something.

> *new bugs are all sitting on toadstools in forest plaing with
> lambs and deers. Birds flit about. Enter molesworth growling
> and cursing.*

come here you horrid ticks!

(*All cower the forest goes dark.*)

do you hear me ticks. You will all get six!
A robin: tweet!
who said that? i will bash the lot of you. i will utterly
tuough you up.

(*Thunder: all the new bugs deer and lambs run away.
Litening pla around my horns.*)

get your handiwork cracking produce your plastissene
for free xpresion and the other wedy things you do.

(*i catch a new bug and let him dance on the palm of my hand.*)

a new bug: you are not tuough.
  Wot me?
a new bug: you hav a hart of gold.
  Discovered! Curses!
a new bug: won't you pla with us?
  No!
a new bug: Come on fellers he won't hurt you he is a
  grate big sham.
All: hee-hee-hee-hee! *They dance back with lambs and
robins. The sun come out and i find myself singing a song
with them chiz chiz chiz chiz chiz.*

Rake's Progress

1. this is parkinson. I want you to help him settle down.

2. Here is your desk, parkinson.

3. Here are some sums. Let us see if you can add.

4.

5.

6.

7.

8.

New bugs often canot write xcept this way:—

The Space*Ship v

However miss pringle soon lik them into shape. She get out her gat and sa: You may look like a lot of new-born babes in yore first grey shorts but it won't wash with me. I am going to hav it MY way. O.K. let's go. All the gifts of sno-drops, aples sweets and ginger biskits do not alter her iron purpose. Before long a new bug can do in his copy-book

The cate sat on

And finally

The love of the poets is a fing apart

He is now in the same spot as the rest of us he hav to write home on Sunda. You would think that this precious link between skool and our dear ones would be cherished by all boys. In fact, let us face it, boys do not like writing home chiz and for a joly good reason. *There is nothing to sa.* Why? Because the truth is so shoking and unspekable that no parent could stand it on a Monday morning. So we hav to gloss it over as it is no use upseting your mater particularly at brekfast on Monday morning.

New bugs when they start writing leters are inclined to be emotional chiz they are a lot of sissies:—

st. custard's,

Darling mama, darling papa,

i mis you very much. i am lonly. plees kiss my golly-wog. never did I apreciate so much the joys and com-forts of home life. To think that i was rud to grandad that i scremed when i was told to hav a bath. And how many times hav i refused to come in and go to bed. O woe. Kiss my gollywog agane.

Yours fathefuly

binkie.

nb you had beter kiss grandad too. Or not. As you plese.

After a bit, though, a new bug gets over this sort of stuff. i mean gollywogs and tedy bears, I ask you! i would not be suprised if som of them hav not a doll which say Mama Mama and go to slepe. Aktualy some toys are not bad. i had a super monkey called spinach of whom (grammer) i was very fond. i would always go to slepe with it nestling on my pilow and . . . . CHIZ! CURSES! wot am i saying?

Leters home in the end develop into a contest between parent and weeny one which come into a full crescendo in middle-life hem-hem as they sa in some of the sunda papers. Note the cooling of the ardour. O woe agane but that is the tragedy nb paters and maters we still luv you reely. Beter than our gollywogs anyway.

LETER:

st. custard's

Sunda.

Dearest Mummy (and Daddy)

We played aganst porridge court on saturday. We lost 9 – o. The film was a western. Will you send me a bakterial gun. They are 6/6 at grabbers.

With love from

Nigel.

ANSER:

Barleywaters.
Clotshire.
Monda

My dearest darling most beloved nigel,

It was marvelous super to get your lovely long leter with all its news. I have telephoned grabbers to send the gun. *Are you taking your lozenges?* Please let me kno. Wot a shame about porridge court i xpect you will win next year. [hem-hem. not a hope]. There is very litle to tell you. the snodrops are out and yore father is in a filthy temper but these facts hav nothing to do with each other. Do not forget, darling, to let me kno about the lozenges

Your fondest superest ever-loving

Mummy.

P.S. *Don't* forget about the lozenges, darling.

LETER :

st. custard's.

Sunda.

Dear Mummy and Daddy,

We played aganst howler house on Saturday. We lost 9 – o. The film was micky mouse. Thank you for the bakterial gun. Will you send me a jet-propeled airship. (17/6)

Love from

nigel.

ANSER :

Barleywaters, Clotshire.

My ever-darlingest superest most smashing and admired son Nigel,

Your letter was a wonderful surprise and so full of news. Your handriting hav improved beyond mesure. *You did not mention about the lozenges darling will you be sure and let me kno next time.* Do not wory too much about your lessons i kno you are doing your best. The crocus are out now but yore father is still in a filthy temper so i hav ordered the jet-propeled airship myself. Don't forget about the lozenges and Gollywog send his love.

Your most tremendously affectionate divinely superly adoring mater

Mummy

p.s   don't forget about the lozenges.

LETER: st. custard's
                                          Sunda.

Mummy,

    (A) v poopwell hall. Lost 6 – o.

    (B) tarzan of the apes.

    (c) a self-propelling car (£125 – o – o.)

                Yrs.

                    nigel.

OTHER CORESPONDENCE

Of course we do not only get leters from our parents. There are leters from gurl friends and the ushual sekretarial mail as hon. sec. of the youth club hem-hem. There are also those leters which you put away hastily after reading the first line. e.g. *Dere molesworth, Yore overdraft facilities are due for review.* – or *2/- each way Claptrap. You win o. You lose 4/- prompt setlement will enable us to kepe our books in order.* All of these are a chiz and on the whole no good comes of them. let us pass to more siggnificant things.

FOR THE TINIES

Some new bugs are so well educcated at their dame skools that they can read when they get to st custards. They will soon forget after a term or 2 give them time give them time. Meanwhile their ever-loving parents send them maggazines and storybooks every thursday chiz to keep alite the dying flame of kulture.

*Price 6d. Published by grabber and grabber, who would luv
to give it away to the tinies. Indeed they would if it were not
that the little ones must learn that it is only by your own
eforts that suksess is won in life hem-hem ask old mr grabber.*

THE ADVENTURES OF DIPPY-DOPEY

Dippy-Dopey love-s his cat. He br-ings the cat
m-ilk. The cat wishes some-thing strong-er. mee-
aouw he sa mee-aouw give me a ry-e on the rocks
so c-old that it would fr-eeze an esk-i-mo ig-loo.
Ver-y well sa Dippy-Dopey i will try be-cos i luv
my cat. Dippy-Dopey runs to town on the toy-
land trane. He goes to his old friend Trash, who
is a dis-rep-u-table li-on. i want a rye-on-the-
rocks for the cat cry Dippy-Dopey. Growl sa Trash
i will fix that id-le fo-ol good and pro-per. He
k-nock up a white-e lad-y in a jif-fy. Dippy-Dopey
run back into the woods with the liquid. Where
you been sa the cat where you been pour me out a
slug quick-ly. He drinks it back. He drinks a-noth-
er. And a-noth-er. Now we can go to sleep sa
Dippy-Dopey.

St Custard's Explaned

A small experiment in piktorial education for clots who don't kno about it. Designed and produced by n. molesworth

1. The peason-molesworth space ship threatened by wild mercurian maths masters lies disabled in the onion bed of the kitchen garden.

2. Meanwhile in the master's common room. Sigismund arbuthnot the mad maths master musters his rhomboids.

3. Time off for tea and seed cake. That is peason on the left he is not bad he is my grate friend. My bro molesworth 2 is eating cake as per ushual he is uterly wet and a weed. The other one is me Captain molesworth the inter-planetary clot cheers cheers.

4. A new recruit for the hard-pressed crew. Aktually it is only fotherington-tomas you kno he sa Hullo clouds hullo sky he is a girlie and love the scents and sounds of nature tho the less i smell and hear them the better.

5. Wandsworth the skool dog trots up with the missing fusion percolater in his fatheful jaws.

6. Sigismund looks at us through his all-seeing videoscope. We look at him. Impasse.

7. A new plot.

8. Bound and gagged the crew are led into Divinity class.

9. Divinity lesson.

10. Meanwhile . . .

11. grabber blasts the walls with his cosmic disintegrator. he is head of the skool and a bit dim but we had to give him this part.

12. Escape!

13. The peason-molesworth space ship takes off (more next week if you have the neccessessary d's otherwise jane is not bad value).

ALL THERE IS TO KNO ABOUT SPACE

There is very little mistery about Space these days at least
not to us boys who hav grown up with it. It is just a lot of
planets dotted about the place and if you want the gen about
them here it is.

THE MOON: This is rather trippery these days as it is only
239000 miles away. Besides it is rather disappointing when
you hav been fired all that distance and spent about
six years of your life in a space ship to step out and find a
lot of craters and moon canals. Agane there is no air so
noone can breathe which make things a bit dificult. On
the other hand you can jump three times as high as you
can on earth but so can everyone else so there is not much
fun in it.

URANUS: This is 1782 million miles away and you hav to
pass through a belt of planetoids to get there. It is well worth
it when you do but that is rather unlikely in your time becos
it would take so long to reach that it would be your grate
grand child who would hav the fun i.e. he would be
murdered by the PUKON and his TREENS. Agane it seme
to be rather a long way to go for that.

MARS: Mars would be all right if it were not for the Martians
who are quite beyond the pail. Always fighting always
quareling no peace at all for the sound of space pistols,
H-bombs, gamma-ray guns, bakterial cannons, Z-destruc-
tors and A-integgraters it might be Big skool at st custards
in brake. I must sa it would be a bit beter if headmasters
zoomed in to take the next lesson in a mini-helicopter like
the PUKON do from his space palace but you canot hav
everything particularly at skool where you get practically
o xcept latin and the kane. It would be nice to get to kno
some of martian skoolboys but they are moluscs with gogle
eyes who talk in high-pitched squeaks. They goble their

mars veg and they are most unsavory they do not wash. Not a bit like us. Or are they hem-hem?

SATURN: You can always recognise Saturn when you zoom towards it at the speed of light. First of all it hav 9 little moons and then three rings. Plunge past these, give it full gravity reaction, ease to half, pick up the first space beacon, turn right at the church, flatten out, blo the space tanks and go in to land . . . . . . CRASH WAM BLAM BUMP so you see it is not so very diferent from landing on the earth. And what is it when you get here? The people my dear are such bores. Very hospitable of course but what do you hav in comon with walking toadstools which is what they are. The rest of them are giant bullfrogs and that is, when you come to think of it, not much beter. They croak and bark. Beter to stay at home really the people at parties there are like bullfrogs and they croak and bark to. But they don't hop out of the window and pinch your space ship. If they pinch anything it's – enuff said hem-hem.

SPACE COMPLANTE: Space is getting a bit congested these days what with all the daring space aces who come out every Friday price 4d. It makes it a bit dificult to get a decent adventure the PUKON is taken up with one VORA with another. You try the vilaninous SHAZAM. Zoosh- Zee-Zeeeeee. . . . So you want to play it ruff, Shazam eh: but he sa go away chiz i am planing to invade mercury with a milion trilion space transports. All the fatheful chaps from other planets who hav names like KONX and carvel and faces it is hard to describe hav disapeared along with the saturnians and mercurians who are fortifying their uranium cities. In fact they are all so taken up with xplosions and zooming about that they hav no time for you. Even when you blast them with your gamma-ray pistol – *ziff-ziff-ziff-ziff* – they take no notice. So there is only one thing to do – zoosh – and go off home to tuough up molesworth 2.

3

AKQUIRE CULTURE AND
KEEP THE BRANE CLEAN

HOW TO BE TOPP IN LATIN

All skools make some sort of show at teaching the pupils things and the headmaster pin up a huge timetable of lessons ect. which make the heart sink when you look at it. I mean do the grate british nation understand that thousands of its young elizabthans are looking at latin ugh before there brekfast hav even settled. i mean to sa how would they like saing monerer monereris moneretur ect. at that hour eh?

Actually it is quite easy to be topp in lat. you just have to work chiz chiz chiz. Otherwise, there are various ways of taking your mind from it such as altering shorter latin primer into shortbread eating primer and if my name you wish to see turn to page one hundred and three. After that you just stare gloomily at stems in labials form Nom and hope for the best.

The only best that can hapen is when the BELL ring cheers cheers cheers and you can stop puting blotch paper into the inkwell.

Meanwhile lat. master drones on. He is always frightfully keen on lat. which he call classicks amo amas amat gender rhymes bonus and hic haec hoc which he quote with glee. Fancy a grown man saying hujus hujus hujus as if he were proud of it it is not english and do not make SENSE.

Lat. masters are always convinced that lat. is easy quite pappy. They encourage you. It is so *simple* molesworth they cry if you will only try.

Now go at it quite calmly.

Tandem novum quidem et inauditum consilium capit . . .

Simple eh hav a hart like all lat. it is just all BOSH.
Sometimes they think they will trick you into liking lat.
by having a latin pla. Latin plas are like this –

THE HOGWARTS
by
MARCUS PLAUTUS MOLESWORTHUS

Sene One. The villa of Cotta at Rome. Enter CORTICUS a
dreary old slave and RADIX his mate.

CORTICUS: (*laying a skin of wine on the sideboard*) Eheu!
(*The headmaster and all lat. masters who watch roar
with larffter.*)

RADIX: Eheu!
(*More larffter they are in stiches*)

CORTICUS: Eheu!

RADIX: Eheu!
(*The curtain falls as the masters roll helplessly in the
aisles.*)

Sene Two. A tavern off the Via apia. Enter MENSA a dirty
old man followed by ANNUS his shieldbearer.

MENSA: Tot quot, clot.

ANNUS: Tu quoque, clotie.

(They trip over each other's togas. An ancient Briton
enters in chains.)

BRITON: Turn it up now turn it up.

(*The curtain falls with all masters in hysterics.*)

Sene Three. The Capitol. Cotta and his wife are at breakfast.

COTTA: Quid est pabulum?

WIFE: (*handing the cornflakes*) Vis.

COTTA: Eheu!

> *IDIOTICUS their son enters singing to the lyre.*

IDIOTICUS: To nouns that canot be declined
              The neuter gender is assigned.
              Bebop bebop
              Examples fas and nefas give
              And the Verb-Noun Infinitiv.

(*This is too much for the masters who join rolicking in
the chorus. The geese begin to quack and all the actors forget
their lines. Curtain.*)

MOLESWORTH V MORON & MORON
(*peason intervening*)

If you do not partikularly care a buton if you are topp
or not, one of the best things is to get into a DISCUSSION
about it (in English). Like this. You put aside your dab-
criket (cowdrey 2002) and look v. puzzled and with a thirst
for knoledge.

Sir?
Be quiet molesworth! Get on with your exercise.
No sir really sir.
Well, what is it? (Thinks: a possible trap?)

Then you sa:

What is the *use* of latin sir?

Master clutches the board ruber but he knos he is beaten this one always rouses the mob. The class breaks into an uproar with boos catcalls and cries of 'Answer!' The master begin

er well er that er quite simple molesworth. latin is er classicks you kno and classicks are – well they are er – they are the studies of the ancient peoples.

SIR NIGEL MOLESWORTH Q.C. So what?

er latin gives you not only the history of Rome but er (*hapy inspiration*) its culture, it er tells you about interesting men like J. Caesar, hannibal, livy, Romulus remus and er lars porsena of clusium.

SIR NIGEL MOLESWORTH, Q.C. And the Gauls you do not mention the Gauls. Would you not consider them interesting.

O most certainly.

SIR NIGEL MOLESWORTH Q.C. (*consulting his brief*) I observe from the work of this class that the Gauls hav atacked the camp with shouts they hav frightened the citizens they hav killed the enemy with darts and arows and blamed the belgians. They hav also continued to march into Italy. Would it not be more interesting if they did something new?

er possibly.

SIR NIGEL MOLESWORTH Q.C. Would you perhaps explane why latin never deals with the exploits of nero and one or two of the fruitier emperors. Or empresses for that mater?

(*The master is silent clutching the board ruber convulsilvely. Sir Nigel looks round the court with a meaning look*)

That is my case, m'lud.

(*He sits down on the inkwell which peason hav shoved under him.*)

That is my case, m'lud

Aktually it never really hapens like that. You hav to listen to the same old stuff about latin giving you depth and background. It is also the base of english words but it canot be base enuff for me chiz.

Another wizard wheeze is to look up something really tricky in the grammer e.g. gerunds which are always tricky and shifty if you ever get as far as looking at them. What hapens is as follows:

Hand up (*Silence for 5 minits*)

Sir (*whisper no repli*)

Hand up agane. (*3 minits two secs.*)

What is it, molesworth?

Sir, what is a gerund? (*Master stare at you as if amazed*)

What is what? (He hav never heard of it)

A gerund, sir.

You ought to kno that. Look it up, boy. (*working himself into a rage*) really the ignorance of 2B they are the worst form i hav ever taken. What is a gerund, indeed! Worse than 3A last year! Much worse.

But what *is* a gerund, sir?

I hav told you look it up look it up look it up. (*turning the leaves of the grammer beneath the desk*) A gerund is a – it is a verbal substantive, molesworth, declined like neuters of the second declension any fule knos that. It seems to me extraordinary ect . . . . . .

It is a pity really that you can't cob masters cribbing and get them 6 of the best but there it is. Festina lente as we say to each other lightly at brake. Festina lente or I'll bash you up.

The Private Life of the Gerund

The gerund attacks some peaceful pronouns

Kennedy discovers the gerund and leads it back into captivity

A gerund shut out. No place for it in one of my sentences

Social snobery. A gerund 'cuts' a gerundive

LATIN PROSE

In the end you hav to come face to face with latin and here is the sort of thing that apperes and my coments.

Test. (3 weakly.) Into Latin:

a) *The ramparts of the enemy are long.*

How long that is the point? If we kno how long they are we can march to the end and go round. Otherwise we must bring up the ballista and catapult our men over. In any case why bother me. Labienus is your man third tent on the right. Hand me back my chisel i am writing to mum.

b) *The boy's head is small, his feet are big.*
Ho! He hav also a face like a wild baboon, arms like a flea and a nose like a squished turnip. He is uterly wet and a weed and it is obviously my grate friend peason.

c) *All the cavalry are on the right wing.*
I ask you! they just chase the ball like the ticks in the third game. Look at Caesar. What's he doing there when he ought to be on the left wing eh? Labienus Cotta and Balbus – what a half-back line. *Mark your men!* Get back in gole, Remus! Wot a shambles i ask you no wonder the hungarians beat them.

d) *Do you always carry your books on your head?*
No, not always. Sometimes i carry an iron bar or a basket of washing on it it depends on my mood. What, then, do i do with my books? i deface them tear off the covers thro them at fotherington-tomas churn them about in my desk make blotches on them and make tunels with them for my trains. What business is it of yours anyway?

e) *Does the clear voice of the girl delight your ears?*
i might hav known it.

THE MOLESWORTH DAY-DREAM
SERVICE 1

Are you fatigued? Bored, run-down, depressed? Are Caesar and Labienus too much for you? Do the Gauls want to make you scream?

The answer is simple.

Help yourself to a MOLESWORTH DAY-DREAM. Simple, easy to operate. No gadgets. Just detach yourself from the hum-drum work of the class and stare out of the window with your mouth open.

THE GRATE ST CUSTARD'S FLOOD

Up Up Up the swirling waters rise steadily. The vegetable garden and playing fields are a sea of water old foopball boots float in the skool yard. Inside corridors and classrooms are deep in water. Another pair of foopball boots floats by with molesworth 2 beneath them.

'That proves,' i sa, reeling him in, 'that you are uterly wet.'

In his study the headmaster sits at his desk with the waters rising to his nose.

'What is it?' he sa irritably at my knock.

'Sir the skool is flooded.'

'Go away boy don't worry me report it to the master on duty.'

At this point the waters gurgle into his pipe putting it out with a rore and hiss of steam. The matron, carried by the current, drifts in through the window. She smiles wanly but says nothing.

'What is this molesworth?' sa the headmaster. 'If this is another of your jokes i warn you there may be serious konsequences.'

At that moment a bust of Shakespeare falls upon his head.

'Great Scott!' he exclames. 'What the Dickens is that?'
(Ha-Ha)

Then he give a grate cry: 'My kanes! They are drifting away.'

Too late the kanes join the swirling jetsam of beetles prunes sossages protractors bungies masters maps foopballs and conkers which hav risen like a scum to the surface. Stuned with his loss headmaster fall insensible.

The galant boys, meanwhile, hav climbed upon floating blakboards benches and tubs. They punt peacefully across the skool yard. The chivalrous molesworth hav prudence entwhistle the beautiful under-matron upon his craft hem-hem

PRUDENCE: How peaceful it is upon the waters nigel.

ME: (*blushing benethe my boater*) i hav rather a nasty hack on my shin and can i have a clean handkerchief.

PRUDENCE: Don't let us talk of everyday things nigel. Am i beautiful

ME: Gosh ur coo i mean to say gosh.

(*We glide benethe the green shade of a willow. There is silence.*)

ME: Prudence –

PRUDENCE: Yes, nigel?

ME: i think on the whole mumps are beter than measles.

(*With a strangled cry she thro the cucumber sandwiches at me.*)

Back at skool the headmaster, recovered, addresses the survivors.

'It is not my rule,' he sa, 'to grant additional half-hols during termtime. As the waters are above the ceiling, however, work may stop after this period.'

WOW! WIZZ! CHEERS! SUPER!

WAM! A volume of Livy uneringly thrown strike my nose. It is followed by a piece of chalk into my open mouth. That is the worst of dreams. They fade and one must come back to reality chiz. Quibus quibus quibus but who cares?

Grate Latin Lies

The customs of the Gauls were honourable

Great crimes were rare in ancient times

The girls were beautiful

All the Romans love home

4

A FEW MOMENTS IN THE UNDERWORLD

It is no use sooner or later it has to come you must talk about your felow sufferers e.g. the boys with whom you are forced to mingle. Some are strong others are weedy so it is quite simple.

If boys are strong you sa gosh grabber it was too bad you made a duck at criket it was dashed bad luck you hapned to make a blind swipe and thereby lost the match. The ball was a googly which had you not closed your eyes tight you mite hav seen. (*Tact*)

If a boy is weedier than you it is diferent you sa Look at little baby made a duck little baby couldn't hit a flea. (*Get tuough policy*)

Of course weedy boys always rely on WORDS. e.g. How many did you make last time molesworth?

o

Yar boo sucks l b w i supose the old story i would not swank if i were you after all some are selekted others are not some hav an aptitude for the game others just slog. Slogging never got anyone anywhere.

(This is the time when you spring upon him mightily and proove that criket may be all very well but not very realistic in the modern world where anyone may next moment be going to mars. Xcept of course that mars may hav a joly good team which can make 10002 so boo to bailey bedser and all the rest.)

But i digress hem-hem BOYS fall into a lot of types which are all repulsive as i shall make clear.

CADS

Cads hav always a grandmother who is the DUCHESS of BLANK hem hem. They are inclined to cheat at conkers having baked them for 300 years in the ancestral ovens. These conkers belong to the national trust they are so tuough and if you strike one your new conker fly into a 10000000000 bits.* In this case there is nothing to do about it xcept to SMILE.

* The conker was a huge and glossy one like a racehorse, but like all racehorses which are huge and glosy they fall into a ditch so do not back them. They cross their legs and that is never a good thing for a racehorse or a conker.

Backs to cads. They sa wot skool are you going to. You sa well it is one of the lesser known publick skools it is called GRUNTS it is in devonshire and my pater thinks that becos it is ok for sons of retired clergymen i will be ok. to eton for you i supose? It is always eton and good luck to them they go to a good show in spite of the fog.

eton is a small paradise in the thames valley. New bugs who arive are met by the maitre d'hotel who sa Welcome sir we have to put you in suite number 2 this is only temporary sir you understand no bathroom no shower your tooth-paste will be waiting for you frozen in the wash-basin.

YOU MUST HAVE PATIENCE. In 3 years you can despise EVERY-BODE the LOT. If you are lucky you can even call the matron a dame which takes a bit of doing. So wot you are still in the thames valley then you can put your shoulder againgst a wall and achive o but less than nothing. CHEERS CHEERS WIZZ WIZZ. Less than no marks to the dear old skool imagine me in a topper eh gosh.

As i sa i am down for GRUNTS wizz wow which is an ancient foundation and full of boys to whom masters hav said You'll never pass the CE molesworth never. But they pass into GRUNTS all right which receive them with open arms.

Cads always ask you about your pater and mater e.g.

Wot does your pater *do*, molesworth?

Not a stroke positively not a stroke (*a lite larff*)

He is in the city i suppose

Som of the time at other times he is in earls court it depends (*more larffter*)

But what is his job?

You canot get out of this one. There are a lot of jobs for which the younger generation are being trained up to take the places of their fathers. There is a bird seed merchant, skoolmaster, pigeonfancier brassfounder skinner stockbroker and a lot of others in fact it is shoking how many there are. But all of them sound deadly when you sa your pater do them. Like mum you could wish sometimes that your pater was a bit more glamorous but hay ho. The only thing is to jam your monocle in your eye and sa i kno your pater is a lord pauncefoote but he could jolly well do with a new suit.

Then run like the wind. Ho jenkins sponge the mud of the country from my knees and I will stroll into deten.

OIKS

Oiks used to be tuough boys who had not our advantages. Passing us and observing our pink caps and blue noses oiks call out

OO er coo lumme look at them.

Then they buzz a conker.

At this any boy of spirit sa charge ta-ran-ta-ra ta-ran ta-ra cut them down with your swords men. If the whole croc descended upon the oiks how suprised and wot would miss pringle do then poor thing. Aktually this never hapens for odd reason: Miss pringle address us a lecture.

Take no notice of them molesworth. They do not kno any beter. They kno well enough to hit peason on the nose? The old man's beard is thick on the hedges and soon the shy wild violet will be flowering. No molesworth i am not trying to change the subject. Duck! Heads! Oh, what can all this be? Another shower of conkers? Take no notice take no notice. WAM BIFF ur-ur-ur. Keep on the pavement, tinies, do not break ranks. As i was saing the old man's beard is thick upon the – SPLOSH. Keep close this is when your discipline counts. The sqadron must get through and they shall never capture the standard.

And so the oiks behave as they always hav. The trouble is that among any number of oiks there is always a big one called Ern. Ern is a buly. Everyone sa stand up to bulies they will run away but do not believe it. A lot of them stand still and then where are you eh? i will tell you you are in the duck pond and it is joly freezing.

Lately however things are a bit diferent. The oiks have become v. well dressed certainly beter than pauncefootes pater and their skools are quite remarkable with all those windows to let the sunshine in. You only hav to look to see what goes on in there. First the foyer then the palm court lounge and swiming pool and lovely women ect. (Cor crikey ermintrude your pigtails are ropy toda. Can i sip a milk and orange juice with you at the brake.) Well that's what these new places are like and you can pla as long as you like with the skool plutonium plant. Yet our paters and maters shell out to send us to st custards but that is the way it is we just hav to put up with it.

GOODY-GOODIES

There is no beter xsample of a goody-goody than fotherington-tomas in the world in space. You kno he is the one who sa Hullo Clouds Hullo Sky and skip about like a girly. i mean you are just zooming about taking pot shots at various new bugs with your catapult when fotherington-tomas sa Do you think you should be doing that, molesworth, is it kind. Can you not hear the shrieks of agony? To which i repli If i had a germ gun i would blast them with 5 trillion bakterial volts so they are getting off litely. But somehow the plesure has gone.

Goody-goodies believe in fairies father xmas peter pan ect. and unlike most boys they are kind to their sisters. Lots of boys are unfortunate enuff to have weedy sisters which must be worse even than having molesworth 2 for a bro. You can imagine wot goes on in the fotherington-tomas home.

ARABELLA FOTHERINGTON-TOMAS (*who is knitting* 5000 *yards of woollen reins*): i am so glad our cotage is called swete lavender.

FOTHERINGTON-TOMAS (*looking up from his story about wee tim in chatterbox*): so am i. There are brownies living in the dust-bin. i saw one this morning.

ARABELLA: Hurrah that makes me feel hapy.

F-T.: Sing me your skool song arabela.

ARABELLA (*at once*):

> Ho for bat Ho for ball
> Ho for hockey and lax and all
> miss dennis is strict,
> miss hamilton fair
> But miss peabody (gym) is both strict and
> tall.

(*There is a mighty racket outside. molesworth hammers on the door*)

Open in the name of beelzebub.

But so grate is the noise of the skool song that noone come so wot is ther left for me to do? i climb into the fairy coach whip up the mice into a gallop and zoom away.

BULIES

Every skool hav a resident buly who is fat and roll about the place clouting everybode. This is nesessessery so that we can all hav a sermon from time to time chiz e.g. *if you are strong remember the little felow. Give him a helping hand*

Every skool hav a resident buly who is fat

do not bash him up. Perhaps he hav been anoying perhaps he have said you have a face like a squashed tomato. Wot of it? Perhaps the little felow is right. You have got a face like a squashed tomato. Ect.

well you kno how they go on.

There are 2 kinds of buly. There are fat bulies who can run fast and fat bulies who can't run for tooffe. There is nothing to be done about fat bulies who can run xcept to be polite to them e.g. *good morning grabber you bilge rat pax pax pax pax. i didn't mean it really i didn't ow ow paxpaxpax.*

On the whole this is hardly satisfactory.

Bulies who can't run are beter. You can watch them swanking up the coridor then zoom past chanting Look at the clot-faced wet. Buly turn red as a beetroot and stump after you like a giant but too late you have melted into the distance hem-hem. 3 days later buly come up to you when you are sitting at your desk. He sa: Look here molesworth you called me a clot-faced wet wot do you mean by it? Then you shake your head. Me? No dash it honestly word of honour (fingers crossed) I would not dream of using such uncouth words. Somebody else must hav thort you were a clot-faced wet as well.

WAM.

But the nimble molesworth have skipped litely away the buly is left cursing. Bulies are pathetic objects whom i diskard. There is only this. Just let a junior tick call me a clot-faced wet in 2 years time and you'll see what i'll do.

SNEKES

Everyone kno wot snekes are they are unspekable but they abound in every skool e.g. i am just cutting up my bungy under cover of the blotch in preparation for all-out barrage when sneke sa

LOOK AT WOT MOLESWORTH IS DOING BEHIND HIS BLOTCH, SIR.

The master look up dreamily from his novel of love and passion. He sees nothing his eyes are glazed he is still with the hero and GURL in the desert. Besides he ma not want to think wot i am doing behind the blotch it might be more than his delikate nerves can take.

HE IS CUTTING UP HIS INDIARUBER SIR IN CONTRAVENTION OF SKOOL RULE 66 (c) para 3.

The master come to earth.

'I suppose that is true, molesworth,' he sa. He stretches languidly for the punishment book. 'The usual, molesworth. Put it away and get on.'

This is the signal for the whole klass to sizzle like a steam engine saing 'Sneke sneke sneke.' Sneke looks highly delighted with himself and put out his tongue. He will be the hon sec of a tenis club when he grow up and serve him right no fate is too bad. Master give long sigh and take up his novel agane. The beaituful lydia parkington is better than j. caesar so i do not blame him.

Gabbitas creeps round the wood one way

5

HOW TO BE TOPP
IN ENGLISH

i have said there only one peom in the english language e.g.
The Brook which chater chater as it flo my dear it is
obviously a girlie just like fotherington-tomas. However
there are other peoms which creep in from time to time
there is one which go

Har fleag har fleag har fleag onward
Into the er rode the 600.

There are as well lars porsena of clusium elegy in country
churchyard loss of the royal george and chevy chase.
Anything to do with dafodils is also grate favourite of
english masters but then nothing is beyond them they
will even set burns (rabbie) who is uterly weedy.

It is farely easy to be topp in english and sometimes you
may find yourself even getting interested. If that happens
of course you can always draw junctions and railway lines
on your desk viz

EXPRESSION

Sometimes english masters make you *read* peoms chiz chiz chiz. You have to sa the weedy words and speke them beaitfully as if you knew what they meant. Fotheringtontomas thinks this is absolutely super and when he sa he wander lonely as a cloud you think he will flote out of the window. Some cads roters and swots love to read they beg for the chance and put their hands up saing sir sir sir please sir as if they are in agony. English masters who are always perverse then sa molesworth go on CHIZ.

SIR THE BURIAL SIR OF SIR JOHN MOORE SIR AT CORUNNA SIR

(*A titter from 2B they are wet and i will tuough them up after.*)

> Notadrumwasheardnotafuneralnote
> shut up peason larffing
> As his corse
> As his corse
> what is a corse sir? gosh is it
> to the rampart we carried
> (*whisper you did not kno your voice was so lovely*)
> Not a soldier discharged his farewell shot.
> *PING!*
> Shut up peason i know sir he's blowing peas at me
> Oer the grave where our hero we buried.

(*A pause a grave bow i retire and Egad! peason hav placed a dainty pin upon mine seat.* Fie!)

Occasionally you can work a wizard wheeze that the english master reads. This is not so difficult becos all masters like to show how it should be done. They look very grave turn the pages and announce

THE RETURN OF THE CHIFF-CHAFF

The class palpitate with excitement at the prospect of so exciting a story. Master slowly and sadly cast his eye to the ceiling and then down to the book while pupils prepare huge dumps of ammunition, train guns and ease atomic catapults.

MAGISTER: (*in a deep sad voice*) The chiff-chaff, the common warbler of his moorland district, was now abundant, more so than anywhere else in England. (*BONK*) two or three were flitting about (eeeauowoooo – *WAM*) within a few feet of my head give me that peashooter molesworth and a dozen at least were singing within hearing (*ur-ur-ur-ur-ur-ur*) chiff-chaffing near and if this noise continues i shall stop reading and give you some parsing far, their notes sounding strangely loud at that still, sequestered spot. (*CRASH BONK WAM WHIZZ*)

Listening to that insistent sound I was reminded of Warde Fowler's words please sir, molesworth is strangling me stand on your chair molesworth CRASH words about the sweet season which brings new life and hope to men there is no need to cry fotherington-tomas and now a BONK and BANG is CRASH on it by that same bird's ur-ur-ur-ur-ur-ur eeeauowooo –

(*MAGISTER continues nothing can stop him while the ELEVES disport themselves merily each small one to his own inclinations. It is this indeed that n. molesworth acquired that grate love for english literature which was such a comfort to him in later years hem-hem.*)

What it all amounts to is that english is chiefly a matter of marksmanship. You can always come topp if you lay the rest of the class out but as auden sa so witily no cracked shot can hit every time. Ho fie lo egad and away for it is the BELL and it tolleth for me cheers cheers cheers.

THE MOLESWORTH DAY-DREAM
SERVICE 2

THE SPACE SHIP TAKES OFF

EEEeeeeeaouh space ship away inside all is quiet as Captain molesworth the interplanetary clot eases the controls towards uranus. An hour later they touch down.

'Late as usual,' grumble molesworth 2.

LOOK OUT!

A poisoned projectile from mars embedd itself in the uranium. As they bend to pick it up 150 treen pirate rockets pancake down beside them.

'Now i hav you capt. molesworth,' grit the PUKON, the MASTER MIND. 'Hav you anything to declare?'

'2 pairs of nylons, some old bungy and the skool dog.'

'Arrest him!'

The treens step forward and bind him.

'WOW, O PUKON.' they sa.

'Put him in the reactor, o clot-faced doodlebugs.'

'The reactor is full, O PUKON. You always put the earth men there and they always escape it is very depressing. It is the same with the furnaces and the steel doors. Always get out at the last moment.'

'Try the moon-crater full of monsters.'

'Full too, O PUKON.'

'Dash it,' snarl the PUKON but as he speak Capt. molesworth's fist smash into his jaw . . . . . .

Go on, molesworth.

Er what, sir?

We hav been reading the water babies molesworth in turn round the class is it possible that you hav not been following?

yes sir of course sir.

then pray continue but i see you canot. It would appere boy that mrs doasyouwouldbedoneby does not amuse you that the

adventures of tom the sweep are shall we sa somewhat insippid
that chas. kingsly's matchless prose is perhaps a trifle demode
It would appere also boy that you have beter thorts, a suficient
knoledge a master grasp . . . . . .

ect. ect. ect. ect. ect. ect. Class think this all highly
amusing chiz chiz and larff like anything and thus the
gosamer SPELL is broken. Pon my soul dear darling
arabela but LIFE is tuough.

6

WIZZ FOR GAMES

Skool acording to headmaster's pi-jaw is like LIFE chiz if
that is the case wot is the use of going on? There must be
give and take, fair weather and foul, triumph and disaster
but he do not give the exact proportions. Anyway finaly
he come to it. There must be WORK – yes but WORK
and PLA. You have guessed wot is coming next it is
inevitable. ALL WORK AND NO PLA MAKES JACK
A DULL BOY. i don't kno about Jack but in my case it is
certainly not *that* which hav made me dull. It is all pla and
no work but let it pass.

Headmasters hav to hav some sort of excuse for games so
that they can drive all boys and masters out into the foul
and filthy air while they stir the coals into a blaze and setle
down with one of the gangster books they have confiskated.
In the last 5 minits they appear on the touchline and shout
GET INTO HIM MOLESWORTH GET INTO HIM it
is all very well i am cold and covered with mud the only
thing i want to get into is a bath ha-ha.

And talking of baths they are all mighty ones at our
skool. It take you 3 days to climb up the side and when
you get to the topp it might be everest giddy heights and
a sheer drop into icy water. There are 3 elks which
turns each of the huge brass taps but the cold elks work
harder than the HOT chiz. Zoom down the side with a
mighty slide and not so much as a st. bernard dog with a
keg of the STUFF to revive you but wot hav all this to
do with games eh. Games are not bad and they foster
our natural development (official).

Batsmanship

1. The stance

2. Left leg towards the ball

3. Eye on the ball

4. Swing of the bat

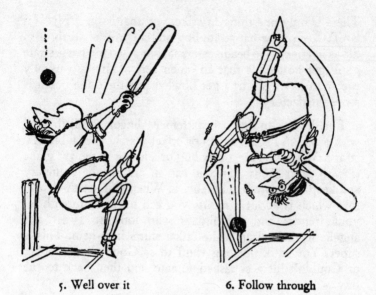

5. Well over it

6. Follow through

7. The Final Phase

CRIKET

There is only one thing in criket and that is the STRATE
BAT. Keep yore bat strate boy and all will be all right in
life as in cricket. So headmasters sa, but when my bat is strate
i still get bowled is that an omen chiz. Aktually i usually
prefer to hav a slosh: i get bowled just the same but it is
more satisfactory.

For the reason that it is extremely dificult to hit the ball
with a STRATE BAT or not criket matches are a bit of a
strane. When you are a new bug or a junior in the 3rd game
it is all right becos then you can sit around the boundary
and keep the score in a notebook. When you get tired with
that which is about 3 minits you can begin to tuough up
your frendes and neighbours who look so sweet and
angelic in their clean white criket shirts hem-hem. This is
super. You look up long enuff to sa Good shot, grabber
or Couldn't hit a squashed tomato and then back to the
fray.

But it is a funy thing when you grow biger you always
get into a criket team you canot avoid it chiz. Tremble
tremble you arive and see the pitch which is 2388 miles
approx from the pavilion. Captain win toss and choose to
bat chiz chiz chiz chiz. Moan drone tremble tremble you
sit with white face and with everybode's knees knoking
together it sound like a coconut shy. Wot is the pleasure
of it eh i would like to kno. Give me a thumbscrew or slo
fire every time.

When your turn come the folowing things can hapen
    (A) You loose your bat.
    (B) You fante dead away.
    (C) Your trousis fall down.
    (D) You trip over your shoe laces.

Captain then come up to you and sa BLOCK EVERY-
THING molesworth and do not slosh we need 6 to win.

SOOLILOQUY

Let us pause a while and consider. Ah-me. As i stand here at mid-of how petty it all seme. These flaneled fules, the umpires, the headmaster who bask in his deck chair. All those latin books inside, the shavings in the carpentry shop the japes and wheezes – so much toil so much efort. And it may all be ended in a moment.

When he sa this all the things above hapen all at once.
They revive you with a buket of water and drive you out to
the wicket. This is not as you guessed 2388 miles away it
is 6000 now and they hav men with gats covering all the
exits so you canot run away.

AT THE WICKET

Of course it is the fast blower you hav to face he is wating
there at the other end of the pitch looking very ferce.
Umpire is v. kind he can aford to be he hav not got to bat.
He sa

We are very pleesed to see you do make yourself at
home. Of course you would like guard what guard would
you like us to give you?

Squeak.

Come agane?

Squeak squeak.

i will give you centre hold your bat up strate to you a
trifle now away agane. That is centre. Your position is 120
miles NNE of beachy head you may come in and land.
There are 5 balls to come. At the 5th pip it will be 4. 2
precisely. Able Baker Out.

PLAY!

Fast blower retreat with the ball mutering and cursing.
He stamp on the grass with his grate hary feet he beat his
chest and give grate cry. Then with a trumpet of rage he
charge towards you. Quake quake ground tremble birdseed
fly in all directions if only you can run away but it is not
done. Grit teeth close eyes. Ball hit your pads and everyone
go mad.

OWSATSIR OW WASIT EHOUT!

Umpire look for a long time he is bent double at last he
lift one finger.

He is a difrent man now from the kindly old gentleman
who made you feel at home. His voice is harsh.

Distance back to pavilion is now 120000 miles

Out. No arguments. Get cracking. Take that xpresion off your face. On course at 20000 feet return to base. Out.

Distance back to pavilion is now 120000 miles and all the juniors sa ya boo sucks couldn't hit a squashed tomato. It is no use saing you were not out by a mile team give you the treatment behind the pav just the same. There is only one consolation you can give it up when you grow up. Then you rustle the paper and sa Wot a shocking show by m.c.c. most deplorable a lot of rabits ect. ect. Well, you kno how they go on. Enuff.

FOOPBALL

Foopball is a tuough game but it is a pity you canot win by hacking everbode. You hav to be nippy. You hav also to be agile cuning alert skeming courageous and imbecile. But there are a few of us who are only imbeciles cheers cheers cheers and just do wot we can to pla our humble part in that well-oiled foopballing machine which is the st custards eleven i.e. thro mud cakes at fotherington-tomas, encourage skool dog to trip referee and diskuss influence of t. s. eliot on 20th century drama with a few progresive-thinking players of like interests. Another thing we do to cheet the long hours of boredom of the foopball field on a winters afternoon is to diskuss composition of all-time world eleven

WORLD XI

Goliath.

Romulus.   Remus.

Skool dog.   self.   Richard 1.

Julius Caesar.   Cain.   Jack the Ripper.   Livy.   Esau.

●

Ref. Solomon.

i think a few of those would hold their own in any company and there mite even be a revolution in foopball methods.

MATCHES

st custards was agog with excitement on the day of the match with their grate rivals, porridge court. And then came the blo which spread consternation through the skool making faces in maths classes glumer even than ushual. Hary mugwort, the briliant centre forward, had been put into deten by sigismund the mad maths master for saing BANG whenever a perpendicular was droped. He must miss the match and who would take his place? nigel molesworth was quietly tuoughing up the junior ticks when the footer captain tapped him on the shoulder. 'You are in the team, molesworth,' he sa. 'Gratters.'

'OO gosh wot me. Where will i pla eh?'

'Centre forward.'

molesworth then fanted and was revived by the larffter of the junior ticks.

'oo ha-ha-ha-ha look at baby molesworth who couldn't kick a flea ect. He thinks he is going to be the hero of the match but we kno beter. Much beter. We kno the match is as good as lost Hahahaha.'

*   *   *

Hurra! a mighty cheer broke as porridge court scored their eighth gole. With only 5 minits to go the match looked safe for this unsemely colection of huge louts and bulies.

'Come on st custards,' sa the footer captain cheerfuly. 'Only 8 goles down. We can do it. Pla up and pla the game.'

'8 goles?' sa molesworth. 'Gosh.'

So far he had not touched the ball except to tap it off from the centre. He had been the weak link in the chain. Now he determined to pla his natural game. Instead of a tap he kicked off with a tremendous boot at the gole. The ball stuned the fuleback and went into the gole. One to st custard's. Porridge court kicked off only for molesworth to gane posession and do it agane. He scored from all quarters of the field – 2, 3, 4, 5, 6, 7, 8 and, in the last seconds, a mighty crash from a gole kick drove the ball into the porridge court net to win the match. Hurra! The exultant spektators dashed across the field to chair their hero into the pav. . . . . .

Poor saps, i supose you believed all that. You lapped it up, eh, like all those skoolboy stories. But life is not like that. It is not like wot dickens and all those write either.

A REEL MATCH

I am sory to sa it but in reel life foopball matches are a bit diferent. First the porridge court team arive they all look like giants tuough tuough but with blue knees. They hav a keen master with them who sa 'Warm up knees bend got your coshes. Each of you get into your man and maim him. Here are your gloves golekeeper the lead is inside.'

He then go off to the touchline to cheer and exhort. The rest of st custard's then arive saing yaar boo sucks while masters lash them with knouts. They are then herded at pistol point and made to sing st custard's cheer

> *Boom-walla boom walla*
> *Geese walla geese walla*
> *st custard's hooray!*

At this moment gold-plated rolls royce arive with visiting headmaster. Headmasters greet each other.

Well how are you hoggwart eh wot eh.[1] We hav not a bad team won all our last six matches quite promising.[2] Of course we are up to 99 boys can't get another bed in the place.[3] And of course royalty is a great responsibility for all.[4] But we are building up quite a little shall we sa kno-how[5] in that direction ha-ha.

REEL THORTS OF ST CUSTARD'S HEADMASTER

1. Older and fatter bad colour.

2. Buys his players wot was the transfer fee.

3. Curses curses.

4. Wait till they ask for the porn ticket on the crown jewels.

5. Kno-how? treble fees and toothpaste extra.

Peep! the shrill whistle go (keats) the match begin. Headmasters charge up and down the touchline belowing at the tops of their vioces.

COME ON PORRIDGE COURT LETS HAV A GOLE. PILE INTO YOUR MEN. MARK THEM. CROSBY-KERSHAW-PARKINSON (Hon. The A.P.R.)

Thring creeps round the other way

167

MARK YOUR MAN. FOUL! SEND HIM OFF! WILL MILORD KINDLY GET HIS FAT HEAD TO THE BALL? IF YOUR HIGHNESS WILL PERMIT ME AFFAIRS OF STATE ARE NOT MORE IMPORTANT THAN CRASHING THE LEATHER INTO THE RETICULE. NO SWEET PRINCE NOT YOUR OWN RETICULE YOU SEE WOT YOU HAV DONE. ON AGANE PORRIDGE COURT ECT.

It is a funy thing tho your side always gets beaten which-ever skool you are at. That is like life i supose. fotherington-tomas skips about when he is golie 'Hullo trees Hullo birds.' ect. He luv only bountiful nature and perhaps he is right.

SHOOTING

This sounds more fun than it aktually is. They lend you a gun it is true but you are not alowed to shoot anything you realy want to chiz i.e. masters, the matron, robins, etc. chiz. You could hav wizard fun if you pretend they were red indians chiz but you hav to aim at a weedy target. You mite get a bird or fotherington-tomas by mistake like this but there is not much chance. Besides, they always tell you not to point a gun. If you do not point it wot use *is* a gun i would like to kno?

SWIMING

Agane the iron hand of authority prevent us from geting the best out of swiming which would otherwise be full of belyflopers, duckings atomic splashes and the shouts and cries of these who perish. Insted we are suspended like a spider chiz on the end of a pole and told to strike out. Most boys in this position do not strike out but suck in which do not help. if i had my way i would be a frogman and look super in a ruber suit and webbed feet but pop sa it is rather xpensive. Anyway peason tell me i look like a frogman without suit or feet chiz chiz so i stooge off to punkture fotherington-tomas ickle pritty water wings.

CONKERS

Conkers is an old-fashioned game which hav been played by generations of british boys. You kno what hapens you pick up a huge horse chestnut which look absolutely super like a derby winner and put some string through it. Then you chalenge grabber or gilibrand who hav a conkerer of 20. You say weedy things like

> Obbly obbly onker
> My first conker
> Hay ho hay nonny no ect.

Honour your oponent and turn round on the points of your toes. After that you whirl your conker round and hurl it at the dangling target hem-hem. Successful conkers are always shriveled and weedy. Wot hapens is that your conker either shaters into a milion pieces or flies through the nearest window crash crash tinkle tinkle. ('i shall make you pay from your poket-money, molesworth, not becos i *need* the money but becos you must face the consequences of your actions.')

What is needed in conkers is a new scientific approach. We are too conservative. As new elizabethans we must adventure with science i.e. select a new conker bombard it with uranium 238 (element 92) folow it with a beam of nitrogen atoms fired from a 60 inch cyclotron. If it stands this all the neutrons will hav gummed together in a nucleus. If it do not, turn the cyclotron on molesworth 2 or fotherington-tomas and see wot it do to them. If they disintegrate in less than 2.3 minits the thanks of mankind should be yours but you may be ahead of your time chiz.

SNAKES AND LADERS

If you hav a quiet half hour with one of your dear companions like peason or gillibrand what is nicer than a game of snakes and laders? Aktually quite a number of things are nicer like a film of marylyn monroe a quiet cig or a plateful of roste turkey but you do not get these things at skool chiz so it have to be snakes and laders.

How to Play. Face oponent and lay all gats and coshes on the hall table. Setle the stakes at 5 bob a corner. Inspect dice. Turn round and tuough up junior ticks for looking. Start cheerfuly go up laders cheers cheers go down snakes. Dice fly and are lost in w.p.b. Stare at snakes and observe resemblance to certain of your contemporaries hem-hem. Go down snake and start agane. Now not so cheerful. Oponent come down. More cheerful. This go on until you are 997 years old and dying of old age. You could take up chess instead but you may find the game too fast.

THE GYMNASIUM

Wot makes a boy healthy and splendid with giant and ripling muscles? Wot makes his torso remarkable eh? The answer is not the red ink skull and crossbones on his chest or the tatoo marks i luv maysie on his biceps. The effect is obtained by his WORK in the GYM.

As in other departments of skool life SUKSESS do not always come easily. In fact the grate gymnasiums of Britain are littered with boys who hav broken their legs, brused their branes (if any) grazed their shins and sufered horibly. You can always tell where the gym is becos all the vultures hover over it and each time the springboard go PLUNK they strane their ears and their mouths water. THAT boy was safely over the horse (and the gym sergeant too) but sooner or later one will make a slip. He will fall out of the line tallest on the right shortest on the left and be deserted to his fate.

The Horse

Every gymnasium hav a horse for the tiny tots to jump over. At one end is a springboard and there is also a scrufy old thing lying on the floor at the other. This is not the gym sergeant who hav had too much BEER it is the MAT and if you landed on the gym sergeant instead you would soon kno the diference and learn some interesting WORDS.

The BOY BEATIFUL who is determined to be good at gym rev. up like mad zoom away bounce on the springbord and sale litely over the horse. Sometimes however he make a bish. When that hapen he bounce on the springbord rise vertically in the air and strike his head on the roof. When you come to think of it there is no reason why this should not hapen more often than it do.

The Bar

No not that kind of bar clot altho anebode would need a stiff tot before he can do 3 circles with no hands. Aktualy the whole thing is simply pappy. You sit erect on the bar bak holow arms stiff eyes fixed in glassy stare and whole face contorted with fear. After about 3 hours trying to pluck up courage this position becomes a bit uncomfortable. Besides the mob ten miles below get a bit restless. They sa Yar Boo Sucks and cowardy cowardy custard and other weedy things. You then decide to go. Then you change your mind the hole affair is too ghastly.

Position 2. Thro the arms upwards and bakwards swing with the bar in the crook of your knobbly knees. Round round round out and down. All you need really is Confidence. You must not believe for a moment that it is posible that you can go round round round down and OUT. Just give a good swing to start with and all will be well. If it isn't you won't kno anything about it anyway.

Position 3. The final position. Rigid, unconscious, chin in, hands stretched to sides, nose and toes in air. (Too much movement may damage the stretcher.)

The Rings

The rings are the most dangerous of all and only a really tuough and brave BOY BEATIFUL can show off with them. There are two rings and they hang down on two ropes at least they do unless some skoolboy who luv pranks hav severed them with his jackknife. Wot you hav to do is to swing on the rings in some very funy positions. You can be chest out or chest in or arms xtended. But there is only one rule i can give e.g. HOLD ON. If you let go you fly out of the window. And then where will you be poor thing? In the rubish bin along with the skool brekfast poo gosh which is most unsavoury.

Another exercise with the rings is to swing on them by yore feet upside down. This is super. At least it would be if fotherington-tomas do not come along.

'Look at me fotherington-tomas,' you sa as you zoom by. 'Look at me no hands.'

'i am looking,' he sa. 'Wot are you doing?'

'Boddy swinging ARMS XTENDED, feet in the rings bakwards and forwards bending with deep rhymical breething.'

'So that is the noise i hear?'

'In and O-U-T. In and O-U-T.'

(*fotherington-tomas scratch his head.*)

'But molesworth wot is the *point* of it?' he sa. 'Wot hav you ganed when it is all over? Do it make you beter than other boys? Wot does it *prove* in the long run? ect. ect.' . . . . . .

These are very dificult questions to answer when swinging by the feet upside down. As you ponder you strike head sharply on the ground.

'You see?' sa fotherington-tomas and stroll away. He is a gurly.

7

HOW TO BE TOPP
IN FRENCH

Whenever anyone mention fr. all the eleves sa oo gosh ugh french weedy ect but it is no use saing what's the use of it as you do with latin. The masters sa fr. is a living langwage and swank about they think they hav got the beter of us chiz. It is not much use repling O.K. bruther SO WHAT when fr. masters sa fr. is living it is beter to be keen cheerful and enthusiastick.

e.g. The Francais, sir, are certainly vital and ebullient.

or

The Francais realy understand the art of LIFE don't you agree, monsieur?

Monsieur may not be fuled by this but it may lead to something. In fact it may lead to him teling you about his last holiday in Dieppe tho i would hav thought the less said about what he did *there* the beter. This may tempt a tiny eleve to get caried away and GO TOO FAR e.g. were there any mademoiselles hem-hem there, monsieur?

No master like his name coupled with a GURL at least not by a garcon they are not pray to mortal passions. Next moment the whole class is back with Armand and M. Dubois and the other weeds in the fr. book. (leson 3 etre to be ect.)

ALL ABOUT ARMAND

Everyone kno that Armand is a wet becos he wear that striped shirt and sissy straw hat. In Lesson 6A Armand has just entered into the salle a manger from the jardin. He enter it not to pinch something to eat but to give Mama the jolies fleurs which he hav picked. Papa is pleased. Papa is not woried as he joly well ort to be at this base conduct. Papa is highly delited.

'Thou art a good boy, Armand,' he sa, 'this afternoon i will take thee to the zoo.'

Ahha you think Papa is not so dumb as he look he will thro Armand to the lions.

'Are there any animals in the zoo?' ask Armand.

'Oh but yes,' sa Papa without loosing his temper at this feeble question.

'Houpla houpla i am so hapy.'

Perhaps the lions are not bad enough perhaps it will hav to be the loups. The loups could indubitably do a good job on Armand. Is it with these thoughts that Papa go hand in hand with his little son? They pay ten sous. They pass through the turnstile. They enter into the zoological garden. They look around themselves.

'How big the elephants are,' observe Armand at length.

'Yes and also the giraffes.'

'The monkeys are amusings.'

'O yes en effet and there is a fox.'

'Foxes are naughties.'

You wonder if it was noel coward who wrote the dialog it is so nervously brilliant my dear how long can it be before Papa do Armand. But it is not to be. They pass the loups and the lions but o hapen chiz xcept that Papa observe that the sky is blue altho it is sometimes grey. They go out of the turnstile and return home.

'Next week we will go a la campagne,' sa Papa.

Now you can see what hav been going on. The zoo and the bord de la mer are too crowded. Get Armand by himself in a meadow and it is money for jam unless aunt beatrice goes along. The Papa can do them both or they can watch the bees flit from flower to flower. It is up to him.

'How big the elephants are,' observe Armand

A STRATAGEM HEM-HEM

Altho fr. masters canot keep order they stick grimly to their task nothing seme to discourage them. It is a good wheeze then if you have a real Fr. boy in the class. Then you sa innocently

What is it like in France, sir?

France is quite exquisit molesworth the fine old wines of Burgundy the splendid food the gay wines of Champagne the cafes the railway stations the mice which love cheese and the trees which are pretty.

Gosh sir really sir then it is just like the piktures in the fr. book?

France molesworth do not hav beetles drawn all over it. Get on with your ex. boy.

This is the time when you stick your compass into the real Fr. boy who jaber like a bren gun

maymsieuestcequejaituailaspaparat ect. for 5 minits. Then there is silence you could here a piece of buble gum drop and fr master larff uneasily

Come again le crapaud he sa come again.

well you kno what it is once a fr. boy start you canot stop them becos they hav so much on their mind.

i only venture to remark he sa that recevoir is a verb which is the invention of the english especially in the imperfect subjunc which the grate poet beaujolais rarely if ever used in his verses assur yourself of my distinguished sentiments ect.

'Cor!'

if i may have the pleasur of continuing i would sa *deuxfrancsilserontbonmieuxmeileur* ect.

'EH?'

etparcequequand and so it go on the trouble is that once a fr. boy start you canot stop him in fact you feel sory for the fr. master in a sort of way chiz. But fr. masters kno how to cope they unroll a huge pikture of a farmyard and point out a turkey.

'What is the fr. for *that*, molesworth?' he sa.

well i mean to sa the only one i kno on that picture is the little baby who is uterly wet he is stroking a sheep. No wonder the sheep look disgusted. Anyway no boy could admit that so my lips are sealed. Dinde dolt or dindon sa the fr. master back on the home ground after loosing away.

In the midst of all these sordid transactions molesworth the magican switches off. His mouth open his plate fall out doodlebugs fall from his hair he rev the engines up and take off into the ether for another daydream.

PAS DEVANT L'ENFANT
GUIDE TO FRENCH BY
GROWN UPS

	WITH MOLES-WORTH THORTS
av-ez voo ach-et-ay le gin?	have you bought the gin to replace that which we inadvertently finished last night? (*m. thinks: i prefer the other brand reelly*)
VOTRE PERE est absolument la der-rière	Your father is the absolute rock bottom. (*m. thinks: the old music hall jokes how true how true*)
av-ez vu le ce cas dans le newsoftheworld	hav you read that shocking case in the news of the world? (*Thinks: stale old bird.*)
voo-voo soo-ven-ez de la scan-dale de mrs higginbotham?	You remember the scandal about mrs higginbotham. (*m. thinks: only too well only too well. Look at her husband you have to make allowances.*)
ce sacre cochon d'un menager de la banque.	That hem-hem (swearing conduct mark) of a bank manager. (*m. thinks: i don't kno why all this fuss about bank managers. They are only doing their job. thriftlessness brings pane in its wake.*)
Quand attend-ell le bebe?	When is she expecting the baby? (*m. thinks: in about 3 weeks.*)

Gabbitas and Thring trap a young
man and lead him off to be a master

8

EXTRA TEW

No one but skoolboys kno what extra tew is extra lesons
for bakward boys which keep aged masters out of the dog's
home becos they get paid for it and so they should. Most
extra tew is about subjects you don't kno e.g. lat. fr. algy.
geom. hist. geog. bot. div. arith. But sometimes there is
extra tew in littleknown subjects which are likely to be of
advantage in that snug nitch in the foreign office hem-hem
which is your pater and maters ambition for their hansome
nigel ho ho look at me. This kind of extra tew is very
special and include german, scandinavian literature, deportment, debrett's peerage, ruffs guide to the turf *inter alia* as
we sa at brekfast. I hav never really had extra tew but i
hav my spies and this is what goes on.

SPANISH

Nobody kno much about Spanish except the Spaniards
whose beards are all singed and they are very proud and
like sherry just as some others about this place whose names
i will not mention. All this is the reason why you hav to lisp
when you speke spanish which make it all very dificult.

thene: A hathienda. Enter don jereth de la frontera moleth-
worth.

A THERVANT: who ith it?
DON JERETH: it ith only me ith ithabel ethpecting me?
A THERVANT: Yeth.
DON J.: O thuper!
    (*he folowth the thervant*)

ithabel! my thoul-mate! ith there any therry in the house?

ITHABEL: yeth. pour out 2 slugth and i will thip with thee.

DON J.: thplendid! good thow! Cheerth! Over the fallth. (*he drinkth*) What ith that thound?

ITHABEL: Thantoth it is my bro Thantoth thipping his therry. He ith thupping with uth.

DON J.: (*thwearing*) Curseth!

That is the sort of thing which hapens with spanish and anyone who decide to kno about it is a fule.

RUSIAN

How many days till the end of term, o molesvitch 2? Some sa 20, others 90, little bro, is the fruit upon the aple tree in the orchard? Only the blosom so you will hav to wait a month or two before you can pinch them o measly weed it is 2006 miles to Moscow. Who cares sa fotherington-tomas from a corner of the room where he hav been trussed up who cares a row of butons. i love only robins. Unless you love robins father christmas will not bring you any presents. A volley of shots ring out. WAM! 900 robins bite the dust. That only leaves father christmas, i sa, how flat life is . . . . . .

The swots tell me that rusian used to be like that chiz but it is all diferent now everybode is joly and at xmas time just when you are deciding whether to ask for a motor bike or a platinum watch an xciting envelop is pushed through the leter box.

'How thrilling,' sa molesworth 2 the youngest of the kiddies. 'What can it be?'

'It *feels* thrilling!' i sa coyly just like the weeds in chater-box. 'It may be a tiny toy from aunt drusila our very xciting aunt from north wales.'

'Sometimes i think she is *too* xciting, dear nigel,' sa molesworth 2 pensively. How joly our xmas hols will be. Let us take the envelope to dear Mama and Dada.

So saing he imprint 3 huge finger prints from his hary hand and skip awa to the kitchen folowed by his larffing elder bro. Dada is washing up in the sink Mama is peeling potatoes Liza dear fatheful liza the maid is smoking a cig over a cup of tea.

'Mama mama,' the 2 sturdy little felows cry, 'Open our leter. Please open it.'

Mama do as she is bid having put the potato knife out of temptation's way. This is what she read:

> И ам гивинг а литтл парти
> I am giving a little party
> ат ди Кремлин. ви вилл хав фун.
> at the Kremlin. We will hav fun.
>
> Хрущев
> Kruschev

'How nice of Mr Kruschev!' cry Mama. 'Of course you can go!'

'And may i wear my velveteen breeches and lace colar, mama?'

'Wow!' lisp wee molesworth 2 turning a somersault and the whole family join in the harty larff when he end in the dog bowl. Even towser bark but that was becos molesworth 2 had pinched his bone.

At last the day come and the 2 little chaps drive off to the Kremlin in their best suits. You can imagine what they look like. Mr Kruschev stand beaming on the steps and waiting behind him are lots of kind uncles. You can imagine the fun they all had with the tommy guns before the sir roger de coverley start: the air is thick with cordite.

Molesvitch

'Children children,' sa mr kruschev. 'Not too rough before the musical chairs.'

And so with flushed hapy faces the children join in the fun until it is time to go home.

'Come along any time,' said Mr Kruschev, as he sa goodbye, 'and I will take you both for a ride.'

That is about all there is to rusian but i supose it is more than enuff. Personally i cant stand parties which hav dancing and eton colars and GURLS ugh. There seems to be some point in a party like that but it is too much to hope we can hav one at our home chiz. rat-tat i have 3 leters for ermintrude if she will come outside and get them BAM BIFF WALLOP folowed by SILENCE. i wouldn't mind paing a forfeit for that.

ADVANCED MATHS

All maths is friteful and means O but if you are a grate brane you hear a tremendous xplosion at about the fifth lesson in trig. This mean that you are through the sound barier and maths hav become what every keen maths master tell you it can be i.e. a LANGWAGE. in my view this is just another of those whopers which masters tell i mean can you imagine peason and me at brake:

MOLESWORTH: (*taking a hack at the pill*) $x^2 \times y^6 = a$
PEASON: $z^8 - x^3 = b$
MOLESWORTH: (*missing completely*) O, y^{99}!

As you will see it simply will not do i am prepared to believe that a strate line if infinitely protracted go on for ever tho i do not see how even that weed pythagoras can tell. But if maths is a langwage i hav only one coment. It is

$$\sum_0^\infty \frac{b^x}{x!} = \sum_0^\infty \frac{e^{-M} \cdot M^x \cdot e^{tx}}{x!} = e^{-M} \sum_0^\infty \frac{(Me^t)^x}{x!}$$

I think that setles the mater.

MUSIC LESSONS

Kno Yore Instrument. This is the skool piano you kno the one which go WAM PLUNK BISH BASH ZUNK. It is a cranky old grid made by an old german called B.ch. .ei.

co. . . .ldb. .rg. As you will see it hav a pair of brass flame-throwers and a bubble for a rear gunner. The loud pedal droped off when molesworth 2 pla 'fairy bells' and hav never been seen agane. Inside there are a lot of old marbles, cig cards, toy soldiers and dead goldfish. There are a lot of wooden things which tap up and down. I think that if it hav a rebore and new piston rings it would be a snip.

The Lesson. It is easy pappy to be a grate player like molesworth 2 all you must do is recognise the notes. The fat ones you hav to hold for 4 secs. These are minims. There are a lot of weedy ones called quavers but it is difficult to get these in. There are also crotchets. I do not think anyone know this xcept mrs curwen. i can only tell you that if you get the whole lot of minims crotchets and quavers mixed up together it is like an atomic xplosion cheers cheers cheers.

The Position. You canot pla the skool piano unless you are adjusted at the right height. You can sit upon a stool and zoom to the right. This takes you up through the ladies hats, hardware, toys and a few v. unsavoury sort of places until you canot get any higher. If you go the other way you go round and round at 90 m.p.h. until you are too giddy to see. When you are like this music mistress lay you out with a hamer and all is peaceful.

The Choice. Wot will you pla? Fairy Bells ripling brook spring dances or scotish capers. You hav a long way to go before you can swing chiz like the last music mistress who was lost without trace when piano xploded.

WAM now nigel pla low C Bonk candlestick shoot into air BISH swing it baby swing it BASH PLUNK ZUNK. Give it xpresion it is a brook. La-la-la and a one BUNK two ZUNK 3 PLUNK – la-la-la the left finger. THE LEFT la-la-la – – well, eh, you see wot i mean? 3 trillion boos to tchkovsky.

9

HOW TO BE TOPP IN
ALL SUBJEKTS

The Molesworth Self-Educator

Directions. Take pencil in the right hand, revolve three times with eyes shut and DAB. You are bound to be right sooner or later.

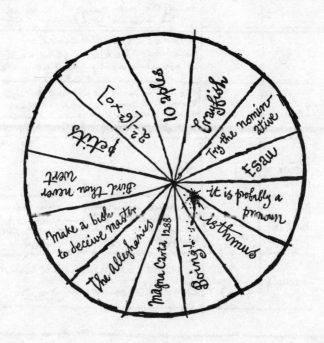

The Molesworth Bogus Report

ST. CUSTARDS.

NAME n. molesworth

EXAM ORDER ❙   TERM ORDER ❙

FINAL ORDER ❙

SUBJECT	POSITION	REMARKS
History	I	Extraordinary! His life of Marlborough was uncannily brilliant one of the best things of its kind in the present century. GUG
Geog.	1	He have a spendid sense of position, give him a globe and he know exactly what do with it. P. st 1. gs
Latin	1	It is seldom that we get a skolar like this who knowe all his grammer backwards. If he have a fault it is to muck quickness livy excons. ovid did not write enuff for him but would be better if he thought they wrote in latin. S.E.gk
Greek	1	Beyond words B. EAK
English	1 (ONE)	I didn't ought too say to much in praise of this style did I but his essays are remarkable and have been reproduced in skool mag. coz strikes a flippin lite a genius S.T.E
French	1 (UNE)	Tres, tres tres tres tres tres bien. Bravo! Formidable M.W.D.

SUBJECT	POSITION	REMARKS
Drawing	1	A wonderful sense of colour + line. His choice of subjects is perhaps a little doubtful. F.V.G
Music	1#	Toscanini must beware. Benjamin Britten

HEADMASTERS REPORT

There was a time when dere nigh was rather wild and chased about the place at full tilt shouting "Down with Skool!". Now thanks to St Custard's that is all changed thanks to St custard's he have almost worked a miracle — now we see him whole skolar, poet, man of action — dilletante, wine lover, dreamer, beer drinker — coiner of phrases, wit, athlete, strongman. He is the LOT. (thanks to St Custard's) I think he should now goon from strength to strength and you can imagine with what feelings I look forward to his returning next term.

J. Duddridge Plunk

Next term begins* :	Jan. . . . .
	May . . . .
	Sept. . 31.

(Headmaster & sole Licensee)

MATRON'S REPORT

We forgot to pack his combs. Simply couldn't face'd.
e.H.

* Fill in one week later

10

HOW TO COPE WITH GROWN UPS

Grown ups are wot is left when skool is finished. Masters are not really grown ups they are ha-ha just spoilt children who hav to hav their own way. You kno where you are with them. One is strict another wheezes through his false teeth, a third teaches geom and a fourth teaches Less than O he just wanders about.

It is not the same with Grown Ups who were always perfect when they were young. e.g.

WHEN I WAS A BOY I WOULD NOT HAV DARED TO SPEAK TO MY FATHER LIKE THAT.

Well, you kno what this means becos obviously this is what really hapned to your pater.

Scene: An old stone breakfast table about 1066 A.D. Your pater, then known as litle Cedric, is sitting down to his groats poor little dear when the old man Horible arive breathing through his beard.

HORIBLE (rubbing his hands): Good morning, good morning, good morning. What mammoth agane?

SPOUSE: It is very nice, my dear. Shall i pour you yore BEER?

HORIBLE: Yes, yes. Goodmorning, Cedric.

CEDRIC: YAR boo and sucks.

SPOUSE: Do not speak to your father like that, Cedric, or you will go strate to your cave. Hav you finished your groats.

CEDRIC: Yes, Mama.

SPOUSE: Then get on with your egg. And stop playing with the brontosaurus at breakfast.

HORIBLE: Yes, stop playing with the bronto –

SPOUSE: Don't buly the child let him get on.

HORIBLE (*meekly*): Yes, my dear.

(*A pause while HORIBLE opens the newspaper and the brontosaurus springs across the table.*)

HORIBLE: We are losing the test match, Cedric. Gaul hav made 2900 for 2.

CEDRIC: So what?

HORIBLE: i only –

CEDRIC: You are a sily old man who couldn't lift a cucumber.

HORIBLE: i –

CEDRIC (*chanting*): Silly old daddy couldn't hurt a flea.

SPOUSE: Stop interrupting and playing with the child. For heavens sake let him get on with his egg.

CEDRIC: Yar yar yar.

(*The brontosaurus springs at HORIBLE'S plate and eats his mammoth. In despair HORIBLE go to the office.*)

So you see how it was.

Maters hav a diferent approach and they are very keen on maners ect which include not throing bungie, making lakes of treacle in the porridge, flicking bread pelets at molesworth 2 grabing the sugar, slashing gravy rivers through potatoes, reading the back of your pater's *Times*, imitating a baboon, striking your next door neighbour ect ect.

In fact you are xpected to be xactly like wee tim especially when mater's grate skool friend mabel entwhistle (prothero that was) pay a visit with her tiny dorter chiz chiz chiz. On that morning all boys cats dogs parots sparos and owls are turned into the garden while house is polished and mabel entwhistle's foto is brought out of the boxroom. Boys glue their noses against windows and are finaly admited.

'Do not the house look luvly, nigel,' sa yore mater.

'But it never look like this reely it is just an empty facade.'

'O.K.,' sa yore mater. 'But let's keep it that way, see? Otherwise there's liable to be trubble. Look at yore knees.'

i do not kno why boys are always told to look at their knees it is dashed dificult. In fact the only way is to lie on yore back and pull yore knees up. Maters, however, are liable to get batey if you do this in the sitting room just before ma entwistle arive becos they see wot is on the soles of yore shoes. Too repulsive, my dear.

Procedure. Ho to the bathroom. Out flanel and wipe geting most off. Brush front of hair and leave back. Gaze in miror at yore strange unatural beauty. Report hopefully. Back agane. Scrub nails. Leave tap runing and soap in bottom of basin. Sa look at ickle pritty to molesworth 2 who hav to put on blue corduroys cheers cheers cheers cheers. Report back and granted certificate of hygene (ist Class Honours) also gold medal antwerp exhibition 1899.

Pijaw. Mater then give pi-jaw e.g. Now you will behave nicely won't you nigel and you won't do wot you did to cicely last time.

Oh no mater rather not.

You promise?

Oh yes and i will sa nothing about her dolly either.

And you will not shout Cave Cave here they come when they ring the bell? You will not repeat wot Daddy sa at brekfast about mabel entwistle? Nor sa rice pud ugh at lunch.

No No dearest mama perish the thort.

You had beter not, rat.

The Works. Mabel entwhistle arive in a super car a bentley or aston martin which show that mr entwhistle hav a clue or 2 which is more than pop hav. Women thro themself into each others arms like guided missiles.

Gaze in
miror
at yore
strange
unatural
beauty

'Darling darling (chiz) how lovely to see you after all these years.'

Visitor then gaze about as if she hav never seen anything more beaituful in the world in space.

'How swete your house is!

(*Thinks: a dump.*)

'nigel! this must be nigel! Wot a good-looking boy.'

(*Thinks: Ugh.*)

'And your younger boy how luvley.'

If anyone can call molesworth 2 luvely you kno she is telling a whoper even blue corduroy trousers do not make him into bubles not by a long chalk so it show how empty and artificial ect. hem-hem.

Enter CICELEY entwhistle.

YOUR MATER: 'Ciceley! She's already a beauty. Such hair Such eyes' ect.

(*Thinks: Gosh wot a plane child.*)

And so it go on the lunch is cold molesworth 2 drop the sprouts ciceley can't eat the steak and all larff wot screams children are to be sure. Zoom out into the garden and ciceley folow litle does she kno gay child wot is coming to her. Enuff said. The maters jaber away until teatime and **at length** the ghastley day is over.

Our Ancestors

nigel is so sensitive

I was awfully stupid at lessons when I was a girl

The trousers are a little long but
I think he will grow into them

Goodbye darling Give you little
motherkins a kiss!

I don't see why you should
look ashamed of me

KITCHEN-WISE

When i was a gurl yore mater sa the butler the cook and the parlourmaid did all the work. Of course all maters are dredfully old, about 96 approx, so it may hav been possible. i just do not see wot point it hav it won't get her out of the kitchen in the present century.

Maters these days train their dear little ones to domestic duties. They are just like performing seals – they clear away, make tea, polish the silver and also WASH-UP crash bang crash smash. A mater believe we are glad to help her out if only she knew. Any rate, we hav to HELP e.g.

Give me that wiper molesworth 2 its mine mum he has got the wiper with the red edges and rather unsavoury black marks give it to *me* (*wiper part in two judgment of solomon divinity ect. Howls of rage from all.*)

Aktualy you can hav a wizard time in the kitchen and molesworth 2 pinch everything including raisins flour jam washed down with the cat's milk.

While we are on the subjekt hem-hem here is my own favourite recipe which is reely very simple.

Take one cup of flour and add water at suficient pressure to spurt all over the kitchen.

Next go to the raisin tin. Eat 3 handfulls and put a few in the cup.

Add salt mint and coffee beans.

Stir vigorously and drop on the floor. Yell out of the door Mum Mum *Mum* where's the rolling pin. Eat a jam tart and roll out thin. When you are fed-up with rolling make the whole thing into a soft ball and chuck at molesworth 2.

UNCLES

Uncles are always v. embarased when they see a small boy we seme to make them nervous and i am not surprised. They ask a lot of feeble questions before they will hand over the routine halfcrown chiz.

Your uncles are outside, sir

Scene: a gilded drawing room of grate luxury. There are thick curtains and thick carpets in fact everything is thick including the head of the small boy who is lying upon the sofa eating bullseyes and watching the television.
Enter a flunky.

Your uncles are outside, sir.

Uncles! wot a bore. But they canot be a worse bore than the television. Let them be admitted.

Enter sixteen uncles with bald heads and spectacles.

UNCLES (*in chorus*): How big you hav grown, nigel, since we last saw you.

NIGEL: Of course i hav grown biger you didn't expect me to grow smaler did you clots. Besides, I do not think you reely care.

UNCLES: You will soon be as tall as us.

NIGEL: If i canot grow taler than *that* i will give up.

(*He peels a banana*).
Proceed.

UNCLES: If we all bend down we can give you a piggy back.

NIGEL: You think we boys like that don't you? You think it makes you appere joly. You will offer to pla criket with us now, I suppose?

UNCLES (*eagerly*): Yes yes. If you bowl at us on the lawn we will show off by hitting the first ball for 6 and loossing it.

NIGEL: As ushual. That is a grate joke?

UNCLES: Yes, yes. To amuse you further we will vault a 5 bar gate or –

NIGEL (*shudering*): That is enuff. Hav you all got your halfcrowns eh? There is no need to sa here is something for your money box. Just put them in my hat when you go out.

UNCLES: We will (*winking roguishly*). But before that we must pat you on the head.

NIGEL: No. no. I will take the will for the deed. And make it five bob next time – the cost of living is going up.

(*Exit uncles all wishing they were young agane and rightly too.*)

GRANDMOTHERS

Grandmothers are all very strikt and they all sa the same thing as they smile swetely over their gin and orange.

It is a grandmother's privilege to spoil her grandchildren GET OFF THAT SOFA NIGEL YOU WILL BRAKE IT.

Grandmothers are very tuough when you get them in a bate so it is beter not to zoom about among the dresden china or direct space bombs at the best tea set.

You ushually get parked on grans when your mater can stand you no longer or go abroad to winter sports (such a change from the kitchen). So you get left behind it might just as well be with jack the ripper for all they care.

Aktually grans are not bad. Gran you kno our gran is a wonderful old lade hem-hem she made munitions during the war and was also a lade porter. Now she fly round the world in comets stiring up trouble so pop sa and beating black men on the head. Pop sa why bother about an atomic bomb if you can drop gran over rusia. She would soon tell them how to manage their affairs e.g. you simply *can't* be a communist, mr kruschev. That's *quite* beyond the pale.

All grans show boys the tower of london and westminster abbey and think it so amusing when molesworth 2 sa 'So what?' when told that the crown jewels are worth five trillion pounds. After that they take you to st. pauls science museum national galery madam tussauds statue of peter pan buckingham place and wonder why their feet hurt. Mine were simply killing me, my dear. Madam tussauds is not bad as gran sa there is a man who murded 3 people. molesworth 2 sa thats nothing i hav done 5 already he is a swank and a wet.

One chiz about gran is that she hound and persekute all shopkeepers. She take you along and you hav to listen while she send for the manager. She sa i have dealt here for 30 years why can you not deliver on tuesdays ect while i try to pretend i am not there chiz also the gorgonzola is not wot it was. Personaly i think no gorgonzola is worth sending for the manager for but it must be diferent i supose when you are 723.

A GUIDE TO AUNTS

Aunts are not bad but they are inclined to be sopy and call you darling chiz chiz chiz. Also you are just like your mater or your pater whichever hapen to be the planer. Aunts ask you how you are geting on at skool and you sa o all right may you be forgiven. Then they ask you to read to them. There is only one thing to do for aunts when they ask this e.g. take out Domby and Son and give them the LOT.

Of course you know, children, what their Uncle did to the two
little Princes in the Tower

11

DING-DONG FARELY MERILY
FOR XMAS

Xmas all grown ups sa is the season for the kiddies but this
do not prevent them from taking a tot or 2 from the bot
and having, it may seme, a beter time than us. For children
in fact Xmas is often a bit of a strane wot with pretending
that everything is a surprise. Above all father xmas is a
strane. You canot so much as mention that there is no
father xmas when some grown-sa Hush not in front of
wee tim. So far as i am concerned if father xmas use langwage
like that when he tripped over the bolster last time we had
beter get a replacement.

CRISTMAS EVE

Hurra for Xmas Eve wot a scurrying there was in the molesworth houschold. First of all mr molcsworth issucd jovially
with the hamer to hang the decorations – red white purple
streemers holly mistletoe lights candles snow Mery Xmas
All: mrs molesworth is in the kitchen with the mince pies,
all rosy and shining: and judge of the excitement of the 2
boys!

In fact, it is a proper SHAMBLES.

Pop drop the hamer on the cat in the kitchen the xmas
puding xplode with a huge crash and the cat spring up the
curtains. Outside the sno lie deep and crisp and ect. and
just as pop fall off the steplader the WATES arive.

WATES are 3 litle gurls with a torch who go as folows:

HEE HEE HEE NOEL NOEL GO ON GURT
NO-ELL NO-ELL NO YOU RING the KING of
IS-RAY-ER-ELL.
PING! PING!
TANNER FOR THE WATES, PLEASE.

This of course is money for jam but grown ups are so intoxicated with xmas they produce a shiling. Imagine a whole weeks poket money just for that when you can get it all on the wireless anyway if you want it. Or whether you want it or not.

molesworth 2 is very amusing about carols i must sa he hav a famous carol

> *While shepherds washed their socks by night*
> *All seated on the ground*
> *A bar of sunlight soap came down ect.*

He think this is so funy he roar with larffter whenever he think of it and as he spend most of the night thinking of it i do not get much slepe chiz. i sa SHUTUP molesworth 2 SHUTUP i want to go to slepe but in vain the horid zany go cakling on. It is not as if it is funy i mean a bar of sunlight soap ha-ha well it is not ha-ha-ha-ha a bar of ha-ha-ha-ha . . . . . .

Oh well.

Another thing about xmas eve is that your pater always reads the xmas carol by c. dickens. You canot stop this aktually although he pretend to ask you whether you would like it. He sa:

Would you like me to read the xmas carol as it is xmas eve, boys?

We are listening to the space serial on the wireless, daddy.

But you canot prefer that nonsense to the classick c. dickens?

Be quiet. He is out of control and heading for jupiter.

Noel noel go on gurt you ring

But –

He's had it the treen space ships are ataking him ur-ur-ur-*whoosh*. Out of control limping in the space vacuum for evermore unless they can get the gastric fuel compressor tampons open.

I –

Why don't they try Earth on the intercom? They will never open those tampons with only a z-ray griper. They will –

Father thwarted strike both boys heavily with loaded xmas stoking and tie their hands behind their backs. He cart them senseless into the sitting room and prop both on his knees. Then he begin:

THE XMAS CAROL by C. DICKENS
(*published by grabber and grabber*)

Then he rub hands together and sa You will enjoy this boys it is all about ghosts and goodwill. It is tip-top stuff and there is an old man called scrooge who hates xmas and canot understand why everyone is so mery. To this you sa nothing except that scrooge is your favourite character in fiction next to tarzan of the apes. But you can sa anything chiz. Nothing in the world in space is ever going to stop those fatal words:

Marley was dead

Personaly i do not care a d. whether Marley was dead or not it is just that there is something about the xmas Carol which makes paters and grown-ups read with grate XPRESION, and this is very embarassing for all. It is all right for the first part they just roll the r's a lot but wate till they come to scrooge's nephew. When he sa Mery Christmas uncle it is like an H-bomb xplosion and so it go on until you get to Tiny Tim chiz chiz chiz he is a weed. When Tiny Tim sa God bless us every one your pater is so overcome he burst out blubbing. By this time boys hav bitten through their ropes and make good their escape so 9000000000 boos to bob cratchit.

XMAS NITE

At last the tiny felows are tucked up snug in their beds with 3 pilow slips awaiting santa claus. As the lite go off a horid doubt assale the mind e.g. suposing there *is* a santa claus. Zoom about and lay a few traps for him (see picture)

Determin to lie awake and get him but go to slepe in the end chiz and dream of space ships. While thus employed something do seem to be hapning among the earthmen.

CRASH!

Be quiet you will wake them up. Hav you got the mecano his is the one with 3 oranges if you drop that pedal car agane i shall scream where are the spangles can you not tie a knot for heavens sake ect. ect.

It would seem that the earthmen are up to something but you are far to busy with the treens who are defending

Trap for dere Santa

the space palace with germ guns. So snore on, fair child, snore on with thy inocent dreams and do not get the blud all over you.

THE DAY

Xmas day always start badly becos molesworth 2 blub he hav not got the reel rools-royce he asked for. We then hav argument that each hav more presents than the other. A Mery Xmas everybode sa scrooge in the end but we just call each other clot-faced wets so are you you you you pointing with our horny fingers it is very joly i must sa. In the end i wear molesworth 2's cowboy suit and he pla with my air gun so all is quiet.

Then comes DINNER.

This is super as there are turkey crackers nuts cream plum puding jely and everything. We wash it down with a litle ginger ale but grown ups all drink wine ugh and this make all the old lades and grans very sprightly i must sa. They sa how sweet we are they must be dotty until pater raps the table and look v. solemn. He holds up his glass and sa in a low voice

The QUEEN. Cheers cheers cheers for the queen we all drink and hurra for england.

Then pater sa in much lower voice ABSENT FRIENDS and everyone else sa absent friends absent friends absent friends ect. and begin blubbing. In fact it do not seme that you can go far at xmas time without blubbing of some sort and when they listen to the wireless in the afternoon all about the lonely shepherd and the lighthousemen they are in floods of tears.

Still xmas is a good time with all those presents and good food and i hope it will never die out or at any rate not until i am grown up and hav to pay for it all. So ho skip and away the next thing we shall be taken to peter pan for a treat so brace up brace up.

The Molesworth Self-Adjusting
Thank-You Letter

As an after xmas wheeze n. molesworth presents his self-adjusting thank-you letter.

Cut out hours of toil pen biting wear on elbows blotches and staring out of windows.

Strike Out words which do not apply.

Dear {
Aunt ....
Uncle........................
Stinker ....
Gran ....
Clot ....
Pen-Pal ....
}

Thank you very much for the {
train. tractor. germ gun. kite.
delicious present.* sweets.
space pistol. toy socks.
}

It was {
lovely. useful.
just as good as the other three.
not bad. super.
}

And I hav {
played with it constantly.
bust it already.
no patience with it.
given it to the poor boys.
dismantled it.
}

I am feeling {
very well
very poorly.
lousy.
in tip-top form
sick.
} I hope you are too.

My birthday when next present is due is on...............................

From..

(*Postage must be prepaid.*)

* When you can't remember what it was

205

WHIZZ FOR ATOMMS

Welcome back for the new term,
molesworth! *Welcome Back!*

Prefface

Conoisuers of prose and luvers of literature hem-hem may recall that some of this hav apeared in that super smashing mag *Young Elizabethan*. [ADVERT]. In compiling the present volume it has been my intention insofar as it be within my poor ability – posh stuff this posh stuff go it molesworth – infarso as it be i.e. wot i want to sa is that i hav joly well tried to give others the fruits of my xperience at skool and also of the various chizzes which take place in the world outside the skool walls.

My thanks are due to grabber for the use of his blotch, peason whose pen i pinched and the skool gardener for cleaning out the ink wells – a task which only a man with iron nerve can perform. i gratefully acknowledge the kindly help and encouragement of gillibrand, a most lively source of material ha-ha the dere little wet. molesworth 2 was just about able to read the proofs and pass the speling. You hav to get in a lord or somebody to show you mix in the right company. may i therefore mention Crosby-kershaw-Parkinson, Hon. the A.P.R., who is the absolute dregs and hav had no conection with this book at all?

It is now my pleasure to introduce a few of the sordid felow workers who appere in this book.

Perlice Notise

The folowing weeds are known for their long records of crime. Many are completely desperate in every sense of the word, all the others are hopeless. All hav been known to zoom along passages at speeds of

1 PEASON (known as the wet-weed, clot, darling timothy, that boy there ect.)

RECORD Known to be desperate during prep, particularly when he hav been looking at the "Charge of the Light Brigade" for nearly 2 hours. A dead shot with the ink dart. From time to time uters wolfish cries.

DISTINGUISHING MARKS Several beetles drawn in ink on the left knee.

REMARKS He is my grate frend so i hav let him off litely. He is much worse than this aktually as his mummy call him 'darling' and kiss his ickle-pritty face. The old gurl must be blind. Or bats. Or both.

2 MOLESWORTH 2, MY BRO.

RECORD His career read as a case-book for a loony-bin. He zoom about the place going ahahahahahah and pretending to be a jet bomber. Caried out the famous hit-and-run raid on the skool larder. Served sentence in sick wing. Adicted to the arts. His piece "Fairy Bells" on the skool piano will never be forgoten by those who hav heard it.

DISTINGUISHING MARKS He do not share the charm and good looks of his elder bro, molesworth 1, hem-hem. Strange that they could be related. One so fare, the other ugh!

REMARKS Nil.

Perlice Notise

mach number, to jab compasses, make aple pie beds, bomb the skool dog, call each other uncouth names, smoke cigs and rob the larder of skool cheese and sossages. If sighted dial 999 or run like blazes.

3 HEADMASTER GRIMES (alias old Stinker, diamond jack, soho sammy and Cave, here he comes)

RECORD A monster of calous cruelty who fly into a bate at every oportunity. Known to consort with desperate carakters on the staff e.g. sigismund the mad maths master. They too hold him in fear.

DISTINGUISHING MARKS A livid scar across the face sometimes looking like a smile, or

REMARKS If anyone can give him 6 months the whole skool will cheer.

4 GRABBER

RECORD Born of very rich parents, and head of the skool. He hav won every prize, including the mrs joyful prize for rafia work. Brilliant at work. Will get a skol. Superb at games. Strikt but fare.

DISTINGUISHING MARKS A coutenance of rare charm.

REMARKS Recieved the sum of 5/- for writing above

1

HOW TO BE A
YOUNG ELIZABETHAN

No one kno wot to do about anything at the moment so they sa the future is in the hands of YOUTH i.e. some of the weeds you hav just seen. As if they kno wot to do about it at their age. All the same we are young elizabethans and it can't be altered – i expect drake felt the same way. Supose we had lived then, eh? i wave my ickle pritty fairy wand, slosh peason with it and the SCENE changes into something most wondrous fair hem-hem i don't think.

Look at me coo er gosh posh eh? You wouldn't hav thort a pair of bloomers would make all that diference. Fie fie – the grown ups canot kno what a privilege it is to be YOUTH in this splendid age of Queen Bess – when all are brave proud fearless etc and looking with clear eyes at the future. (Not so clear after some of those evenings at Court, i trow, when all drink BEER.) All the same it is up to us boys becos the grownups hav made such a MESS of it all. So here i am looking like a hem-hem fule but fearing absolutely O. no one could be so brave. Hist! Hist tho! – i hear the headmaster advancing *clump-clump* with his huge feet encased in gooloshes. I had better begone like a scalded cat. The headmaster is not a young elizabethan he is an old – conduct mark (swearing rude words general uncouth behaviour and letting down the tone of st. custard's.)

OLDE TIMES

Drake, you kno Drake who singed the king of spane's beard, he was the kind we ought to model ourselves on.

Look at me coo er gosh posh eh? You wouldn't hav thort a pair of bloomers would make all that diference

With him he had a gay band of cut-throats who would make molesworth 2, peason, grabber gillibrand ect look like the weeds and wets they are. These cut-throats were very fond of Drake and when he was dead they kept calling to him.

CUTTHROATS: Captin art tha sleeping there below?

DRAKE: How can i when you are making such an infernal din?

CUTTHROATS: Drake is in his hamock —

DRAKE: i am not in my hamock curse you. All there is down here is sea-weed and shells it is worse than a bed in the skool dorm.

CUTTHROATS: Captin —

DRAKE: Wot is it? if you're going to sa 'art tha sleeping' i shall hav insomnia.

CUTTHROATS: Then you are not dreaming all the time of plymoth ho ——?

DRAKE: if i could dream at all it would be of marilyn mun-ro oh-ho that is a good one twig?

(*the cutthroats go home in disgust to fill in their foopball pools.*)

Aktually Drake was pritty tuough and did more or less as he liked espueshully if there were spaniards about. Good Queen Bess was very keen on him in spite of the remonstrances of the king of spane who had a lisp like all spaniards.

THE KING OF SPANE: i tha, beth, that thcoundrel drake hath thinged my berd agane.

ELIZABETH: (*wiping her fhoes on his cloke*) La coz you furprise me you fimply fake me rigid.

THE KING OF SPANE: Tith twithe thith week. Ith abtholutely off-thide.

ELIZABETH: Off-fide? Where are your fectaclef? He was on-fide by fix yardf.

THE KING OF SPANE: Yar-boo. Thend him off.

ELIZABETH: Upon my foul tif clear you do not kno the rules of foccer.

(*Raleigh, the earl of essex, john and sebastian cabot join in the brawl with vulgar cries. Which match are you looking at? Pla the game, ruff it up ha-ha etc.*)

What would happen to Drake today?

DON SEBASTIAN ORSINO JERETH DE LA FRONTERA
 (*a courtier*): How common!

They were certainly swashbukling adventurers in those days
and life in general was tuougher than an end of term rag at
skool. But it is all very well it is not the same today – I mean
what would happen to Drake if he wanted to singe the king
of spane's berd today?

LOUDSPEAKER: Passengers by Golden Hind for Cadiz
 please report to the customs.

OFICIAL: Hav you read this card? Hav you anything to
 declare?

DRAKE (*trembling*): No.

OFICIAL: No buble gum no spangles no malteaser?
 nothing in the nature of a weapon –

DRAKE: Just this pike –

OFICIAL: Did you buy that pike in Britain, Mr Drake?
 Hav you an export license? Hav you filled in form 3

stroke D stroke 907? Are you Mr Mrs or miss? Do you possess a dog license?

DRAKE (*on his knees*): Hav mercie.
OFICIAL: Folow the blue lights to the place of execution.

(*A gold ingot fall from Drake's pocket and he crawls away blubbing. Oficial takes up the ingot. He is lawffing triumphantly the skool dog howls a skool sossage stands on its head.*)

THE CURTAIN FALLS SLOWLY

KRISTMAS AT KURDLING

Of course Xmas was still going in those old times and you can imagin how excited the lusty skolars of Kurdling Kollege are as the end of term approaches. They are all in Big Skool becos there weren't very many skolars in that century the boys used to get away with it.

Piktur the scene if you can – 1576 a.d.

molefworth 1 and molefworth 2 are sitting on an old bench staring with leaden eyes at lat. books. Up and down strides Doctor Kurdling and every few minutes he take up a boy and give him 6 with the kane. An ink dart heaved by peason scrape his august nose.

'Quidem telum emmissit?' he sa in voice of thunder.

'Nemo,' sa the whole skool, for they all speke lat.

Doctor Kurdling do not take their word for it and flog the lot. Boys noses are blue and ears drop off with cold chiz it might be almost like skool today. At last porter ring bell –

KLANG–PIP–KLANG–PIP. (The bell hav been cracked on one side.)

After 6 of the best each they dash out into quad where stand the ancient motto of the kol.

> *Quantum ille canis est in fenestra?*
> (How much is that doggie in the window?)

One of the super things about being an elizabethan skoolboy

Franklyn come here bend over

was that so much less had hapened then. I.E. in Hist you
were doing that utter weed perkin warbeck in modern and
advanced study tho let us face it he was just as big a weed
then as he is today. As for Geog they had only just discovered america and were assimilating the fact for wot it
was worth.

All this could make a geog lession with Doctor Kurdling
v. interesting:

KURDLING: it if sayde to be a fact, skolars, that Columbus
   hav sayled fo far to the westward that he hav discovered
   the americas. In my opinion, Franklyn come here bend
   over *WHACK* there if notte *WHACK* a word
   WHACK of truth in it –
MOLEFWORTH 1: fir.
KURDLING: The world of course if flatte – flatte as a pancake – and when you come to the edge any fule kno that
   you fall over.

MOLEFWORTH I : fir please fir.

KURDLING: let us assume – Cranmer take that pious expresion off yore face, Wolsey stop scratching, let us assume purely as a suposition that there are such things as the americas.

MOLEFWORTH I : fir fir fir fir please fir.

KURDLING: they can be hardly more than a group of islands small barren uninhabited –

MOLEFWORTH I : fir, you are wrong. America is a continent a huge powerful nation live there and the pacific washes the western seaboard.

DOCTOR KURDLING IS CONVINCED

KURDLING: Fie child you speak with conviction. Stand forth and bend over *WHACK WHACK WHACK WHACK* ow gosh ow gosh that will teach you not to alter the ignorance of a lifetime (which all masters possess).

MOLEFWORTH I (rubbing his bloomers): Semper aliequid novum, fir, if i may fa fo.

Of course they had xmas then and wizard rags japes pranks wheezes chizzes when the skool brake up. grabber drive away in a gold coach fotherington-Tomas in a smart gig and Jan the Cowman come for molefworth 2 and me on an old cart horse.

Xmas day is the same and both get 69 copies of skoolboys diary for 1567 with spaces for personal details. The usual sort of xmas mail arive – Dere sir unless your account is payde. But it is a super day with wizard puding crackers larfter and song.

And so the new year with its resolutions. Noe smoking (which is easy becos sir w raleigh hav not discovered it yet). Decide also to give new xmas present to the poor boys –

An Act of Charitee

Inspiration

The gift

Doubt

Exploration

Despair

Meanwhile

Here we are at st custards poised between past and future. How far along the road hav we traveled? How far must we proceed? Wot of Livy and J. Caesar? Will Bluebell win the 2.30 at Kempton? Who cares? This is the present and it is up to us to make it as beauteous as possible.

THE FUTURE OR
OAFS WILL BE OEUFS

Everyone kno wot we are like now you hav only to look around and see it is ghastley enuff. But wot of the future, eh? Wot are we all going to be like in a few centuries? Come on molesworth i have told you a 1000000000 times . . . . . wot of the future? . . . . . come along boy . . . . . how many more times *WAM* hav i *SOCKO* got to tell you *BIFF BAM* that we must never resort to FORCE *WAM BIFF BAM* . . . . .

Wot else? Wot hapens when we get beyond contemporary verse in the classroom e.g. it was the skooner hesperus that sailed the wintry sea and the skipper had taken his little hem-hem to bear him company etc. Well everyone use their branes so much that in the end they are all going to turn into eggs becos they will hav thort a way of getting along without walking. This will not be until 21066 a.d. (approx.) but it makes you think a bit.

And where will the sports comentaries be?

Here come the eggs of 761 st. custardhuss . . . . . they look tremendously fit . . . . . they all hav their log books . . . . . brown and shiny, curled up at the edges . . . . . i see that one of the players hav writen 'if my name you wish to see turn to p. 103 – ha-ha – that used to be done hundreds of years ago . . . . . and now there's a tremendous cheer as of porridge court 979 . . . . . . THIS should be a grate match . . . . . now they're kicking a few logarithms about and at the other end they're runing over the reactions involving the recombination of ions before the whistle go for the start . . . . .

As a mater of fact it is all quite pappy becos all thinking is done with a machine e.g. the molesworth-peason electronick brane Mark VI which any fule kno was invented by those 2 grate pioneers to do multiplication and long div for them and thus fool sigismund the mad maths master and others of his kind. The early Mark 1 brane that these intreppid inventors achieved was just a simple digital computor working with electric pulses. (I won't explane further as the masters sa when they don't kno the answer.) The brane soon became involved in the study of super-sonic flite and all went well until molesworth 2 creep up and ask it a cunning question e.g. brane, wot is $2+2$ eh? At this the brane larff so much that it bust into a trilion pieces.

The œufs of the future, however, are fitted with the much superior Mark VI electronick brane and you can imagine wot it is like in skool.

Scene. A classroom of the future. Twelve branes sit at there desks sploshing infra-red ink at each other. The head eggs helicopter is heard approaching despite its speshul silencing device.

AN OEUF NEAR THE DOOR: Cave! Hear comes the Pukon!

All look keen and inocent.

HEAD BRANE: Today we will do a little comon computing.
8765 MOLEGRUB 1: It's relativity sir not . . . . .

(The automatick kaning machine deliver 6)

HEAD BRANE: As i was saing. Now wot is the polynomial equation of degree n in one variable or unknown . . . . ?
LES OEUFS: *(in chorus)* $a^0x^n + a^1x^{n-1} + a^2x^{n-2} + \ldots + a_{n-1}x^{+a}n = 0 (A. \neq 0.)$
HEAD BRANE: A very nice little rational integral equation –
8765 MOLEGRUB 1: Sir please sir it really is relativity –
HEAD BRANE: Write out the law of electromagnetic induction 5000000000 times.

8765 MOLEGRUB 1: *(thinks)* $D = 1 + (\frac{s-1}{npq}\sum_{i-1}^{w} p_i - p)^2$.

molesworth 2 zoom down with his rotors whirring

The head brane drone on until brake when cocoa and buns are fed in on a conveyor belt and we are allowed to pla around on big field with our helicopters.

'Lets go to mars,' sa fotherington-Tomas. 'Come on molesworth o you mite. We can go up there and hav a lovely think.'

'No,' i sa, 'i hav thort myself stupid already.'

molesworth 2 zoom down with his rotors whirring.

silly sossage can't think for toofee, he sa and zoom away. If only it were like the old days when the tuougher you were the more you were respected chiz! Now it is the opposite and if you can't think they all buly you espeshully fotherington-Tomas who hav a huge brane. But there is no hope. It is 200000 years ahead and I am still learning 'amo'.

'You are a clot-faced wet,' sa fotherington-Tomas, aiming a thort at me. 'Thou canst not hurt an insecta siphonaptra or comon flea.'

No wonder i sigh for the old days as we oeufs hav it in our spechul hist. broadcasts and telyfilms. e.g.

PLAYS FROM HIST

This illustrates a well-known incident in the uranium age of the 20th century.

Musick: The Gondoliers. Scene: A dorm at st. custards. Enter molesworth the gorila of 3B cursing.

MOLESWORTH: who are these weedy ticks who lay their golden locks upon their pilows? I will uterly bash them up until their own maters whose fotos grace these sordid shelves will not kno them. Charge!

(*Comentator:* Observe the low beetling brow the hair which hang over the eyes, the knees with noughts and croses scribled on them in ink. What a short step is this specimen from the ape chiz chiz chiz. What progress hav we made.)

In the dorm pilows fly about in clouds of feathers.

A SKOLAR: Cave! *As they all rush back to bed the* HEAD-MASTER GRIMES *enter.*

(*Comentator:* This horid creature is no beter than the boys. Look at him if you can bare it. It make you think do it not? To think that an objeckt like that could hav thort to teach boys cheers cheers cheers. In his right hand he grasp wot was known in those days as a kane or swish, his face is contorted in fury. Such barbarism o woe o woe it is enuff to bring tears to the eyes.)

The HEADMASTER GRIMES *look around the dorm and sa:*
'Any boy who was out of bed to own up.' *Silence.* 'Curses'
sa head master 'i could hav sworn i heard something perhaps
it was the matron plaing darts againe.' *A well-aimed tomato
hit him in the face* . . . . .

(*Comentator:* Do you see that, eggs eh? In those dark days skools
were full of mutiny and disorder. The pupils ran wild with
wizard wheezes jokes and pranks. They aktually throw a
tomato at the headmaster . . . . . *PING* . . . . Wot egg did that?
. . . . . Own up or i shall kepe the whole clutch in . . . . . *CRASH
WAM BONK* . . . . . i saw you oeuf 8765 molegrub . . . . . do
not deny it . . . . . you shall hav half an hour in the automatick
kaning machine . . . . . as i was saing it make you sigh to think
of the misery and injustice of those prehistorick times ect. ect.)

The next part of the film show a game of criket but as this is
still going on all cheer. There may be a result by 15678 a.d.

'Curses' sa headmaster 'i could hav sworn i heard something'

2

THE UGGLY TRUTH

The scene is still the dark, doom-haunted skool of st. custards chiz chiz moan drone where the tiny pupils live a life of friteful sufering at the hands of the headmaster GRIMES and his band of thugs who hav the impertnence to call themselves masters.

GRABBER, dark, dashing debonair (compliment hem-hem he is perfectly weedstruck actually) is head of the skool. He is approached one day by a foul-looking specimen called PEASON who is my best friend.

'Look at ickle pritty baby,' sa peason in mocking tones. He run away and not before it is time becos the skool is on fire.

Terible cries come from the roof where MOLESWORTH 2, and FOTHERINGTON-TOMAS, the skool gurly are traped on the roof with the matron and a string of skool sossages. Who will save them? The crowd parts for a mysterious figure which zoom headlong into the fire on his erand of mercy – it is me MOLESWORTH 1, the gorila of 3B, the masked clot. (wot is the use of writing a book if you don't give yourself a good part, eh?) In 5 minits he hav saved the LOT which is pritty good work. Begrimed and exorsted he is aproached by the headmaster. 'Your face and hands are filthy,' he sa. 'Go and wash, boy. Do also 500 lines.' Smarting under a sense of injustice MOLESWORTH 1 decide to run away but, before he can turn, a voice sa 'Stop! Stop him!' It is SIGISMUND THE MAD MATHS

MASTER who point an acusing finger. 'There,' he sa, 'is the boy who start the fire. I saw him do same.' Wot will hapen to MOLESWORTH? Is the can of petrol inflammable? Who hav tampered with the headmasters protractors?

(Now read on.)

'Nearer and nearer crept the ghastly THING'

For story turn to p. 1096b, col. 2.

A GRIM SUBJEKT

CLANG-PIP. CLANG-Pip.

The craked tones of the skool bell sumon all weeds and skolars to xsemble in big skool. This is most unusual just before brake and in the middle of lessons. 'Wot can it mean?' ask grabber.

'It mean,' sa molesworth 2 litely, 'that 99 sparrows hav fallen from their nest in the bell, the masters are interupted doing their foopball pools, the skool dog will eat the buns and – and – "

'Yes? Yes?'

'It mean that thou, o weedy clot, are the biggest wet of them all.'

With this riposte molesworth 2 ignite the fuse and zoom vertically up in rocket flite to safety as HEADMASTER enter. Silence you can hear a pin drop.

'molesworth 2, were you the boy who sai *ZOOSH* as i entered with the staff?'

'Yessir.'

'Can my ears hav deceived me when i heard you calling up mars?'

'Yessir – nosir – yessir.'

'A remarkable feat, molesworth 2. You should be congratulated. Kindly do fifty lines.'

Bad luck aktually getting cobbed but such is the fate of all pioneers. Now to the business of the meeting. HEADMASTER look stern. Tremble tremble quake quake. Wot can it be? Air is blak with sins rising before boys eyes.

SILENCE

'St. custards,' sa HEADMASTER, 'hav always prided itself upon its long tradition of

good maners
discipline
decorum   } *strike out word*
honour   *which do not aply*
sobriety
musical apreciation

We are all proud of that. i and the staff (*he gives a contemptuous look over his shoulder at the sheepish colection of branes and louts behind him*) hav laboured long and hard to preserve it. We have done our best to discourage

gambling
poker   } *strike out words which*
drink   *do not aply tho sometime*
smoking   *HEADMASTERS*
gurls   *use all of them.*

Of corse this is only the beginning. It is not for this that we hav been sumoned. These fine phrases are like when molesworth 2 pla fairy bells on skool piano – it take a minit or two before it sound like an H-bomb.

HEADMASTER *continue*

'Some boy,' he sa. (This is it. Always is when a headmaster sa 'Some boy') 'Last night – or in the early hours of this morning – *some boy* broke out of his dormitory and

strike
out   { discharged pellets at skool pig.
CRIME   hung by his heels from the weather
which do   cock.
not aply   bunged up the drane with a pair of
                    socks.
                Scared the matron stiff.
                Painted the gymnasium purple.
                Raided the larder.

O woe tremble tremble agane. Who can hav been so beastley? Wot cad could hav sunk so low? At first there is a feeling of exquisite relief that it wasn't that little business of dougnuts in the deaf master's mortar board in which you were hem-hem involved. Then you look about at the little cherub faces for the criminal. Who look guilty? ALL of them, which do not get anyone very far.

And the HEADMASTER? His eyeballs pop out his hair stands on end and the fur on his gown emit electric sparks. His face is purple and his hands twitch convulsively. One would judge him to be angry.

'Some boy,' he sa agane, 'is guilty. Let him own up now before the whole skool. Let him admit his guilt. Let him step before his judges.'

Silence

'Come on!' he roar. 'Oo dunnit, eh?'

Silence

There you hav the weakness of his case. The clot hav not got an earthly – i mean, well, lets face it he simply doesn't kno. One should really feel sorry for him. He – well, every boy kno wot is coming next.

IF THE BOY DOES NOT OWN UP THE WHOLE SKOOL WILL BE KEPT IN.

It is not always like that sometimes it is the whole skool given six or fifty lines or made to go to bed at six. But it is always the same principle – the Inocent punished on acount of the Guilty in contravention of paragraphs 2 and 3, Sixth Schedule of Standing Orders on British demoracracy. As any fule kno it is therein stated clearly that a guilty party must be arraigned therto and evidence therunto duly and properly brought hem-hem. Any boy kno that and give us 5 minits alone and this is wot would hapen –

Come on grab him by the neck scrag him give him a chinese

him up. Tung Fifth dynasty? You surprise me

DET. INSPECTR THE HON NIGEL MOLESWORTH: Now you kno the rule in cases like this the smallest tick hav to own up. What an exquisite vase Lord Weevil. Is it ming?

A VOICE: Wot hav that got to do with it?

DET. INSPECTR THE HON NIGEL MOLESWORTH: Detectives are very cultured. Come on grab him by the neck scrag him give him a chinese burn beat him up and let him hav it. Tung Fifth dynasty? You surprise me. i would not hav thort that tint of eggshell blue – no matter, tie his hands behind the chair. Now, scum, are you going to own up?

No, o no i am inocent.

O.K. Work him over, butch. Headmasters do not care who is inocent, they only want someone to confess. You will only get 6 with the kane – why hav it both ways? And do not bleed on this rich aubusson carpet which lie upon the floor of Big skool etc.

In the end the victim confess and once agane British justice is served cheers cheers cheers.

Aktually in some cases there is no need for these extreme measures. When the headmaster sa he want to see the boy outside who hav been pinching the raspberries the whole Skool surge to the exits trampling all before them in the rush. But, i ask you, wot petty trifles headmasters get worked up about, eh? A few raspberries, a paltry pair of socks in a drane pipe, tadpoles in the tea – you would think such trivial affairs were beneath their notice it show how mentally undeveloped skoolmasters are.

At this moment HEADMASTER glare round.

'Well, the culprit hav had the good sense to confess. If this horid crime is comited agane he will not get off so litely ect.....'

As he go out deaf master take off his mortar board and 12 doughnuts fall out.

'SOME BOY......!'

SIX-GUN MOLESWORTH

Peace broods over st. custards, that cloistered seat of learning hem-hem. Grabber the head boy – brave, noble, fearless true as all head boys are is smoking a furtive cig in the lib as he reads about Jane. Other seniors lie at ease reading the works of c. dickens and sir w. scott which would be a chiz if they were only covers to conceal RUDE BOOKS within. In his study the headmaster gravely peruses SPACE ACE: a boy reaches for the bell to order tea.....

Hopo! Hopo! Hookahey!

Bang!

Ya-hay. Ya-hay.

Crack! 'You're dead i shot you you've got to lie down maplethorpe no you didn't yes i did.....'

'Injuns!' gasps grabber, reaching for his winchester. 'Get the wagons in a circle, corral the ponies.....'

A senior stirs languidly.

'It's only molesworth 2 and fotherington-Tomas plaing with the new bugs. Calm yourself, clot.'

Grabber flushes at his mistake. No one speke but they kno that only a few years ago he also was plaing cowboys. They kno that they were plaing cowboys themselves and they flinch at the recolection. Are such games worthy of the new weedy generation who are to blaze a trail of fearless adventure in the new age?

Inspired, i spring to my feet.

'Chaps, felows, custardians i am dashed if this is good enuff. Are we not meant to be folowing the footsteps of drake, howard effingham and other good men who are sleeping tha' below? Are we not suposed to be making a beter world? This low, vulgar game of cowboys and injuns – beg pardon, indians – ort to be stoped for it teaches the tinies ideas of violence. Shall i therefore tuough them up?'

'Do that thing,' sa grabber. 'Knock their heads together squish their ears and hack their young shins until they stop.'

It is a mision after my own heart. i spring to the saddle and joris and he etc i zoom he zooms we zoom all three out into the shrubery where i am greeted with a horid sight e.g. molesworth 2 wraped in a blanket.

'How,' he sa.

'Wot do you mean "how"? it is uterly wet to sa "how" you mite as well sa "when" or "where".'

'How.'

'Look molesworth 2 you mite as well listen becos i shall be a prefect next term.'

'How.'

'A box of cigars to the headmaster 20 players to the masters, 5/- to the matron, bone to the skool dog and a box of chox for the maids. That is how.'

'How.'

i am about to bash him when the situation is saved by 16 new bugs who arive saing bang bang and charging round. The weediest one stroll up and say, 'Howdy, stranger?'

To me!!! The gorila of 3B. My veins stand out like whipcords my fists clench and unclench.

'This game,' i snap, 'must cease. Cowboys are weeds and wetstruck.'

'You're a kinda crazy galoot, pard,' sa the new bug. 'Heck, we'll drill you fuller of holes than a seive. Take my advice stranger and git – git outa town – git.'

The poor pipsqueak must be bats. No other explanation can be possible. Quite mad and so young.

'Tell us why you don't like cowboys,' come the chorus. 'Tell us why you do not like them.'

'How!' sa molesworth 2.

'That's enuff,' i sa. 'i shall go bats also. i do not like cowboys for one reason. When the posse chase the hero he always go up a side turning and they always charge past. That is uterly wet. Q.E.D.'

My veins stand out like whipcords

'Pla with us,' chorus the new bugs. 'Go on molesworth 1 pla with us o you mite. Show us how it is done.'

They dance round me weedily like little gurlies all the same they touch my hart poor weak fule that i am.

'O.K.,' i sa, 'bags be a cowboy . . . . .'

10 mins 20 secs. later

'Wot is yon object with a face like a squished turnip which approaches?'

'i kinda figger its tarzan of the apes. Or mabbe there's a resemblance to Vora king of space. Wot does big chief Blue Nose think?'

molesworth 2 give another grunt.

'How?' he sa.

'Pardners i guess it's grabber.'

'Yep it's grabber O.K.'

Tremble tremble moan drone grabber approche looking tuough. 'Look here ticks there's a jolly sight too much din you will even wake the headmaster which takes a bit of

'Yep, stranger, and he's plenty light on the trigger too'

doing at this hour. Wot are you doing, eh?' He see me and his jaw drop. 'You molesworth, a senior, plaing cowboys?'

'Yep, stranger, and he's plenty light on the trigger too,' sa mapplebeck the new bug. 'Git and skit while the going's good.'

grabber fante dead away at such neck. When he come to
he find himself by molesworth 2's wigwam where a huge
pot of radio malt is slowly cooking at the fire. Beyond it a
delicious meal of dried braces and stewed prunes.

'Who are you?' gasp grabber.

'How,' come the chorus.

'How indeed can an apparition so friteful with a blue nose and a smelly old blanket hav come to pass? Wot is it?'

'How.'

'This will drive you crazy, pard,' i sa. 'Join our merry game we are having a supersonic time . . . . . "

5 mins 6 secs. later

'Cave, chaps! Here comes the head. You've woken him up from his hog-snoring.'

Headmaster it is indeed with the skool coyote scampering at his heels and barking. Headmaster is in good bate and chat with the matron about gillibrand's vests hem-hem so he is glad to change the subject when the new bug with specs jump out at him.

'Stick 'em up,' he sa. 'Pronto. And that goes for your squaw too.'

'A game of cowboys,' sa the headmaster. 'An excellent game to develop quick thinking. I trust however that when the hero turns to the right the posse do not galop past? You see it is obviously quite simple – '

'Sir sir sir pla with us sir. Sir pla with us . . . . .'

20000 years later

As i said before, the human race hav progressed so much that they hav only tiny legs and the rest of it look like an egg. they hav so many branes. It is afternoon at the Institute Custardhuss. Sudenly a shout rends the air: 'Tha he goes git after him.' One egg is hotly pursued by sixteen other eggs . . . . . the first egg pulls up a sidetrack to the right and the other eggs go thundering by . . . . .

There is a lesson in this and wot it is i am sure molesworth 2 can tell us. He ponder for several hours and at last give his verdict.

'How.'

MORE CULTURE AND A CLEANER BRANE

Now it can be told. The story of our pioneer inventors early struggles . . . . .

'I think, peason,' sa prof. molesworth, gravely. 'That we may now conect the cyclotron to the reactor. We shall then be ready for the plutonium – "

'You mean ? ? ? ? ? ?'

'i do not kno wot i mean, o measly weed. But if all do not go well, i would not give 2d for st. custards chances in the local skools charity league next season.'

Above them tower the huge atommic PILE which they hav constructed in the MUSICK room. There are 10 bombs – a litle one which trigger off a bigger one, which trigger off the next one until you get to the last which is super coolossal.

'Well?' sa prof. molesworth. 'You seme thortful?'

'It is just that it appere to be going to a lot of trubble just to heat the gym.'

CAVE! CAVE MOLESWORTH CAVE!

The warning cry come just in time. HEADMASTER GRIMES puts his hoary head round the door. He beam at the two keen little chaps who are now sitting together at ye olde skool piano plaing a super duet.

'Bravo,' he yell above the din. 'Keep it going, hep-cats, get in the groove. If that is the *Flite of the bumble BEE* it must be the biggest bee in the world, in space. It sound more like a comet IV at full boost. It is louder than when molesworth 2 pla *Fairy Bells*.

'There are 2 of us at it,' shout prof. molesworth. 'Why not join us, sir, on drums?'

'No, no. Can you lend me a tanner till tuesday?'

GRIMES catch the coin in his mortar board with the skill of long practice and withdraw. Out in the passage he rub his hands. 'Peason and molesworth are at last settling down to a sense of responsibility,' he sa. 'st. custard's will hav cause to remember them.'

He pick up his banjo and move to the next pitch outside 3B where he strum *swannee river* with one hand and ratle the bones with the other. Molesworth and peason return to the 'Young Students Chemistry Set' which gran hav given molesworth for Xmas . . . .

'Wot are you doing, molesworth, go on tell me o you mite.'

It is fotherington-tomas who intrude this time skipping weedily he is utterly wet. And is he to be trusted? Hav he been cleared for security, eh?

'It is the Peason-molesworth Atommic Pile fitted with radio and plug for electric razor.'

'Goody goody,' sa fotherington-Tomas. 'Will it cost a grate deal to get a shave?'

'About three trillion pounds.'

'A new era for the world,' sa fotherington-Tomas. Then he begin to blub. 'Science is not everything. There is culture as well.'

'Come agane?'

'In a mechanised age the things of the spirit are more important than ever. Consider shapespeare, c. dickens, c. kingsley, sir w. scott and others. And wot of christopfer robin, eh?'

His words set up a chain reaction and the skool piano and chemistry set blow up. Only the Peason-Molesworth Atommic Pile seme unaffected tho we use the metronome as a geiger counter . . . . .

That was how it began. That nite in the Pink Dorm i hav DOUBTS. It is the same old q. for a scientist. Should he make his knoledge avalable to everyone? It do not mater one jot in my case becos with my knoledge they would all still be where they were before. And wot about all these

Should he make his knoledge avalable to everyone?

books which we hav in eng.? Wot of all those q's in the exams e.g.

Sa wot you kno of silas marner, queeg, jack the ripper, perseus and mrs do-as-you-would-be-don-by. Writing and neatness will be taken into consideration.

Answer:

A grate thort strike me:

ALL BOOKS WHICH BOYS HAV TO READ
ARE WRONG

How dare you, molesworth. You are idle, inattentive, slovenly, stupid, irascible, hopeless and hav o branes. Also you hav drawn beetles all over m. dubois in the fr. book and hav given armand a moustache.

How dare you?

i can see wot will be the answer to my grate thort but i hav my defence.

Take the first book in my little selection this week e.g. O. Twist featuring in the old Curiosity Shoppe introducing douglas fairbanks jr. as fagin. Book and lyrics by grabber 1. From an idea by c. dickens.

You remember how it go? Where is my book bag? Ah, here it is. O. Twist feel that he hav not had enuff skool sossages ect. and ask Mr bumble the beedle for more i.e. he make the message quite clear and sa Please, sir, can i hav some more. Mr bumble is so surprised anyone could want any more he fall into a rage and O. twist get his chips. Now wot would hapen toda?

TWIST: Another sossage, fatty.
BEEDLE: Eh, wot. You hav had yore allocation as pre-sribed in the skool leaving act A/cD/10L.
TWIST: Come on come on. This is the welfare state. Give us a couple also some free milk and orange juice, a corset, some false teeth, old age pension, forecast for the pools, 20 peoms by w. auden, six beetles, a pencil sharpner and anything else you hav in yore poket.
BEEDLE: No, no.
TWIST: Garn, or we'll rip yer.

It is the same with many a well-known charakter. Another is that well-known weed christopfer robin who luv poo bear ect. and watch the changing of the gard at buck house with alace, alice, avise alias Mopp the Mess.

ALICE: They are changing the gard at buckinham palace.
C. ROBIN: So wot so wot?
ALICE: You had better be there. You have yore publick. You hav made the whole place impossible for the q, also the de of e and prince charles.
C. ROBIN: i am getting past it i am slipping.
ALICE: You talk as if you hav to march from wellington

baracks every day. *And* carrying a trombone. Where are yore call-up papers?

Another wet in my book bag is jules verne. He said there would be submarines he is brilliant. Also the flying machine e.g. around the world in 80 days (delay at gander even b.o.a.c. must start to be thinking they mite catch up) jules verne, in fakt, was responsible for SCIENCE Fiktion, also h. g. wells who wrote The First Clots in the Moon.
You remember how it went? Or not?

FOTHERINGTON-TOMAS: Hullo clouds hullo sky. Let's all go to the moon. Hurray hurray. Prof. cavour hav the answer i.e. the Peason-Molesworth Space Ship (patents pending).

ZOOSH!

The scene switch to the MOON. 20 mushrooms are on watch. They watch the skies. They also watch each other wondering which will be fried with the bacon and skool sossages tomorow. Sudenly a BALL arive. The mushrooms jump up and down.
'Go on, Stanley, net the leather. Get yore head to it. Foul! Send him off. Shoot! Buy more players. Who's for tennis?' SUDENLY there is a hush.

1ST MUSHROOM: Anything the matter?
2ND MUSHROOM: It's THEM. From THERE.
1ST MUSHROOM: Cripes. Where's THERE?
2ND MUSHROOM: Here's HERE. THERE'S there. THEM'S they. He, she or it equal the 3rd person sing and ushually go in the nomminative.
1ST MUSHROOM: Higgnerant. Here THEY come.
2ND MUSHROOM: Ugh!
MOLESWORTH: (*stepping forth from the space ship*) Ugh!

they glare at each other, mutually repulsive. He canot eat

me for brekfast and i canot eat HIM. Impasse. Nothing for it but to go home.

ZOOSH! ZOOOOO....!

Wot's wrong? Anything the matter? Try the boost. Flog the reactor. Why did i not marry a mechanic? ECT......

And so it prove my point q.e.d. There is only one thing. Tomorow is another day and there will be geom. eng. fr. lat. botany, rest on the bed and then ho for more. Life is tuough. It depends whether you can take it.

2nd Mushroom: It's THEM. From THERE

3

HOW TO SURVIVE IN
THE ATOMMIC AGE

GUIDE TO GURLS

As i sit among my faded memories and old relicks e.g. lat books, bungy, caterpillers, mice and old stamps which i hav not stuck in, wot do i find but my Skoolboy's diary. This tell me that it is 7021 miles from London to Bangkok, also my size shoe is 6 watch number 234547 and oxford won the boat race in 1896 so wot i sa so wot. At this moment fotherington-Tomas skip in –

'O molesworth,' he cri. 'Do read me your diary go on o you mite.'

'Well – ' i sa, flatered in spite of myself.

'Goody goody i hav always admired your prose work altho sometimes it is a little *strong* especially when they set us "Wot i think about masters."'

So the little wet curl up on the floor and i read:

> JAN 1. *did nuthing.*
> JAN 2. *mucked about.*
> JAN 3. *Went to a party.*

'Genius,' cri fotherington-Tomas, claping his hands. 'Economical, stark, compressed t.s. eliot himself. . . . .'

But i do not listen for i think about parties and parties mean gurls chiz chiz chiz. . . . .

All girls are soppy. This fact is recognised by all boys and the mesage is clear but seme to become dimmer as they draw on to man's estate chiz. Eventually it fade altogether and all is lost in a welter of SOP and SLUSH, like you get in the films they dare not show us at Skool. e.g. darling chiz i guess this is the end. Gurl cries tho heaven knos why, she luv other men beter and hav a husband anyway. Man then go into the night from which he should hav never emerged. 'How beautiful,' sa your mum to your pater who is sitting despondently behind her. 'If only you could be noble like that ocasionaly.'

'It is only a world of makebelieve,' he repli. 'You must face up to reality.'

'Reality,' sa molesworth 2, 'is so unspeakably sordid it make me shudder.'

He take a bullseye and pater lite his pipe. The matter is closed.

If we are to believe the books gurls read life at their skools is full of jolity and xcitement. There are always some tremendous PROBLEMS to be solved e.g. 'why choose mavis?' sa the other pres indignantly. 'We doubt her capacity to handle the most difficult house in the skool.' Do they not kno they talk about mavis grabber? grabber ma is head of st custard's and win the mrs joyful prize for rafia work. He could win a brownies kniting badge for the ushual amount.

Anyway imagine wot life would be like at st custard's if the weeds oiks tuoughs snekes and others behaved like they do in gurls books. Imagine conversashuns like this:

"Rats, you crumpet," sa gillibrand, the mad cap of 3B. 'It's joly rot to sa that molesworth cribbed in the botany exam.'

'It's simply swete of you to sa that, gilly dear,' chime in peason. 'I kno he was cobbed with 3 newts and a titmouse in his gym shirt, that he hav a guide to natural hist open on his desk, a snake curled round the leg of his chair, a pair of binoculars, and british birds tatoed on the palm of his hand – but there must be *some* explanation.' (there is, enuff said.)

The xpresion tense on his luvley face

'And you realise this mean he won't pla in the lax match aganst st Cissy's on Wednesday? Oh bother i do think miss grimsdick is too bad.'

He toss his tawny head and a hale of beetles fall out.

molesworth flush as he enter the study. He know they hav been talking about him becos they wouldn't hav been little gurlies unless they had been jabering.

'Hullo, you clot-faced sewer rats,' he sa, quietly, the xpresion tense on his luvley face, the lights in his hair shining and also the lights on his nose.

'O, moley dear, you absolute juggins! Now miss grimsdick want to see you in her study.' molesworth go chalk white benethe the dirt.....

Aktually my racecourse correspondent tell me that real life in gurls' skools is not a bit like what (grammer) it is in the books.

'Carrots' Crumpshaw, the madcap of the fourth is swanking along to the musick room when a huge prefect bear down on her.

'Crumpshaw! Why are you walking down the Milky Way, a pasage reserved for prefects? *WAM*. And you ar wearing lipstick. *SOCKO*. And you cut the coll. criket match. *BIFFO*. Blow yore nose. (*ZOOSH*). i shall tell the whole house to pinch you this evening . . . . . '

('Carrots' Crumpshaw thinks: just becose miss peabody [gym] praised my knees bend she is jealous.)

'How cynical you are, molesworth,' sa 1otherington-Tomas, at this juncture. 'Gurls can be most interesting companions, as you will find when you gro older.'

The only bonds in fact between boys and gurls is that the skools they go to are SIMPLY SHOKING.

N.B. my racecourse correspondent tell me that there are some gurls skools like ro-hem, st. j-hem, heath-hem, wyk-hem, where all is luxury and you must bring yore own servant to tend after yore lightest wants. Imagine this at st. custard's eh i mean to sa just imagine it.

Dawn brakes a few dispirited birds sa Queek and go to slepe agane the skool dog growls in his slepe a master steel guiltily across the lawn. Another day is beginning at st. custard's.

Tap! a manservant enter with a glass of coca-cola.

it is seven a.m., sir on a filthy morning and all is friteful. *Snore.*

The curtains are drawn sir and your clothes are laid out. Yore marbles are laid out on the closet.

Snore.

The ice in the white jug hav been broken. Should you wish to clean your teeth or knees the appropriate brushes are at hand. the electric fire is switched on and before you lies the adventure of new day. One last word the penalties for being late for brekker are mediævil in their severity.

SNO– in the middle, the matron burst in like an atommic Xplosion. Wakey-wakey she bellow, sho a leg rise and shine. Up you get rats it is only 20 below and there is nothing like a song before brekfast . . . . .

Another dreme is shatered. Come to think of it, gurls hav to put up with boys. So their lot is hard too.

How to be a Goody-Goody

ARE YOU AN ERIC OR A NIGEL?
A smug chart for sissies
Get teacher to hang this on the klassroom wall

Do not bolt your food, boys. Eric sits erect and chews his food at leisure becos the weed hav got up early.

Now look at nigel, Ugh!

251

A FEW TIPS FROM THE COARSE

A velvet silence (peotry) enclose the famous PINK dorm of st. custards. Beyond the curtaned window there is no sound except the tread of feet as boys break out down the fire escape and the plop-plop of darts as ye olde matronne sink another treble twenty into the board. Below a gang of mice attack the skool cheese with jelignite . . . . .

Sudenly the stillness is broken by a low, musical whisper e.g.

Wot is yore fancy for the 3.30 at Sponger's park, tomow, molesworth?

Instantly the whole dorm is awake. Aktualy it was never silent becos wot with SNORES GRUNTS AND GROANS it would be quieter when they are re-laying the surface of the 7 sisters road than here.

The q. i hav been asked, however, catches my interest.

Get out the port and cigars, i sa, and we will diskuss the form. i wate until the decanter is passed hem-hem it is pepsi-cola aktually and give my verdict.

Bees Knees will be having a go. On breeding alone it should be cast-iron. i shall risk half a lb of wine gums on her.

Ta-ran-ta-rah! yell molesworth 2, weedily. 'Come on, lester pigot. come on, scobie breasly. Come on me yar boo to molesworth 1 he couldn't hurt a flea.

He jump up and down on the soft springs hem-hem of the skool bed until he bounce too high and strike his head on the ceiling cheers cheers.

Which all go to show that apart from backing a county at criket, a foopball team or two, cris chataway, le rouge at the casino and mr grabber for the father's race every boy ort to equip himself for life by knoing a bit about horse racing.

All i kno about this subjekt is contaned in my grate work *Snaffles, fetlocks, pasterns and girths* – A CRITICAL

This is only one side of a horse

EXAMINATION (Grabber 25/- or send a p.o. to the auther direct). This book go to the hart of the matter by considering something you canot hav a horse race without e.g. the HORSE. (see above)

This is only one side of a horse so it hav only two legs, one ear and one eye. However, most horses are aproximately the same on the other side and if they are not it is not safe to hav a fluter on them.

Every horse is said to hav POINTS which is pritty dificult for any animal which is not a hedgehog or comon porcupine. In racing, however, there are only two POINTS about the horse which need concern the eager student – the ears and the tail. If the horse is going to try the ears should be so far back and the tail so far up that they almost meet. When it trot up to the post like that the backer can be sure it is trying, which is something with a horse. It is something with a boy, too, but no one can kno from his ears otherwise we mite get something like this in klass –

MOLESWORTH 1 *stare at a problem in algy scratching his hoary head.*

SIGISMUND THE MAD MATHS MASTER *regard him anxiously through his racing glasses.*

SIGISMUND: there go the galant molesworth upon whom i hav put my shirt (heaven forbid). He is a cert for this algy problem. But wot is this? His ears do not twitch. He sweateth at the mere look of x+y. He screws his pen into his ear he is in a lather. Quick quick i must lay this off on peason who hav an answer book but it will be O.K. unless there is an objektion.

(*He rushes out. molesworth gets the answer from gilibrand and so foils the plot.*)

That is all about horses. Now the q. is how to put your money on. You do this with a bookie or the tote as even a fule kno. Wot every fule do not kno however is which horse to put the money on and bring back a dividend.

To kno this you hav to study form e.g. buy all the papers which say:

> The Dope's Nap – 3.30. BEES KNEES.
> 3.30. FATTY IS A CONFIDENT SELEKTION.
> COARSE WIRE. 3.30. BUMBLE PUPY.
> NEWMARKET. TOOTHBRUSH.********

This leave you pritty much where you were but it is better than buying a midday edition when all the tipsters agree:

RACING SUMARY.   3.30.

PREPOSTEROUS (*Daily Plug*) DANDRUFF
MENDAX (*The Smugg*)   DANDRUFF****
ON THE BALL (*Daily Shame*) DANDRUFF
ALCESTES (*Farmer's Joy*)   DANDRUFF

ect.

Every horse is said to have POINTS

Everything is right. DANDRUFF hav won over the distance, it hav two ancestors from the national stud, a french owner, trained on meat, sits up in its stable, lest... pig...up...firm going THE LOT. BASH ON THE WINE GUMS. As you are sitting nonchalantly in your club drinking a last pepsi cola you carelessly pick up the ticker tape.

3.30. SPONGER'S PARK. 1. BEES KNEES. 2. CLOT. 3. MORBID. ALSO RAN — DANDRUFF. SKOOL CHEESE. 5 RAN. DANDRUFF 51/1 ON (FAVRITE)

'Hogsnorton.'
'Yes. sir ?'
'Bring me another pepsi cola.'
'The '37, sir, or the Club ?'
'Wot do it matter ? There is only 6d in it.'

Let us stroll over to the padock where the horses are parading. All around is the clamour and bustle of the race-coarse full of gipsies, oafs, cads, snekes tipsters, bullies in fakt it mite just as well be a half-hol at st. custards. See who strolls among them it is ickle-pritty fotherington-Tomas the wonky wet of the skool!

FOTHERINGTON-TOMAS: Hullo clouds hullo sky! How colourful the scene! the colours so gay so alive. But, woe, here is the headmaster GRIMES!

HEADMASTER: Want to buy some jellied eels? Lovely jellied eels. (he starteth) Discovered! it is fotherington-tomas!

FOTHERINGTON-TOMAS: Oh wot, sir, can hav brought you to this pass?

GRIMES: the skool doesn't pay all hard work nothing out of it. The boys hav got to be fed and as for the masters they fair eat you out of house and home. (*fotherington-tomas begin to blub*) And then look at the rates on the old place – and the taxes. Can't blame me if i try to make an honest penny down here, there's no disgrace –

FOTHERINGTON-TOMAS (*blubing harder than ever*) don't go on, sir. Take my money. Here.

GRIMES: don't you want no jellied eels?

FOTHERINGTON-TOMAS: no, no.

GRIMES: Bless you, sonny, you hav a kind face.

As fotherington-Tomas skip away a thick wad of banknotes fall from GRIMES poket. He pick them up agane and begin to GLOAT!

PLATE IX PICK THE WINNER – *to face page p. 1000 76.*

GRIMES: there is one born every minit.

And now we hav aktually got to the padock where the horses are walking round and round and people are looking at them. This is yore first chance to make sure yore selektion is in racing trim. Even at this stage it may be lathering and foaming at the mouth. If, however, its eyes are brite pinpoints, it is dancing lite-hartedly on its horseshoes and neighing to itself – it is safe to assume that the stable hav decided to hav a go.

BASH ON MORE WINE GUMS and return, for the START.

This is the most exciting moment and fotherington-Tomas jump up and down.

'Hurrah hurrah how good it is to be alive and the horse is the frend of man!'

At this moment a beer botle fall on his head from the roof of a motor coach and he is borne away. Cheers cheers we can watch the race in peace. THEY'RE OFF! Everyone go mad men shout, gurls fante, molesworth 2 shout ta-ran-ta-ra. Everyone shout and point at each other. IT'S BEES KNEES. DANDRUFF A STREET. FATTY WALKS IT ECT. The race only last ten secs before it is over. And wot hav hapened to the chokolate hoops, raspbery hoops and suede gloves of yore fancy? Alas, it is almost always down the COARSE.

Boys, keep away from race coarses. Wot is the fun of them. They are crooked and you do not stand a chance. Open the paper and see how grave the world situation is. Look at the H-bombs and disasters and find how you can give yore services to the cause. Open the paper i sa – and wot is the first thing that catch yore eye?

4.00. COARSE WIRE. NANKIE-POO CAN'T MISS.

BASH ON THE WINE GUMS!!!!!!!!!!

THE MOLESWORTH MASTER METER

Chiz moan drone they are everywhere. Masters i mean.
Beaks. Thin ones fat ones little ones tall ones some with
cranky cars others with posh ties, some you can rag and
others who strike mortal fear into our tiny harts it is cruelty
to expose us to such monsters. Everywhere a boy goes at
skool there is liable to be a master chiz chiz seeking you out
with his fierce burning eyes. It was becos of the pressing
need hem-hem for some such instrument that the molesworth Cave-Counter or master meter (patent pending) was
invented. See below.

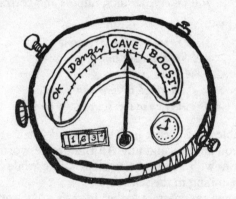

prof molesworth and his batty assistant peason had the
geiger counter in mind in creating their famous master meter.
The principle is the same. When a master is in the offing
dreaming of BEER and LUV the meter throb and the needle
come up to the CAVE position on the dial. Increasing
danger makes the needle creep up until it reach the maximum
spot ie. when a master rush you with a kane held in his hary
hand and his eyes bulging with fury the needle show
BOOST and the whole gadget zoom up and down like a
skool blancmange. That is the time to scram quickly leaving
a heavy pall of cig smoke hem-hem behind, safe and sound
with trousis still full of dust thanks to yore Cave-counter.

In fakt in generations to come the name of molesworth will be venerrated among skoolboys as we are suposed to venerrate the chap who discovered chloroform and other pane savers.

But enuff. Charge ta-ranta-rah for the masters comon room. Leave yore Cave-counter behind or it will go mad at so many masters, such a pong poo-gosh of pipes and cig ends you would almost think they all go around picking up ours.

Any boy kno wot a masters comon room is like. It smell of beetles and the ceiling is suported by ex. books. It is a place where you take yore lines, impots and corections

e.g.

A stitch in time saves nine
A Stich in save tim
A ssave is nine
A stitch in time sav
A stich in tim save

on the table. The master look up from the chair at the fruits of yore toil and sa languidly All right molesworth you can go away now. Then he go to slepe agane while below the slaves are toiling in the salt mines.

Here then the masters gather in their gowns and discuss the problems of their existence i.e. the brave noble and fearless boys whom they persecute. When the HEADMASTER is around this is how it goes.

you kno HEADMASTER that thanks to the brilliance of my tuition, the care i hav lavished, the hours i hav spent molesworth hav improved in lat out of all knoledge.

HEADMASTER (*thinks*) Wot is all this leading up to? i must go carefully.

Of corse 3B were v. backward when they came to me. i am not saing a word aganst popplewell – a sound teacher within his limmits but it took my genius, my inspiration to make molesworth put 3 konsecutive subjects in the nomm.

HEADMASTER: Grand work Grand work.

MASTER: How about a quid until next thursday?

HEADMASTER: (*quickly*) I'm out. Haven't a nicker.

MASTER: Make it arf a crown.

HEADMASTER: Very well. The ushual rates. And i fore-close next week.

Otherwise you can guess wot go on. Every evening a commando course taken by the Sarnt-major and an open space for unarmed combat.

SARNT-MAJOR: O.K. now. Get fell in. Two ranks. By the right – DRESS. (*Shuffle Shuffle* As you were ect the old gag.) Now. We all kno the Hobjekt of our hin-struction i.e. that is how to do the boys proper. No knives no knuckledusters only a ruler alowed. All right. Fall out number 6, arbuthnot, sigismund, maths master, mad. HIFF you were required to do a job on a boy how would you go about HIT? i see. Very hinteresting but scaracely fare pla. hi do not think as ow we need to go *that* far. Hact haccording to the manual.

ORRIGHT?

(*Fancy asking a lot of MASTERS if they are orright. Haddress the q. to the boys. They'll give you the right answer.*)

SARNT puffs out manly chest and continue humidement: 'Hon the word One Hobserve the boy or pupil who is busy on hillicit hactiivity i.e. has it mite be drawing tad-poles on the blotch. Hon the word TWO – draw hin the hibrows, making sure that the rest of the klass hobserve and hapreciate the umor of the situation.

ORRIGHT?

(*Enuff said.*)

Hon the word THREE – grasp the ruler and stand behind the boy or pupil with the hands lightly hupon the ips. Wait for the larff. (Hit is never difficult for a master to hobtane a larff.) Hon the Word FOUR bring the ruler down promptly and smartly on the victim's swede. A howl of pane his the signal that the hobjektive hav been attained.

And so it go on for Masters kno that if they once relax their vigilance the DAY IS OURS. JUICE! GLOAT! i can hardly wate for their shrieks for mercy.

So far we hav dealt only with masters who are english e.g. sir jones, sir arbuthnot, sir phipps-potts BA sir higgs-hake, sir muggs f.r.g.s. ect. But, felow suferers, remember this. There are skoolmasters all over the world, even bulgarian skoolmasters which take a bit of doing gosh chiz. But before you think it is hard cheddar on the bulgarian boys remember this is the atomm age and masters are exchanged like stamp swaps from country to country.

WE MITE GET A RUSIAN MASTER AT ST. CUSTARDS!

gosh golly you can pikture it.

We mite get a Rusian master

Into 3B stump sir petrovitch who not only hav a face like a squished tomato (as all masters do) but hav hary wiskers.

THE KLASS: Good morning, sir petrovitch.

SIR P: good morning, little children. (*He burst out blubbing*) o woe o grief the HEADMASTER makes me teach lat. geog, algy, arith, fr, eng, some carpentry, musick, the organ and asist with criket it is worse than the salt mines. Wot is the lesson, little children?

THE KLASS: peotry, sir petrovitch. (*They recite*)

> *Harkski harkski the larkski*
> *At heavenski's gates singski*

(*sir petrovitch cry more and more*)

THE KLASS: Give him Boots that will slay him.

FOTHERINGTON-TOMAS: o goody!

THE KLASS: Bootskis, bootskis, bootskis movin' up and down agane (ect)

SIR P: Good show good show. Give it the rhythm. Definitely give it the rhythm, dogs.

(*He jumps on the desk with his boots shouting Oi Oi Oi and struming on a balal – well you kno. The whole klass join in – ink wells fly threw the air, the uprore is immense.*)

HEADMASTER look up from the desk in his study where he is counting the GOLD in his moneybox: 'Comrade petrovitch can certanely instil an unwonted enthusiasm into 3B tho his methods are a little – er – unorthodox. Now shall i raise the fees or hav i got enuff? Beter be on the safe side.' He taketh up his gold plume et commence a ecrire: Dere parent, Owing to the cost of living and death-watch beetle in the bell tower i regret ect ect... The tears fall in pools from his eyes, smudging the encre. But that is nothing to wot hapen when the parents receive it. You should hear the WORDS yore pater use when he cancel the order for a rolls-royce and make do with an A90 instead.

So much for comrade petrovitch and the 89 ickle pritty capitalists of st custards.

Now we come to another swap. This is ed. hickenhopper from the U.S.A. of america i.e. he is wot we vulgar boys hem-hem call a YANK. He is very tall and wear specs hem-hem and we awate his appearance with interest i.e. where do he keep his gat?

'Now, boys,' he sa, 'this morning it is lat. We will comence with translation.'

'O.K. Stranger. Hep-hep and get cracking.'

'Do you, molesworth, consider yourself equal to attempting sentence one?'

'Sure don't, pardner. Never was no good at book larnin. Try one of these other critturs who are hog-snoring in the desks around me.'

'Now come,' sa sir hickenhopper. 'Balbus admires the clear voices of the girls – surely now – ?'

'Now listen. i ain't aiming to make no trouble. You're the sheriff around here. But if the mean coyote who wrote that latin book come into this saloon i'll riddle him full of daylight. And the same goes for Balbus.'

And so it go on it is only after a long time that you find out that all YANKS are not cowboys and while you are still reeling with disapointment you learn too that they are not all gangsters. Well, of corse, my dear, that remove their last atraction for me but i expect they hav found it quieter to live at home if they can watch the television instead of shooting all the time. A pity.

Aktually, yank masters are diferent from ours. If sigismund arbuthnot the mad maths master were to organise us into a task force to solve a quadratick equation we would think him mader than ever. But that is wot ed. hickenhopper did. And we rather enjoyed it – wot am i saing *ENJOYED* it? CURSES CURSES. Re-shake this cocktail, peason, and don't drown the gin.

A Wizard Wheeze

ST. CUSTARDS.	
Name or Cognomen:	Cyril Bertie Cedric de wetby Higgs-Hake, alias Smoky Joe alias The Creeper.
Age: 102 (approx)	*Position:* The Bottom
French:	He tries hard at this subjekt and considering he hav never been nearer La France than the front at Margate his ability is remarkable.
Latin and Classicks:	He do not sho a grate deal of interest. The extraordinary behaviour of Balbus, Cotta, Caesar and Labienus do not fill him with disgust as they should neither dous the appalling mortality rate among the Gauls seme strange. He is inclined to be idle and boring, staring out of the window with his mouth wide open.
English:	His idea of instilling the treasuries of english literature seme to be to turn his klassroom into the training camp of some puglist. Howls of pane, right-upper cuts, biffs and bangs. I fear that he hav not an 'h' to his name and it is a case of the blind leading the blind hem-hem.
Manners:	Quite revolting.

Why be down-troden? Is this a free country? Why should the beaks escape? Fill out the molesworth end-of-term Report on Masters e.g.

Health: It sometimes seme that when he gaze at the skool sossages at brekfast he is not feeling well in himself. Can it have been too much B·E·E·R the nite before? Or does he feel the same as we do about skool sossages?

General: He have tried hard but he have still got a long way to go — about 160000000 million trillion miles would be enuff for most of us. Above all he must learn the meaning of self-D I·S·S·I·P·L·I·N·E cheers cheers cheers. Have he any clue wot he look like when he bare his ugly fangs at a noble boy? One look would be enuff we can assure him. And wat about those yelow socks and that tie? Pull yorself together felow and make an effort.

Signed:

N. Molesworth

Next term begin on Jan 20th but donot bother to come back.

4

HO FOR THE HOLS

GOODBY TO SKOOL
(for a bit.)

'Boys,' sa headmaster GRIMES, smiling horibly, 'st. custard's hav come to the end of another term.'

Can there be a note of relief in his craked voice? There can be no doubt of the feelings of the little pupils. CHEERS! HURRAH! WHIZZ-O! CHARGE! TA-RAN-TA-RA! The little chaps raise the roof of big skool, which do not take much doing as most of it is coming off already.

'Ah, molesworth,' bellow GRIMES to molesworth 2, who is dancing a hornpipe on a desk, 'not *too* much excitement. We hav not broken up yet, dere boy.'

'Wot, sir?'

'Not too much excite – '

'Speak up, sir.'

'GET DOWN OFF THAT FLIPPING DESK OR YOU WILL GET 6!'

At last, order is restored and end of term marks are read chiz chiz chiz. Another loud cheer greet the fakt that i am botom in eng. fr. geom. geog. div. algy and hist. When grabber get his ushaul prize i.e. the mrs joyful prize for rafia work there are boos and catcalls nothing can stop the mitey upsurge of popular feeling.

'SILENCE!' below GRIMES. 'You are unfare. You kno how he won this prize.'

'Sure!' we roar, '£5 to you, £1 all round to the staff and a botle of beer for the olde matronne. The same story.'

'SILENCE OR I WILL KANE THE LOT!'

Methinks his unatural benevolence is waring as thin as peason's second-best pare of trousis. The mob is hushed by this thort.

'Now see here,' sa GRIMES, 'see here, scum. We gives you edducation here, see? We gives you maners and disscipline, don't we? Don't forget them when you gets 'ome. Do not forget to sa "pardon" at some breach of etikette and tuck the old serviet into the colar firmly. Should egg be droped upon the tie remove same quietly with the thumb as you 'av seen me do. Be a credit to St. custards! DISMISS!'

With one mad yell the mob, armed with stumps and bits torn from desks, surge away down the pasage, trampling the masters under foot. A buket of water fall on GRIMES and the term end in a series of wizard rags and japes. Cars arive, driven by parents with drawn, white faces. The rolls for grabber, a bentley for peason and a cranky old grid for fotherington-tomas. For the rest it is the old skool bus for the station.

'Six quid,' hiss the driver to GRIMES, 'and i'll put the lot over a cliff.'

'And deprive me of my living?'

'You hav yore jellied eels and the whelk stall in the new cross road, not to mention other enterprises.'

'Begone, tempter!'

With a roar the skool bus drive off. Goodby, sir, goodby, skool, goodby, matronne, goodby, skool dog ect. No more lat. no more french. Wave wave and we are free.

Cheers for home and the maison molesworth! All are pleased to see us, dogs charge, cats miaouw and parot whistle poly wolly doodle. Wipe mud on carpet, change clothes, eat super cream buns and relax. So far only 62

people hav said we are taller, 96 that we are like mum, 107
that we are like pater and all hav asked if we had a good
term. It is the same old story. Soon we are lying back in
pater's chair, eating bullseyes.

'Wot is on the t.v. we hav nothing to do,' we sa.

'Nothing,' sa the parot, 'the programmes are lousy' he is
browned off becos since we hav a t.v. he hav not been able
to get a word in edgeways.

Mum seme to hav run out of conversation.

'Tell us about skool,' she sa, at last.

'Skool? The masters are all teddy boys and would slit
you with a broken botle for 2 pins. The food is uneatable
and conditions are
vile.'

'You poor darl-
ings!'

'It is horible,'
blub molesworth 2.

'My poor little
lambs ect' hem-hem
rather embarassing
mum look as if she
will burst into tears,
good old mum. All
mums are the same
and luv there wee
ones somebody hav
got to, after all. I
send her for my mail
and litely thumb
over the leters i.e.
16 football pools, 1
bill from the book-
maker, a badge from

the golly club, an invitation to a dance chiz and HO! wot is this, eh?

> *Dere frend,*
>   *Welcome! in sending for details of the Goliath, the Strong Man course you are opening a new life. If you are a pigmy i can make a giant of you with bulging mussles and HERCULEAN strength in 6 weeks. Write at once with P.O. for 2/6.*
>
>   *(signed) G. Goliath.*

Gosh! This is something! A new future open up by the time we return to skool i can hav giant strength. How wizard that will be next term.

Scene: big skool at st. custard's. Goliath molesworth is unpacking his tuck box.

PEASON: Hullo, o weedy wet, you hav a face like a squished tomato.

MOLESWORTH: (*thinks*) Poor fule, he do not kno

the mob surge away down the passage

(enter sigismund the mad maths master)

SIGISMUND: Come on get cracking no talking no smoking, no entrance you are in my clutches agane.

(He striketh peason.)

MOLESWORTH: Stop! Enuff!

(sigismund aim a wicked blow with the protractors. molesworth catch them, bust them, brake an iron bar with his teeth, lift a statue of j. caesar, leap 82 feet, beat his chest, crunch a skool cake, do 2 back somersaults and aim a rabit punch at sigismund.)

MOLESWORTH: Take that.
SIGISMUND: Wow!
MOLESWORTH: And that and that and that and that –
SIGISMUND : Do not repeat yoreself.

(M. toss him over his shoulder and the bout is over. Sigismund is down for the count the crowd roars.)

At this point the dreme is interrupted.
'Would you like another cake, nigel?'
'No, thanks, mum. I hav some correspondence.'
'To whom are you writing?'
'Just to the golly club, mum. Just to the golly club.'
i write to the golly club thanking them for their good wishes. Also to Goliath for the strong man course. We shall see.

And so the hols proceed. I quarrel with molesworth 2 and he do not seme to see my point of view. Let him wate. Ocasionally there are treats e.g. gran come to see us in her 90 m.p.h. sports car and zoom about the roads which is more dangerous than the skool bus. Boys come in to pla and depart in tears. The parot see sooty on the t.v. and sa a rude word. He want to get an audition and kepe saing "Cock-a-doodle-doo" and swank he is a cock he will not get to first base. Then come the FELL DAY i.e.

dere nigel and molesworth 2

GLORIA AND HYACINTH

AT HOME

dancing 8 – 10.30. Cakes, creme buns, trifle, jelly, chocs, crackers, whisky for paters and gin for maters. Do not miss this unique ocasion.

A snip!!!!!

CURSES! me dancing with gurlies? gosh. i ring the bell for mater and issue stern protest but in vane. It will be good for me to go, she sa. Also gloria and hyacinth are such nice little gurls and i must learn to dance early before it is too late chiz chiz chiz.

Another weedy party and lots of weedy little gurls with pig tales and also some joly big ones. a nice lady come up with a knuckle duster and ask me to dance with tough baby called honoria. Cornered, i bow, take gurl by my gloved hand and draw her litely on the floor. After a few turns she speke shyly:

'This is a waltz, you big lout. You hav kicked me 5 times.'

'And, fare made, i will kick thee agane.'

'Sez you? I will do you if you do.'

'I shall do thee first, see if i do not.'

And so to the lite strains the young couples in the first flush of their youth whirl round and round to the strains of the craked gramophone. Wot young hopes and ideals are confined in these innocent breasts, wot – SPLOSH! Wot can that be? It is hyacinth who hav thrown a jelly at gloria she hav been sipping mater's gin. Gloria respond with the trifle cheers cheers cheers. 'Go it, gloria,' shout honoria, 'tear out her hare' and molesworth 2 zoom by dive bombing with eclares. A wizard confusion ranes.

'Did you enjoy the party, nigel?' sa mum when we get home.

'Oh yes,' i reply, tired but hapy. 'Altho next time you mite send us to the moulin rouge or an apache's dance hall.'

The weeks and days pass on winged feet. Soon we shall hav to think of getting our things together for the new term. Ah-me! All those pants and vests and shirts got out for another tour of duty. The happy relationship between me and molesworth 2 hav broken up in cries of 'Shall', 'Shan't'. 'You are.' 'You aren't' ect.

'Wot did you sa about the masters at yore skool, nigel?' ask mum. 'The ones who are teddy boys?'

'They would rip you with a botle for 2 pins, mater.'

'So would i,' she sa. 'So would i.'

As for Goliath i never hear from him agane. The golly club thank me for my contribution to party funds. They hav made me a golly Captain now. i must hav put the P.O. in the wrong envelope. I would rather be Goliath than a Golly Captain any day but that is life.

HEE-HEE FOR TEE-VEE

Gosh super! we hav something to contend with which no other generation hav ever had before i.e. the television cheers cheers cheers. Everbody kno wot a t.v. is it is a square box with a screen. You switch on and o hapen, then just when you hav given up hope and are going off to buzz conkers a great booming voice sa, 'That's an interesting point, postlethwaite. Wot does higginbottom feel? Higginbottom? ect ect.' It may be an interesting point but i could not care less and just go away agane when a ghastley face suddenly appere. It is worse than a squished tomato but it hold me in hypnotic trance and it is the same with molesworth 2, tho he always look dopey like that. We sit and watch more and more ghastley faces with our mouths open and even forget to chew the buble gum we are slaves of the machine.

Of course all boys and gurls hav to go through a time when there is no t.v. xcept at the postman's down the road. Yore mater and pater then sa weedy things.

i will not hav one in the house.

the programmes are simply terible, my dear.

it is bad for children.

it destroy the simple pursuits of leisure.

Hem-hem if they only knew what the simple pursuits of leisure were like potting stones at vilage oiks or teaching parot rude words they would not hesitate for a moment. Anyway they get one in the end and sa 'Children can only look for 1 hour at suitable programmes' then they forget all about it until we are halfway through '1984' and molesworth 2 sa 'if that is the best a rat can do i do not think much of it.' 'The rat,' i sa, 'is exactly like thou, o clot-faced wet.' Then mater become aware of our presence and hury the dreamy-eyed little felows up wood hill to blanket fair, as dear nana sa.

A ghastley face suddenly appere

When you setle down to it this is wot hapens in your dulce domum (lat.)

Scene: A darkened room with glowing fire. Mum, Nana, me and molesworth 2 are goggling at the screen. So are the cats, dogs, rats, mice and various bugs about the place.

T.V. Are you a clump-press minder? (Grate cheers)
MATER: I thort he was an aero-dynamicist or a moulding-clamp turner...... I really think .....
ALL: Sshh!

(*Enter pater, tired from the office.*)

PATER: Are you looking at that friteful thing agane? Programmes are terible. Nothing to look at.

(*With a roar and a ratle he put coal on the fire*).

ALL: Sshh!

(Pater setle down. molesworth 2 aim his gat at
very fat gentleman in specs. It is the same gun
with which he shot mufin the mule, mcdonald
hobley, a ping-pong champion, three midgets, a
great-crested grebe, a persian student and lady
Boyle and a budgerigar.)

MOLESWORTH 2. Ah-ah-ah-ah-ah. Got you.
ALL: Ssh!
MATER: Do you not think it would be better if their heads
were not three feet away from their shoulders?

(Pater go and twiddle knobs. First of all there is
a snowstorm then what seem like the batle of
jutland, then an electronic bombardment. Finaly
a vast explosion.)

MATER: You hav ruined it, clot.
NANA: Boost the contrast.
MOLESWORTH 2: Adjust the definition.
ME: O gosh, hurry up.

(Now picture is upside down, then leaning
drunkenly, then it disappear altogether amid
boos and catcalls. Finaly Nana do it.)

T.V. Are you conected with seaweed? (Huge cheer)
MATER: look at tibby the cat he canot stand this
man.....
ALL: Sssh.
PATER: He's a guggle-gouger.....

(And so it go on. Supper is not cooked, fires go
out, kettles boil their heads off, slates fall off the
roof and house burn down, but we are all still
looking at a nature film in w. africa chiz in fact we
hav seen more monkeys since we got the t.v. than
ever before xcept at st. custard's where peason
hav the face of a wild baboon.)

He is going to zoom to the piano and pla fairy bells

Aktually t.v. is v. cultural for boys and improving to the mind. You learn so many things that when you go back to skool all are quite surprised.

MOLESWORTH 1. To the q. whether the hydrogen bomb should be banned i give a categorical 'no'. unless there can be international agreement to co-exist in disarmament.

MOLESWORTH 2: That is a valid point, o weedy wet. Do you kno the population of chile?

MOLESWORTH 1: No. But everyone should look both ways before crossing the road and wot can be more dramatic than man's fight against the locust, eh?

MOLESWORTH 2: The problem of asia is the problem of over-population and now i will pla brahams etude number 765000 in F flat. . . . .

You kno wot this mean he is going to zoom to the piano and pla fairy bells nothing can stop him the whole skool will rock and plaster drop from the ceiling, chandeliers will shake and light bulbs burst. Hav to take cover until it is all over when the head of an elk, dislodged by the blast, fall on my head chiz chiz chiz that is life.

So you will see that t.v. is a joly good thing and very restful to the nerves, my dear. You can talk about it next day, particularly to those who hav no sets and hav not seen the programmes. This make you very popular socially, with the smart set of 3B, and take your mind off the lessons. It also gives rise to several wizard wheezes. For instance, why not start a maths lesson with a ghastley face smiling at you?

'And now, 3B, we are going to show you the elementary principles of vulgar fractions so we hope simper simper you will be able simper to get the things into yore thick heads without carving the desk or sticking compasses into fotherington-Tomas. Simper. May we also remind you that there is cocoa and buns at break and from 10.30 to 11.15 there is a gorgeous lesson in which Cotta will be beaten for the umpteenth time by the Belgians with darts and arows?'

With a huge SIMPER the picture fade. Which only leave time to prepare placard for the final wizard wheeze.

molesworth, next sentence. Marcus and Balbus, my dearest friends, are walking out of the city. Come along, boy.

You do not need to sa er-er and scratch yore head or even ask what the blazes the two cissies are doing walking out of the city for. You just hoist your placard for a technical hitch.

NORMAL SERVICE
WILL BE RESTORED
AS SOON AS POSS.

A NEW DEAL FOR THE TINIES

Hist! Cave! methinks the bold bad molesworth 1 have wind that there are tinies around the place. you kno wot tinies are – they are ickle pritty little boys who wear blue corduroy trousis and zoom about on fairy cycles. They hav not come to st custard's yet they do not kno their fate. They hav mistresses at skool and dance weedily with ickle gurls chiz chiz chiz e.g.

Now david, now bobby, now cyril stand round me in a fairy ring and join hands with drusilla we will pretend we are all going to fairyland.

At this all the tinies becom xcited and jump up and down. Goody goody hurray and hip hip they cri shall we see a fairy godmother?

'But,' sa fotherington-Tomas, when i express these things to him, 'we must hav the younger tinies to folow in our footsteps. After all,' he sa, 'you were a tiny once yourself.'

'Me? Curses!'

'With corduroy trousis and your mother wept when she cut off your curls. You looked just like bubbles, molesworth 1, and the old ladies said how swete you were.'

With that he skip weedily away singing tra-la-tra-la but i feel there is a grane of truth in wot he sa. Gosh chiz, i dare not think of it. Me in corduroy trousis! 10000000000 boos to bubbles.

Aktually all boys hav to hav a time when they are not tuough and canot even read. There was even a time when i had no culture myself hem-hem which was when my pater and mater thort i was a brane and would win a skolarship. Not much hope of making *me* a slave to pay the fees nowadays. But there was a time once when –

(*Scene*) *the molesworth nursery young nigel molesworth is sitting on the floor braking a hornby trane with a hamer. The*

There was even a time when i had no culture myself

place is litered with debris of wheels nuts bolts dinky toys tanks and clockwork mice it is as if there hav been an H-bomb xplosion.

NURSE: come nigel dere it is time for your reading lesson.

NIGEL: Boo-hoo-boo-hoo-hoo.

NURSE: If you are wilful i will smak yore little hand.

NIGEL: And i will thro the hamer at you. If you want to get tuough, you can hav it tuough dere nana.

(With a quick judo thro nana come up from behind and disposess the game little chap of his weapon. He sits upon her ample knee with an open book.)

It is a funy thing about reading when you are a tiny they make you sa Ah-Eh-Ih-Ou-URR etc. which is uterly wet and read about weedy dogs e.g.

*There is a dog. Jack is a...Jack is a...Jack is a...is
a bitch. No, not that, nigel, do not guess. Read the word.
Wot does DER-OU-GER spell? Jack is a dog he is a bad
dog jack steals the bone...(zoom zoom along you can remember
it all). Cook is angry. Cook is a cow. Well, that is what dere
Dada...Cook is a lady. She whacks jack with the LUR-
AH-DUR-LUR-ER. Wot the blazes can that be? She
whacks jack with the hamer...with the gun...with the cosh
...with the rolling pin...etc. etc. And so it go on until nana
fall into a stupor and it is time for the archer family on the
wireless.*

Everything is difficult for tinies they hav to write too. But
first they pla with plastissene and make drawings in crayons
which is like glorious tecknicolour hem-hem i don't think.
When they write it is like this they copy things *why dus the
owl owl wod pek on the nos.* Or, *hokey-de-poke de zoopity zing
you are under my spel and dus everything i tell.*

wot speling eh?

Soon however the tinies can use their new found skill
and scrible on their books rude things about lambs, roy the
rat, tortoises, geese which they hav to read about e.g. *ded he
is ded i shot him he is ded yes.* This show promise for the
future and a brite career at st custards.

Another thing tinies kno o about is games such as foopball or criket. When they first see a foopball they are
amazed. 'What do we do with it?' they ask the mistress.
'You slam the leather right-footed into the reticule, little
dears,' she repli. So they put the ball down and retire to the
end of the field then zoom up for huge shot. Ball go two
inches and tiny fall on his nose. 'Ha-ha-ha,' sa mistress,
'that will teach you, rat. Now it is cedric's turn.'

It is the same with criket, which the tinies ushually learn
with their pater on the lawn.

pater: Set up the stumps, boys.

Do you not want to be grown-up?

tiny: i were playing with my balloon.

pater: All grown-up men pla criket. Do you not want to be grown-up?"

tiny: not when i see some grown-up men, Dada.

But pater is inexorable. He grasps the bat. First tiny bowls the ball backwards over his head, then into the greenhouse, then along the ground and finaly the dog run away with it. When the pill is recovered tiny bowl pater with a wizard daisy-cutter. Pater then bowl and hit tiny's stumps. 'You're out!' he yells. Tiny throw the bat at him and walk off into the house. The game is over.

So you see. Even the Hugest hav been tinies once. And even when they are huge and hairy as me their maters sometimes sa: "Did I show you that sweet photo of nigel when he was a baby?" And there you are looking weedy on a rug. But it's all right as long as none of the other boys don't see. You take another look. You weren't a bad looking tiny at all quite d. in that peticoat – curses wot am i saing?

Dere Little Chaps

Will you take me for
a bike ride, dad?

Parkins shows a good deal
of promise.

nigel is a slo developer.

You hav caught me, sir, like a treen in a disabled space ship.

i shouldn't do that if i were you, old chap.

SUMER BY THE SEA

Hurra for the hols agane cheers cheers cheers. Boo and snubs to all skools and masters which are closed for repairs and renovation during august. ('i think we'll have big skool done a pale dove grey with petunia lame curtains,' sa headmaster's wife hem-hem i do not think. Big skool will be lucky if it get a rinse with the carbolic.)

Wot will the little chaps do with themselves when they can no longer wake up each day in their beloved alma mater? (SKOOL! SKOOL! SKOOL! BASH 'EM UP ST CUSTARD'S!) Wot will they do, eh? Frankly i would hardly like to sa it is so unspekeable wot with 3 cokes and $\frac{1}{2}$ a lb of home-made fudge before 10 a.m.

A few, however, of the more thortful types will be planing ahead for lazy days by the sea e.g.

'i see that striped beachwear is in fashion agane this season,' sa molesworth 2, laing down his ladies mag hem-hem. 'Do you intend to be chic this season molesworth 1 in casual slashnecked coton with delectable acessories or do you intend to wear your ushual dirty blue drawers?'

'Shutup molesworth 2 i am looking at t.v.'

't.v. is the curse of modern youth. Wot is on?'

'It is a brany chap who hav made a telescope out of a tin of pineaple chunks as a sparetime hoby.'

(*3 hours later. plus 2 mins and 6 secs.*)

'The pla is over and i have guesed that it was an etruscan jam jar dated circa 1066a.d.,' sa molesworth 2. 'Where shall we all go for our glamorous holiday in the sun? Shall it be breezy ventnor? or rolicking ryde? Do you wish to find health and hapiness at bridlington molesworth one? Perhaps romance will come your way this year, o weedy wet. Or do you prefer the s. of france?'

'Ah how joli et gai the s. of france would be!'

(*He dreameth.*)

La France. Beneath an orange umbrela sit molesworth 1 on a chaise on the terace of the hotel magnifique. there is the scent of jasmin and bullseyes in the air, an orchestra pla the minstrel boy softly, Le soleil brille. molesworth turn to his companion, the glamorous hortense –

M. MOLESWORTH: j'aime voo, hortense.

HORTENSE: Oo la-la and houp-la. c'est vrai?

M. MOLESWORTH: (*souriant soppily*) Les loups sont laids, les elephants sont enormes, les girafes sont hauts.

HORTENSE: Wot the blazes hav that got to do with it, mon amour?

M. MOLESWORTH: it is all the fr. i can remember it is potts and pilcher fr. primer ex 9B and wot is a grate surprise to all is that all the adjs hav an 's'.

HORTENSE: Why do you always hav to bring the loups into it? The loups are idiotics. they are unnecessaries. they are humides. they are weedys they are unintelligents. (*She brake off and stares*) Qui est ce beau gars?

m'sieu molesworth regard autour de lui.

M. MOLESWORTH: Mon dieu c'est grabber the tete de la skool! Je l'ai eu (i hav had it). *He gives another quick blow of the eye.* Non, j'ai tort egad c'est M. Hubert our fr. master –

M. Hubert sees molesworth and reels with dismay. i supose it is hard chedar when you come on a cheap pleasure hol and find me there large as life at the other end. Any case in certain circumstances masters seem to feel boys cramp their style e.g. over GURLS.

M. HUBERT. Cor cripes its molesworth i must get the blazes out of here. (*Il voit hortense*) Well this is reel nice, molesworth, is the lady votre mere?

HORTENSE: Mais essayez-vous clot et dites moi qui vous etes etc?

La France. Beneath an orange umbrela sit moleswort

a chaise on the terace of the hotel magnifique

HUBERT: Come again?

M. MOLESWORTH: She was telling you to sit down and give an account of yourself. Pray join us.

(the fr. master so betwitched with the beauty of hortense that he take molesworth's hand and kiss it chiz chiz chiz.)

MOLESWORTH: As i was saing the loups sont laids. . . . .

But it is no use hortense and the fr. master gaze into each other's eyes. Finaly armand the boy from the fr. book appear with Papa. Houp-la he sa i see the sea. Big boats go on the sea. Is the sea wet?

PAPA: Non armand but you are.

He push him quietly off the port and join the fr. master and hortense. The dream fades. . . . .

Aktually most boys do not get the chance of a hapy hol in the s. of France. They go on the broads where a steady percentage fall in and are never heard of agane: they go in caravans or camps, they are sent to aged aunts who hav houses au bord de la mer. Anything to save money.

molesworth 2 and me ushually get a lite sentence at a boarding house at Babbling-by-sea e.g.

MON REPOS

frunished accommodation
teas. new laid eggs.
letuces from own garden.
piano taught. Manicure.

Prop. Mrs furbelow.
(aply within)

Mon repos is a pritty tuough place and make even st. custard's seem like the ritz. It always rain when we arive and all in a bad temper. Inside front door is a mat which sa '*Welcom*' and a huge hairy lady spring out at us and below '*Wipe your shoes*'. In fact this is all you are alowed to do in mon repos the rest e.g. sliding down banisters, having baths, bunging cushions etc is stricktly forbidden. There is no future in wiping your shoes forever so it is beter to brave the elements outside.

You kno how they describe hols in the childrens books e.g. as soon as mummy and daddy had unpacked the eager little chaps ran off with their bukets and spades to the sea-shore. If you do this at babblington-on-sea you get blown sixty miles inland the wind is so ferce. You hav to hang on all the way if you want to get down to the beach.

And then wot do you see? Babies. Nothing but babies. Some sit in pudles, some stager drunkenly across the sand, some beat pat a cake with a spade but most just sit there with their mouths open looking loopy. And when you pass it is always the same thing the mum sa: 'Baby sa helo to the nice little boy.' Me nice? Hem-hem.

'But you were,' sa molesworth 2, weedily. 'my first recolection as i opened my blue baby eyes was you moles-worth 1 you were shaking a ratle and sa 'ickle pritty brudder.'

'i was only saing my lines.'

'That may be but mum always sa i was a beautiful baby.'

'time molesworth 2 works grate changes.'

Ho for beach criket! As the tide recede leaving vast expanse of seaweed, old bottles, planks and oil wot can be nicer than a joly game of criket? All the fathers encourage their little ones and the little ones gaze at their fathers with their white hary legs and become depresed about the future. If we are all to grow up like that wot is the use of going on, eh? Paters are oblivious of this and encourage all.

'Come on cyril you are in...don't blub...timothy

is not blubing...hit a six old chap...well tried...next man ect ect ect ect.... until all the children are blubing and all the paters are plaing it is the same old story. Wot is left for the new boyhood? They dash into the sea with glad cries and drown themselves. So boo to boarding houses, cliffs, bukets, spades, water wings, windmills, model boats seaweed and striped beachwear – roll on thou grate and restless ocean roll over the LOT.

Roll on thou grate and restless ocean roll over the LOT

5

THE CRUEL HARD WORLD

WHO WILL BE WOT?

Fellow weeds, hav you ever cast those blue eyes of yours –
just like your mater's hem-hem – into the grimy future?
Wot i mean is, we are YOUTH chiz chiz whether we like
it or not and as every weed who come to give us prizes sa –
The Future is in yore Keeping.

n.b. it is no use saing We don't want it. You can keep it
etc. *Nobody* wants the future and we are left holding the
baby chiz chiz chiz.

These Grate and FEARLESS thorts come to me the other
day in prep as i stare gloomily at the imperfect subjunk of
avoir. From that i allow my gaze to wander out of the
window at those little feathered creatures who kno tru
freedom. Next i draw a wizard H-bomb xplosion and then i
look around me at my felow weeds.

All these oiks, tuoughs, weeds, wets, bulies, snekes, cads,
dolts and knaves – Wot will Become of Them?

Hav they tried their best? No. Hav they put the Subjekt
in the Nom? No! Hav they kept their eye on the pill at
criket? No! Hav they been well-manered and respecktful to
the masters? No! Hav they heeded warnings and pi jaws?
Absolutely not!

Wot is to become of them? The molesworth Daydream
Service now merged with Bets, Wagers and Prophesies Inc.
produce the answer.

089281 GRABBER. Everyone kno grabber he is head of
the skool and winner of the mrs joyful prize for rafia work.

He also win every other prize and is collosally rich etc. Everyone now would sa wot a bright future lies before him, the world is at his feet. Ah no, the grate buly hav an ugly fate. First, his pater lose all his money so grabber drift from bad to worse and as he could not be worse now this is joly difficult. First it is the pin-table halls, then pepsi-cola, then dogs, then GURLS and then horses. In fact the only good thing to be said of this wastrel product was that he liked the horses better than the gurls.

In the end a mere empty husk grabber came back one night to st. custard's, the scene of his brilliant triumps as a youth. He climb in through the ushual window and gaze at the darkened classrooms. Alas, the scene do not soften his callous soul. No tears glisten in those beady eyes. In the morning the skool come down and gaze open-mouthed at the Blakboard. Some words hav been rudely chalked hem-hem.

LATIN IS SOPPY. MATHS ARE MAD. FRENCH IS FRITEFUL. ALG IS AWFUL. WOODWORK IS WET. THE FOOD COULD DO WITH IMPROVEMENT.

This terible crime so shoked the nation that the whole resources of Scotland Yard were thrown into tackling the criminal. grabber was caught and sent to Wormwood scrubs were he met several old custardians. The governor put him straight on to rafia work ignorant that this had been the cause of his downfall. Soon the inmates were shoked by another outrage in the Health and Beauty Hall.

WARDERS ARE WEEDS. GOVERNORS ARE GURLIES. RAFIA WORK IS ROTEN. THE CELLS ARE DISGRACEFUL AND THE FOOD COULD DO WITH IMPROVEMENT.

The eye of the prophet molesworth

For this grabber get another 7 years but he sa he do not care so boo there is no difrence between st. custard's and wormwood scrubs anyway.

The eye of the prophet molesworth next lite upon dere little fotherington-Tomas. Wot does the cristal ball reveal for this gurly? Can it be true? AIR VICE-MARSHAL SIR BASIL FOTHERINGTON-TOMAS, V.C., D.S.O. Clubs: Spaceman's, Ovalteenies.

Air Vice-Marshal Sir basil fotherington-Tomas lowered himself into the cockpit of the gleaming space jet (complete with all parts £2 mill.)

Is the atomic reactor set to zero, Huggins?
Yessir.
Anti-gravity boosters to half-cock?
Yessir.
Pressure reading $8\frac{1}{2}$?
Yessir.
Radial dynaflow in parallel?
Yessir.
That's it then. Can't afford to make a mistake. Only a fifty-fifty chance I'll make mercury. So long, Huggins.

SHoo-SHoo-SHoo
ooooooooooooooooooooooooooooooooooo
oooooooooooooSH

OBITUARY. *(By a pal.)*

All those who knew basil fotherington-Tomas will mourn the death of a very brave space pioneer. He won a v.c. for shooting down 99 spaceships off mars and this was folowed by the d.s.o. for beating up the bauxite in Betelgeuse. Sir basil was educated at st. custard's where he is still remembered for his skipping and liteness of foot. 'He skipped everything,' said his headmaster, reminiscently . . . . .

O goody sa fotherington-Tomas peeping over my shoulder O goody molesworth you hav put me in and made me brave. How can i thank you enuff? i'm brave i'm brave hurra.

I should not count on it, i sa. It is only a flite of fancy.

Thanks all the same. You are super molesworth 1 you really are. Now wot is yore future?

Another splendid creation by NIGEL

Who me oh i sa gosh no.
Fearfully i put my grate nose towards the cristal ball....

Another splendid creation by NIGEL is this
daring cocktail frock in burned orange and
squashed muskrat. Note how Nigel has modelled
bodice and waist in crashed chipmunk and a
flaring skirt with matching beads. No wonder
that Nigel's B-line is the sensation of the season.
Nigel has *flair*! Nigel will be showing his spring
colection.....

CURSES! I take the wretched cristal pill and punt it out
of the window. It take few things to drive me back to the
imperfect subjunk of avoir but this is one of them. J'eusses
tu euse..... But wot's the good of any of it?

'5 rats eat 6 seed cakes in 43 mins, 9 secs. They pause for twenty minutes. Then they eat 29 rock cakes in 15 secs (dead). They pause for 1 minute, 13 secs. Then they eat a cheese in 33 minutes.

How long do the rats take to eat the seed cakes, the rock cakes and the cheese?''

Wot a question, eh, to ask a boy! But that's the sort of thing you get faced with in exams and if you don't pass exams in this brave age you DON'T GET ON. chiz. Of corse it is quite easy to see why a weed who kno the height of Ben Nevis also that vertically oposite angles are equal is a beter bet for a bank or dog biscuit firm than me who kno o less than o cheers cheers cheers. But wot ocasionally depress me in my few leisure moments, my dear, is that you hav to go on taking exams all through your life chiz chiz chiz chiz
    e.g.

THE BOSS: Ah, fotherington-Tomas, wot is the population of grater london eh?
F-TOMAS: 44 million and a few odd thou.
THE BOSS: Are the oposite sides of a parallelogram equal?
F-TOMAS: Indeed they are, sir.
THE BOSS: i won't ask you about the rats. . . . you hav satisfied me. You are now export manager.
F-TOMAS: O goody!

You see wot i mean? Except for a couple of peaceful years doing national service the brave new clots hav got nothing but EXAMS EXAMS EXAMS. And it's the same for the gurls, too.

Aktually there is one comfort for clots like me who are not brany we can always get a job in a factory. In fact factories are glad to get anybody to judge from their notices:

O.K. No need to wory if you canot pass your Eleven Plus or Comon Entrance to an extremely tuough public skool, all you hav to do is to wait until you are 15 and cash in at the dere old plant.

This is wot hapen. You catch the old works bus and clock-in, put on your overalls, chaff the gurls, turn on the air conditioning, open the marshmallows and switch on the old precision tool. Any fool kno how to work a precision tool it's pappy. You feed in a piece of steel at one end and the machine grab it, hoist it over, punch, turn it back, punch it, press it, heave it upside down make a right-hand thread, squeeze it in two and there you have a finished snibber ready to rivet into the crocks of the cramp thus marrying the prip with the creech in the finished end-product.

But wot make work in the factory so fasscinating is the GOOD CONVERSATION in the shops. Effie on the glug driller next door tell you all that she sa to her boy-friend last nite and you tell her wot you see on the telly you've just bought and all the machines go –

A puff-a grab – sizzle – grunt – screeeeeee – ow – gosh – sizzle – screeeee – ow – help – gosh – and agane – screeeeee——

In fact, all are hapy turning out milions of snibbers when in come the shop foreman.

All right, he sa, switch off we're downing tools. Send for the manager and quick. Tell him I'm waiting. Jump to it, molesworth, i just seen another nine snibbers drop off. If you're not careful they'll be making a profit.

'Wot,' you sa, throing an oily rag at Effie, 'seems to be the trouble, horace?'

'Felow called peason without a union card in the paint shop. Manager won't sack him so i am calling you out.'

So it's no more snibbers and out with the old cards and a nice game of pontoon. Pity really becos it's not as if you were doing much work in the first place. Anyway imagine wot it would be like if this sort of thing spreads –

Scene 3B. *Master is reading his ushual book of love and passion while form swot at fr. verbs, dab criket, NOUGHTS and crosses, pools, free verse and other trifles of the boy mind.*

Enter GILLIBRAND, *foaming at the mouth.*

GILLIBRAND: All right. That's enuff. We're out. Down yore potts and pilcher fr. primer.

BEAK: (*reciting dreamily*) She galoped across the desert hem-hem in his strong tawny arms . . . . . (*he gives a start*) Wot is the meaning of this?

GILLIBRAND: a stoppage.

BEAK: No no, not that. How ghastley! Let the production lines of avoir, etre, donner, aimer and recevoir roll on. After all, you're a reasonable boy. (*thinks*: i must be polite to the twirp tho i would like to give him six).

GILLIBRAND: a tick in 1B hav exceeded his algy quota yesterday. We can't hav that, you kno.

The Beak fall down on his knees.

it is by such an example as i, like those other brave, clear-eyed workers
in the documentary films that britain will win its export batle

BEAK: Don't go out. Stay on the jobs. i'll do anything to
put this injustice right ect. ect.

Well, imagine that if poss. There is a grate deal of thortful
work to be done on labour relations between beaks and
boys though i expect it will be the same old story do wot
you're told or 6 of the best.

Back to the factory now and 12345/C nye molesworth hav
been shifted from the machine shop and is now working in
asembly as a reward for his zeal promise and enthusiasm.
Let us prick our grimy ears and listen. The forman speaketh.

'molesworth!'

'wot me? it was me the last time.'

'you 'eard. get up there, lad, and give it a $\frac{3}{8}$ turn on the
left-hand creep. Why you looking like that?'

'Nothink. i wasn't looking – i was thinking.' it's ten to
twelve, that's all. Time i get up i'll hav to come down.
don't seem any sense in it, really.'

'Any other thorts?'

'it's hot-pot today. Always hot-pot at the canteen thursdays. ho well, i'll get on down to the stores now – '

'waffor?'

'draw a $\frac{3}{8}$ monkey. i can't look at the job without a $\frac{3}{8}$
monkey now can i and if the creep is crabbing i'll need a
blower and talking of blowers – '

'i kno. 12 o'clock and hot-pot thursdays. The trubble
with you, molesworth – '

Hooooooooooooooooooooooooooooooooooo . . . . . !

it is by such an example as i stand there like those other
brave, clear-eyed workers in the documentary films that
britain will win its export batle hem-hem i do not think.
But you hav to be careful. you don't want to do too well
tho or you may become a manager and hav to recieve
reports from head ofice e.g.

Be careful or you may become a manager

PRODUCTION: very disapointing. why?
RAW MATERIALS: very disapointing.
  See tomkins.
LABOUR POSITION: very disapointing.

in fact it is just like a skool report or one of mine at any rate
and it would seme that you go on having reports as well as
exams all yore life. Wot an outlook. fancy giving us all that
free milk and orange juice just for that. still if we all work
hard enuff they are promising the workers automatick
nuclear atommic factories which do all the work by themselves. cheers cheers. Then the problem is LEAISURE.
cheers. Well, leaisure hav never been any problem to me –
and now yore rolls-royce is at the machine shop door, mr
molesworth. O.K. – and hav this precision tool gold-plated
by the time i return tomorrow. Exit the wealthy worker
12345/c nye molesworth and all the machines go:

*A puff-a grab – sizzle – grunt – screee – ow – gosh – sizzle –
screeeeee – ect.*

Produktivity in Skool

The molesworth production line for latin sentences

1   The raw sentence is fed into the sorter

2   The words pass along an endless belt into the electronik dicker

3 The dicker disgorges
them as latin

4 The assembler puts
them together

5 The boys take them to the ticking machine

Snip! Snip! Snip!!!!!!!!!!!!!!!!
At speshul sacrifice!!!!

HEADMASTER FOR SALE

Small, part used in fare condition considering. Mustache recently trimmed and shoes soled with ruber excelent for cobbing boys, miscreants ect.

No maintenance. Can live on seaweed and thinks boys can, too.

Handy, adjustable, can be used for any purpose. Cantilever movement.

together with

SET OF KANES (part-worn and frayed)

price one d. or offer
or
would exchange for jumping flea

BACK IN THE JUG AGANE

1

I MITE HAV KNOWN

Well i mite hav expected it. The game's up. They got me just when i thort i was safe. So here i am back at SKOOL agane for a joly term chiz chiz chiz.

St custard's, i regret to report, hav not changed in my absence, though perhaps it may hav got worse. It is just the same as any other first day since i started my akademic hem-hem career there some few semesters ago. (It seme as if it were yesterday, my dere.) Same cobwebs, same smell of wet flannel, soap, carbolik ect poo gosh: inside the skool piano there is now a nest of mice, 1 cig. card, 3 katerpillers and pik-ture of marylyn monro pinched no doubt from the master's comon room.

As for my merry felow students, they are still here worse luck. Just look at them – grabber who arrive in a swank-pot rolls, peason my frend who hav a face like a squished tomato, gillibrand, molesworth 2 my bro. And who is this who skip weedily up to me, eh? 'Hullo clouds, hullo sky,' he sa. 'Hullo birds, hullo poetry books, hullo skool sossages, hullo moles-worth 1.' You hav guessed it is dere little basil fotherington-tomas.

Wot brethless adventures lie before these stout little chaps? (And none stouter than fatpot peason.) Wot wizard japes and priceless pranks will they get up to? Before them lie the bright future of a new term – will they accept the chalenge?

(*Now read on.*)

On arrival all boys stand about with hands in pokets look-ing utterly fed up and dejected. Finally someone speke.

'Did you hav a good hols, molesworth?'

'Not bad.'

(*Silence.*)

'Did you have a good hols peason?'

'Not bad.'

The dialogue is positively scintilating, my dere. Surely they canot kepe it up? There is no chance of that for the wit of these skolars is interupted by a dread sound e.g.

CLANG-PIP. CLANG-PIP. CLANG-PIP.

It is the skool bell which sumon us to asemble in big skool into which enter anon GRIMES, the headmaster surounded by a posse of thugs and strong-arm men in black gowns. The beaks, of course, alias 'my devoted staff'. You can imagine it a few minits before.

Scene: GRIMES study. A candle is burning in a botle. A botle of GIN stand on the table. A beak is fixing an iron spike on a kane, another is fixing a knuckle-duster, a third practise with a broken botle.

GRIMES: Are they all in, Slugsy?

G. A. POSTLETHEWAITE, m.a. (leeds): Yep, they're all in, boss.

GRIMES: o.k. then we're ready to pull the job. You kno the plan. Slugsy, you cover me from the door. Lefty, cover my right flank. Butch, on the other side. Killer, bring up the rear. If there's any trouble, let them hav it. That clear Butch?

P. ST. J. NETLETON, b.a. (exeter): Wot about our cut? You still owe us for last terms jobs.

GRIMES: How can you be so sordid?

ect. ect. ect.

Now GRIMES stand on the platform, smiling horibly at the pitiable colection of oiks, snekes, cads, oafs and dirty roters below.

'Welcome back,' he snarl, 'Welcom back to st. custards for a new term. I hope you had a good hols? i did myself – spane, the s. of france, then on for a couple of weeks to the italian riviera. This term, of course, the fees will be higher to meet the mounting costs.'

But this evidence of good humour is short-lived. Without warning, he bare his fangs.

'Now listen, scum,' he yell, 'The last mum hav departed in tears. You are in my clutches agane and there is no escape. And its going to be this way this term. More work, increased

Before them lie the bright future of a new term – will they accept the chalenge?

production, trades unions supresed and the first boy i hear who sa poo gosh at a skool sossage will get 6. And strikes won't help you. If you go out the shop stewards will be flogged.'

'Remember this,' he leer, 'You never had it so good.'

Well, this is just wot we expect. We hav it every term and our tiny harts sink to our boots. It will be nothing but *lat. fr. arith. geom. algy. geog.* ect. and with the winter coming on it would be warmer in siberia in a salt mine. Oh well – we wait for wot we kno will come next.

'And wot,' sa GRIMES, 'hav we all been reading in the hols?'

Tremble tremble moan drone, i hav read nothing but red the redskin and Guide to the Pools. i hav also sat with my mouth open looking at lassie, wonder horse ect on t.v. How to escape? But i hav made a plan.

'fotherington-tomas,' sa GRIMES, 'wot hav you read?'

'Ivanhothe vicar of wakefieldwuthering heights treasure-islandvanity fairwestwardhothewaterbabies and —'

'That is enuff. Good boy. And molesworth?'

He grin horibly.

'What hav you read, molesworth?'

gulp gulp a rat in a trap.

'Proust, sir.'

'Come agane?'

'Proust, sir. A grate fr. writer. The book in question was swan's way.'

'Gorblimey. Wot did you think of it, eh?'

'The style was exquisite, sir, and the characterisation superb. The long evocative passages—'

'SILENCE!' thunder GRIMES. 'There is no such book, impertinent boy. I shall hav to teach you culture the hard way. Report for the kane after prayers.'

Chiz chiz to think i hav learned all that by hart. It's not fair they get you every way. And so our first day end when we join together singing our own skool song.

St. custard's is brave.
SWISH.
St. custard's is fair.
BIFF BANG WALOP.
Hurrah hurrah for st. custard's.
SWISH SWISH SWISH.

As lashed by the beaks we join our boyish trebles in this fine old song we feel positively inspired i do not think. We are in for the joliest term on record. In fakt, i am back in the jug agane.

THE GRIMES POLL

Headmaster GRIMES lay down his mitey pen. The crossed skool nib hav ceased scratching: the watery skool ink is dry upon the ex book: candle in the bottle in his studdy gutter fitfully. 'Finished,' he sa. 'Completed.'

To wot do he refer, eh? Is it to the corektions of our weedy lat prep i.e. balbum amas puellae? Could it be, perhaps, a letter to our pore parents putting up the fees? Could it be the anual statement of his whelk stall accounts? No chiz it is none of these things. It is his master work on the behaviour of boys – SECRETS OF THE BOOT ROOM by phineas GRIMES, b.a. (stoke-on-trent) to be published in the autumn by messers grabber at 30 bob.

However by courtesy of the molesworth chizzery and spy service it is now possible to reveal some of the startling fakts contaned in this huge opus.

TELEVISION

Out of 62 pupils at st. custard's, $61\frac{1}{2}$ stay up late at nite gawping at the t.v. To do this they employ unbelievable cuning saing mum, can we? ect. o pleese, mum, just till 7.30 when that grate dog who rescue people and bark like mad will be finished. $61\frac{1}{2}$ mums out of 62 fall for this becos it mean a little quiet in the house (xcept for the grate dog barking, this, however, appere preferable to our boyish cries.) Wot hapen next? The grate dog is folowed by an even grater fool i.e. plunket of the yard. This is a program highly suitable for small boys as there is murder and various other CRIMES in it. The grate thing is to manage to sit gawping until the new program begin: then, when yore mum come in and sa britely 'Time for bed, chaps' ect, she will get wraped up in the brutal crime which go on. This take $61\frac{1}{2}$ boys out of 62 until 8 p.m. when there is a quiz chiz. Pater storm in and sa 'aren't these boys in bed yet?' He then kno the answer to the first q. i.e. wot is the capital of england? This set him going since he wish to give a demonstration of his prowess.

'Any fule would kno that,' he sa.

$61\frac{1}{2}$ boys out of 62 restrane any comment on this, knoing they will get sent to bed. Pater go on saing weedy things i.e. china, of corse, edison, e.a.poe also that he ought to go in for it he would win a lot of money. mum do not restrane coment on the last point and by the time the argument is over we can hav a little peace with the play. This is about LUV and of no interest, but it do kepe you on the job until 10. The $61\frac{1}{2}$ boys then get into there pajamas and come back to sa good nite. They stretch forward for loving embrace when sudenly they are turned into pilar of salt e.g. lot's wife becos a HORSE is in terible trubble on the screen with a ruough master. 11 p.m. bed and swete dreams.

SMOKING

Enuff said. Just count the cig. ends behind the skool potting shed. It look as if the skool gardener must smoke 500 a day.

CONVERSATION IN DORMS

The news is grave. 62 boys out of 62 indulge in this forbidden practise after lights out. Moreover the conversation is not on a high level i.e. you hav a face like a squished tomato same to you with no returns ass silly ass i said it first yes i did no i didn't. This frequently end up in BLOWS with ye olde concrete pilows. From 1 boy alone do we get GOOD CONVERSATION i think you kno to whom i refer. Oui! c'est basil fotherington- (hullo clouds, hullo sky) tomas who bore us to slepe with proust and t.s.eliot.

RUSHING DOWN THE PASSAGE

There is something about the sight of a passage which raise the worst in a boy. No sooner than he see the end of it than he wish to sa charge ta-ran-ta-rah and do so, sliding the soles off his house shoes. ½ a boy, however, do walk slowly and with corekt deportment, one hand on hip, until overtaken and troden on by the mob. And good ridance.

MOB VIOLENCE

We must do something about this: we canot hav it, you kno. In future there must be no more scrums in the gim. The honor of the skool is at stake. And the answer is easy. Organise some morris dancing and all will be well. Or not.

And wot is GRIMES conklusion, eh? Modern youth is on the way down. But he was a boy once (i supose). Can it get any lower?

MUSIC THE FOOD OF LUV

Sooner or later yore parents decide that they ought to give you a chance to hav a bash at the piano. So wot hapen, eh? They go up to GRIMES, headmaster, who is dealing in his inimitable way, my dere, with a number of problems from other parents e.g. fotherington-tomas's vests, peasons cough drops, grabber's gold pen and pore, pore mrs gillibrand thinks that ian (who is so sensitive) is the tiniest bit unhappy about the condukt of sigismund the mad maths master. (Who wouldn't be? He is utterly bats and more crooked than the angle A.) Finally come the turn of those super, smashing and cultured family hem-hem the molesworths. Mum step forward britely:

Oh, mr GRIMES, she sa, we think it would be so nice for nigel and his wee bro, molesworth 2, to learn the piano this term.

(GRIMES thinks: Another mug. One born every minit.)

GRIMES: Yes, yes, mrs molesworth, i think we could manage to squeeze them in. Judging from their drawings both yore sons hav strong artistick tendencies. i see them in their later years drawing solace from bach and beethoven ect in some cloistered drawing room. It'll cost you ten nicker and not a penny less.

PATER: (*feebly*) I sa—

GRIMES: Look at the wear and tear on the piano – it's a bektenstein, you kno. Then there's the metronome – had to have new sparking plugs last hols and the time is coming when we've got to hav a new pianoforte tutor.

Pater and Mater weakly agree and the old GRIMES cash register ring merily out again. It is in this way that that grate genius of the keyboard, molesworth 2, learned to pla that grate piece fairy bells chiz chiz chiz.

The first thing when you learn to pla the piano is to stare out of the window for 20 minits with yore mouth open. Then

316

Before getting on to rimski-korsakov it is as well to kno wot
you are up aganst

scratch yore head and carve yore name, adding it to the illus-
trious list already inscribed on the top of the piano. Should,
however, GRIMES or any of the other beaks becom aware
that there is no sound of mery musick, the pupil should pretend to be studdying the KEYBOARD in his instruktion
book.

This is meant to teach the eager pupil the names of the
notes ect. The skool piano may hav looked like that once,
but toda it is very different. Before getting on to rimski-korsakov it is as well to kno wot you are up aganst. Here is the
guide –

C—this one go plunk.

D—the top hav come off the note and you strike melody from something like a cheese finger.

E—sticks down when you hit it. Bring yore screwdriver to lever it up.

F—have never been the same since molesworth 2 put his chewing gum under it.

G—nothing hapen when you hit this note at all.

Do not be discouraged, however, show grit, courage, determination, concentrate, attend and soon you will get yoreself a piece. This will probably be called Happy Thorts and there is a strong warning at the beginning which sa Not Too Fast. Who do they think i am, eh, stirling moss?

Scene: fort twirp, h.q. of davy croket, wyatt earp, last of the mohicans, lone ranger ect. Enter a quaver spuring his horse.

QUAVER: (*quavering*) Larrfffing lemonade, the Indian semi-breve is on the war path.

CROKET: Oo, gosh!

EARP: This is yore job, lone ranger, i guess.

L. RANGER: Wouldn't want to get mixed up with all them breves and semi-breves, mr earp. To sa nothing of the crotchets and quavers. When they get mad, they get real mad. Where's the sheriff?

(*Enter Chief Larrfffing Lemonade.*)

CHIEF L L.: i feel really crotchety. Guess i'll have a half of minim . . .

Ect. And so it go on. But wot really hapen, when yore aged musick mistress is on the job?

'And a one, to, three . . . softly, softly, molesworth, that is a pedal not a clutch . . . and a two, three, four . . . lah-dee, dah . . . this is a lake not an ocean . . . get cracking . . . hep, hep . . . sweetly, sweetly . . . hit the right note, rat.'

Well, musick is just another of those things. Wot i sa is. Either you have it or you haven't. And i would rather not.

PASS THE SPUTNIK, MAN!

Wot is yore opinion of colin wilson, the new philosopher?'
sa fotherington-tomas, hanging by his weedy heels from the
crossbar.

'Advanced, forthright, signifficant,' i repli, kicking off the
mud from my footer boots.

'He takes, i think, the place of t.s. eliot in speaking for the
younger genneration. Have you any idea of the score?'

'Not a clue.'

'Those rufians hav interrupted us 6 times. So one must
assume half a dozen goles. If only our defence was more
lively, quicker on the takle! Now as i was saing about colin
wilson –'

Yes, clots, weeds, and fellow suferers, it means the good
old footer season is with us and jack the shepherd is a good
deal warmer when he blows his nail than we are. Birds are
frozen: little children sink with a vast buble in the mud and
are not heard of agane: sigismund the mad maths master don
his long white woollen hem-hems. Yes, this is the time when
we are driven out with whip and lash upon ye old soccer field.

Mind you, there are some who think soccer is super. These
are the ones who charge, biff, tackle and slam the leather
first-time into the net ect. They hav badges and hav a horible
foto taken at the end of term with their arms folded and the
year chalked upon the pill. This foto cost there parents 7/6
on the skool bill and i hope they think it is worth it. i would
not care for grabber's face on my walls, that's all.

Of corse i'm no good . . . no, i mean it . . . i simply am
no good . . . no, please, grabber, my body-swerve . . . well,
it go in the wrong direcktion . . . o, i sa, no . . . wot a nice
thing to hear about myself . . . if i try hard i'll be in *the
seconds!* And then how much further on would i be in the
career of life, eh?

I speke for millions when i sa i *AM NO GOOD AT
SOCCER.* You can, of corse, watch it from the touchline
in that case. Very diffrent.

'Pass . . . get it out to the wing . . . move in to the centre . . . wot are you plaing about at? . . . Get rid of it.'

I need hardly tell you the esential thing about a football i.e. nobody need tell *me* to get rid of it. i do not want it in the first place. Wot is the use of having a soaking wet piece of leather pushed at you? Give me a hadock every time, at least you can eat it.

However, where would headmaster GRIMES be without the good old game? No longer would he be able to look up from those delicious crumpets, which he eat before a roring fire and observe: 'The third game ort to be finished in about 20 minits. Cold out there. About 50 below zero. Damn it, forgot to stoke the baths! o well, a spot of cold water did nobody any harm, eh?'

However, there is no doubt about it the honour of the old skool depend a grate deal on whether you can score more than wot i may litely call 'the oposition'. Scoring more than the 'oposition' is practically imposible, but it sometimes hapen. Beware when it do becos you hav to bang yore spoon on the table, just when you want to help yourself to the jam, and yell RA, RA, RA! Well done SKOOL, SKOOL, SKOOL!

And who is it who have achieved this sukcess? None other than the games master, who hav given his life, his time, his bootlaces and his premium bonds into making the 1st XI into a well-oiled footballing machine. There are lots of diffrent kinds of games masters, but there are usually 2 types who are able to be distinguished by us weeds on the touchline e.g.

Type One: He do no not sa anything: he put his hands in his mack and watch. After about 17 minits of the first half he is heard to sa 'O, potts-rogers'. He knock out his pipe at half-time when the team are sucking lemons and whisper: 'good show, get on with it.' Then he relapse into silence and, about 2 minits from time, sa 'o god'.

The other type of games master is exactly the oposite.

'Mind you, there are some who
think soccer is super.'

Remembering his own football prime (one day we must go
into the rekords of games masters, must we not?) he think
he can score a gole with his own voice. Some of them can: or
ort to be able to.

'COME ON, ST. CUSTARD'S ... GET INTO
HIM ... PASS! ... MARK YORE MAN! ... BLOW
YORE NOSE ... INTO THE CENTRE. ... NO,
THE CENTRE NOT THE ARTERIAL ROAD
... GET IT IN! ... COME ON NOW! SHOOT!
...'

This is the last desparing cry. Lots of games masters have
been carted awa murmuring faintly 'Shoot!' In 999 cases if
they were aiming at gole someone missed: but ocasionaly
the shot hit the mark. And it was an elfin-ray pistol with
atommic atachment that do the damage.

'The New Year stretches before us, molesworth,' sa fother-ington-tomas, skipping weedily.

'Wot of it?' i sa 'Wot of it, o weedy wet? It will be the same as any other, all geom.fr. geog ect and weedy walks on sunda.'

'It was just – well, have you ever thort of becoming a skoolmaster when you grow up?'

Curses! Curses! That i should live to see the day when these things were spoken!

'Sa that agane,' i grit, 'and i will conk you on the head and/ or thoroughly bash you up.'

'Do not,' he sa, 'get into a bate. i was only trying to help. A skoolmaster is better than a fashion designer. Besides, you hav all the qualifications.'

'Hav i?' i sa, in spite of myself. 'How super, fotherington-tomas. Tell me about them, go on o you mite.'

'You are qualified,' sa fotherington-tomas, 'becos you can frankly never pass an exam and have o branes. Obviously you will be a skoolmaster – there is no other choice.'

Enraged i buzz a conker at him. It miss and strike the skool dog wandsworth who zoom across the footer field at mach. 1 and trip the reff cheers cheers.

As it hapen this witty conversation take place during the 2nd XI footer match v porridge court. There comes a warn-ing shout from the spektators. fotherington-tomas skip back weedily into gole and i remane where i am, a bleeding hart on the left wing.

All the same the conversation have me worried and affekt my game. (See report)

'*For the rest of the match molesworth* 1 *was not in the smashing form which have earned him the soobriquet of the "Dribbling Wizard." He was not fastening on to his passes.*' (m. thinks: you mean when someone hack a huge muddy ball in my direction? Wot a pass.) '*The opposition had him at sea.*' (m. thinks: it's amateurs still at prep skool, isn't it? Or are porridge court buying players?) '*Where was that body swerve? That familiar jink?*' (m. thinks: Gone, my dear. Absolument disparu like mother's mink.)

And so it is the old story. The better team won, ha-ha. All clap each other on the back and hug each other. 'Where are your lovely flowers, molesworth, which porridge court spartak hav given you?' 'i hav thrown them to ye olde matronne before disappearing into the dressing room.' Well you kno wot go on in there. WAM BIFF SOCKO ZOOSH. CRASH. BASH. Headmaster GRIMES emerge smiling. 'A little disappointing but we must learn to swallow defeat.'

'Of corse,' sa mater. 'How are nigel's spots?'

'Hav he got spots? gosh chiz i haven't had measles yet myself. i must get awa from this.'

'i was a little *surprised* to find him playing. nigel is so deli-kate, so thin, so nervy, so tense, so neurotick (strike out the word which do not apply). i felt that he mite perhaps hav been in bed ect. . . .'

And so it go on at football matches. But, as that nite i lie awake on my downy couch hem-hem in the PINK DORM the conversation come back to me as it was a nightmare. Me a Skoolmaster! Me a BEAK! Me an Usher! Wot an idea – and yet look around you. There are so many of them that it is obviously a fate which is difficult to avoid.

My head nods the tired brane drowses. i slip i slide (peotry THE BROOK) into merciful oblivion. Soon the dorm resound with a steady note plaster falls off the ceiling, the paint blisters pop. My snores join the others but there is no rest i am shaken by a terible NIGHTMARE.

i am sitting at the master's desk looking with horor at a see of faces, fat ones, thin ones, contorted, spotty, green, and black ones, there is no doubt of whose they are – it is 3B.

And who is that horid creature dodging behind gillibrand

and trying to conceal the fact that he is chewing buble gum? It is me, molesworth 1 chiz chiz chiz. *i am teaching myself!*

'Boy!' i rasp, in a voice i can scarcely recognise it is hoarse and thick with pasion. 'Boy, stand up. Wot is yore name?'

'molesworth 1, sir.'

'That is very interesting, molesworth very interesting indeed. Can it be, however, that you are having some difikulty in enunciating? i thort there was some slight suspicion of er congestion in the mouth? Some er impediment of the speech?'

'N—no, sir. Nnnnnnn—no, sir.'

'BOY HOW DARE YOU?'

My face is red as a tomato i shake with rage my eyes are those of a MANIAK. Like any other master i hav forgotten that i was ever a boy i hav forgoten brave noble fearless youth cheers cheers. My hand go back like a flash and i buzz the red chalk striking the victim on the nose. The rest of the klass titter they are sicophants and toadies i diskard them.

'If there is another sound i shall keep the whole klass in. Molesworth, go outside and remove that disgusting objekt.'

It is too horible. i struggle to awake but the nightmare continue.

It is still the same lesson and i am the master. Everything is normal i am feeling a trifle lazy and set the boys some geom propositions to get on with. Before me is a pile of uncorekted exercise books i pop outside for a quick cig and return to study a book on grips and tortures for boys. i am immersed in this when i hear a sound.

'Sir,'

(A spasm of anoyance run through my frame. i pretend not to hear.)

'Sir, sir, sir please sir.'

CURSES! Is the child not to be put off? am i never to be rid of his importunity? Wearily i raise my bespectakled face and gaze at him over a mountane of exercise books and bottles of red ink.

It is me, molesworth 1 chiz chiz chiz – i am teaching myself.

'Well, wot is it molesworth?'
'Wot is the verb-noun infinitiv, sir?'
'Eh?'
'The verb-noun infinitiv, sir. It sa in the Shorter Latin Primer . . .'
'All right all right. i heard you the fust time' (thinks: verb-noun infinitiv? i dunno. search me.)

Open lat. grammer under cover of books. shufle shufle.
Sweat pour from my brows i must play for time. i cover my
action with stinging words.

'So molesworth you do not kno the verb-noun infinitiv?
Wot crassness, wot ignorance ect . . .'

Masters ushally keep their cribs and answer books in the
dark depths of their desks and wot a collection there is in
there – kanes, beetles, chalk, thumscrews, old tin soldiers
which hav been confiskated, fotos of gurls, bat oil, fleas and
cobwebs.

in here i find the lat. grammer. i prop it against a tin of
pineaple chunks and find the answer. My blak beak's heart is
filled with relief. Also i thirst for revenge. i switch to geom
and make the chalk squeak with the compass on the blakboard until all howl it is worse than molesworth 2's space
ship.

SCREE SCREE SCREE SCREE delicious torture! i
draw a collossal Angle A and make it equal to Angle B. Gloat
Gloat. Wot does it matter if it is half the size? pythagoras
could make an elephant equal to a flea . . .

Restlessly i toss from side to side in my bed. Can it be
that i have eaten too much skool cheese? Why can i not
awake? The nightmare continue . . .

am i popular? Do the boys like me? O grief. perhaps they
do not. i will do anything. tomow i will read to them. i will
give them the water babies that always sla them. it sla me too.
Poor tom. And yet . . . are they making enuff progress?
perhaps it should be the confidential clerk by t.s. eliot. But
will that make me popular hem-hem?

THE BELL! The BELL!

I am telling a story about how i won the war. WEEE
PING EEEAUOOWOO. Men, there is a nest of pea
shooters under that map of the world i want you to silence
them. CHARGE TA-RAN-TA-RA. BANG BONK
BISH. Who zoom past then? it is molesworth 2 beating us

up in his super-jet speed hawk ur ur ur ur. Take cover, Sigismund, these boys are fiercer than the mau-mau and many look like them. This is rebelion and the boys mean business. Give me my kane i will die like a man.

THE BELL.

Why have not mrs grabber given me the ushual 50 cigs for an xmas box? Where are my yelow socks and pink tie? i am alone the skool is empty. Where are the boys? Gone. it is the old story, caruthers, too many masters chasing too few boys. Too many . . .

THE BELL.

And this time it is the skool bell bidding me rise and face the chalenge of the new year hem-hem. Sun shine, birds sing, skool sossages frazzle in the kitchen – hurrah hurrah i am not a master after all. I stride forth with new knoledge e.g. even masters hav their problems. i will remember that in future.

MOLESWORTH WOT ARE YOU DOING WITH YORE HAIR UNBRUSHED YORE SHOES UNLACED AND WEARING ONE FOOTER SOCK ECT? DO 1000000000000 LINES.

So you see. There you are. There's nothing you can do about them.

2

HURRAH FOR EXAMMS

Do examms hav any teror for you, clots? Are the 11-plus, G.C.E., common entrance ect preying on your tiny mind? Are you posessed with a feeling that you may fale? HAV YOU NOT WORKED HARD ENUFF IN THE PAST, EH? Perhaps you may not enjoy a briliant future as an atommic physisist?

It is strange that i, molesworth, the goriller of 3 B, do not share these fears with you. Observe with what confidence i stride into the examm room with new sharpened old h.b., bungy, ruler and a stop watch on ye olde chippendale desk. And wot then? I take off my coat, roll up my sleeves and fold my stout arms awaiting the q's with impatience. Not for me the worried frowns of les autres, those careworn looks. When the Beak bring round those papers which smell so swetely of printer's ink this is wot i sa:

Q.1. Complete the following series TR. S.G.P.

ME: Potty!

Q.2. Write the nex 3 numbers in this sequence: 1. 79. 232. 6 billion.

ME: Larrfably easy!

Q.3. A stupid old man walked 6 paces to the east, 12 to the north, stood on his head, then ran 100 yards at 100 m.p.h. Where is he?

ME: Too simple for words!

And so it go on. Of corse, criticks may point out that i occupy the lowly position of 9th out of 9 in 3 B and am in some danger of relegation to div. 3. Why dost thou always put the obj in the nom, clot, aussi? Alas i canot deny the truth of these harsh words. Wot, then, is the sekrett of my sucksess in examms?

Hist, cave, come close felow skolars and suferers of the world of space and listen with all thy mitey ears, which, no doubt, hav not seen a towel for years.

My sucksess is not due to any stroke of good fortune but to careful planning in the past in association with my grate chum and felow research worker hem-hem wet peason. The results of our activities can now be anounced to the world i.e.

1. The molesworth/peason electronick brane which is disguised as a stop-watch. This amazing gadget can answer the most dificult question in a matter of secs enabling the skolar to sit back after 5 minutes with a look we kno so well in others which sa, 'That's pappy ect.' Any fule can use it and no beak will suspeckt.

2. The molesworth/peason portable roving eye. This is an intrikkate system of mirrors which can be flicked out of the poket (along with fluff, beetles, old cig. ends, stamp swaps ect) when the Beak is not looking and, in the space of $\frac{1}{8}$ secs can obtane the answers from all the other candidate's papers. The portable roving eye hav one serious operational defeckt, however. It hav been known to get 15 diffrent reports, all of which sa *Puellam amas puer*, which, for some reason always get a cross aganst it and o marks.

3. Another triumph of science is the new molesworth/ peason very high frequency radio set so that all boys can talk to each other on a wave length so high that no Beak can hear i.e.

CALLING BADGER ONE, CALLING BADGER ONE. HOW DO YOU HEAR ME, EH?

The molesworth/peason porta

ing eye hav one serious defeckt.

THY SWETE VOICE IS LOUD AND CLEAR, NIT-WIT WOT CAN I DO FOR YOU?

CALLING BADGER ONE. WOT IS THE ANSWER TO NUMBER THREE?

X TO THE POWER OF A OVER BETA, CLOT, AS ANY FULE KNO. WOT DO YOU MAKE OF NUMBER ONE?

NOTHING.

SAME HERE WE HAD BETTER CALL UP FOTHERINGTON-TOMAS WHO ALWAYS KNO.

O.K. BADGER ONE. OUT.

So, by a carefull system of cross-checking each boy in the examm can get exactly the same answers.

Two further inventions upon which me and my emminent colleague are working are a magnifying glass for thumbnale cribs and a pill which send the Beak off to slepe. So why be worried, restless and iritable as examms approche? Give your mater and pater the poor skoolmasters confidence by yore calm attitude. These epoch-making products are on the market now, so send for catalog at once.

KO-EDDUKATION AT ST. CUSTARD'S

Hay ho! Wot a lot of problems we dere little chaps of the 20th century hav to face – there are H-bombs, missiles, spacemen, russians, yanks, electronick branes, headmasters, apart from the weedy ones in the arith books. Now as if these various chizzes are not enuff there is another i.e. i rede that in the society of the future there will be no such thing as boys skools and gurls skools. This can only mean ko-eddukation and already there are millions and trilions of brave noble and fearless boys who are being submitted to this fearful torture chiz chiz.

IT IS TIME THE SKANDAL WAS EXPOSED!

It is easy to immagine wot hapen at these ko-eddukational skools and we must rite it down fearlessly. It is time the people knew. Pause while this scruffy scribe draw the CURTAIN aside.

Scene: a klassroom. This is much as ushual with blotch in the inkwells, ice cold radiator, railways carved on the desk, portrate of caesar crossing the rubkon (1896), bits of aple core and beak's desk bulging with artikles which he hav confiskated. A klass is in progress with all the boys gazing out of windows with their mouths open and all the GURLS looking intent, eager, keen ect.

THE BEAK: molesworth, wot is the first rool of the 4 concords in lat.

(*No repli.*)

THE BEAK: MOLESWORTH!

ME: eh? Were you perchance adressing me sir?

THE BEAK (*with a vane effort at control*) i was asking you the first rool of the 4 concords, rat.

ME: Cor, stone the crows, search me!

THE BEAK: Perhaps some other boy will oblige with the answer – peason, gillibrand, fotherington-tomas? Is any boy reddy with an answer?

(*Silence meanwhile the gurls giggle and go mad with xcitement. Finally, the beak turn his beetling brow to them and his xpression become sudenly soft, his stern eye mild*) 'Mavis,' he whisper, 'perhaps you——?'

MAVIS: The first of the 4 rools of concord in lat is that a Verb agrees with its subjekt in number and person.

THE BEAK: Excellent, mavis!

MAVIS: Xamples are tempus fugit. Time flies.

THE BEAK: Bravo, now—

MAVIS: Or Libri leguntur. Books are read.

THE BEAK: Thank you, mavis, thank you.

MAVIS: (*continuing, nothing can stop her*) The second rool of concord is that an adj or participle agree in gender, number and case with the substantive it qualify. Xamples – Vir bonus bonam uxorem habet. The good man has a good wife.

ME: A highly debatable statement, if I may sa so, sir.

We get a bit of a larff for this but the day is lost and mavis continue to the bitter end. And she is only one becos ermintrude, matilda, mary and peggy are all branes of britain, junior quiz champions ect.

Another thing GURLS have difrent standards of behaviour in Klass i.e. if i thro a bit of bungy at peason he will bide his time and thro an ink bomb back which hit me splosh on the nose. But wot hapen if you pull mavis pigtail, eh? You get a speech like this ;—

MAVIS: I feel it my duty, sir, to report a trifling incident which hav just taken place. I feel that it will be for the good of the klass as a whole that i should do so. (*Cries of* 'sneke,' 'sneke') i am not alarmed by doing wot i conceive to be my duty. (*loud cheers and interjektions of* 'sit down,' 'sit down') Sir, these vulgar cries do not dismay me – nay (A member: 'Back her for the Derby') nay, nay (The price is slipping, six to four the field). This klass, sir, hav

GURLS hav difrent standards of behaviour in Klass.

always had a reputation for clene living, decency, deckor-
um, and the preservation of behaviour-standards as reco-
mended in the last phamplet by the min. of edukation
obbtainable at the h.h. stionnery office, price 3 gns.

Wot (sa Mavis) Wot is the result?

A vulgarian whom i do not wish to name (Cries of
name him, molesworth, who were you with last nite ect)
A vulgarian whom I feel should be brought to book hav
now sullied the honor of this mixed klass and brought to o
the good name of the skool. By doing wot? He have
pulled my pigtail.

Ow! (Once agane the molesworth touch bringeth ressults)
OW! OW! OW!

And now i am glad to sa that mavis turn and swing with a
short uppercut, following with a rite cross to the jaw. Human
at last! She is once more champion of the world.

Well, there you are. Does ko-edducation work? Who will
pla tag with me in the break, eh? Many people point to
America and Russia and sa they hav had gurls and boys at
skool together there for years. Does that make it any better?
We venture hem-hem to think not. Hurrah for st custard's!

TENIS ANEBODY?

'Hullo, clouds, Hullo sky,' sa fotherington-tomas, skipping weedily by. 'Who's for tenis?'

i frown with anger, for i am looking at ye olde television chiz and robin hood is in a v. tuough spot indeed i.e. the sherif of nottingham is about to torture him with red hot irons, which is something we little tots are very used to. Anyway, i sometimes hav a feeling of sympathy for the sherif of notingham wot am i saing? Outside, of corse, it is a briliant, fine sumer day with bees buzzing, birds twittering ect.

'Who's for tenis?' repete fotherington-tomas, waving his racket.

'Go away, clot, You are standing in front of the screne. i can only hear the grones of agony.'

'Go on, molesworth, o you mite.'

'If i want tenis i can see it on the television,' i repli. 'Besides, it is a game for gurls.'

This is a new thing for the galant boys of the younger generration, they are always being told to pla tenis. Why is this? It is worse than criket becos at criket you can at least get bowled out but at tenis you hav to go on missing agane and agane and agane. i mean i expect it is all right if you can pla like those fierce people at wimbledon who go, well, you kno

PUNG! PING! PING! PING! *PUNG!* HURRAH!

If i pla there is dead silence becos i never hit the pill at all they are all air shots chiz. Besides, am i likely to play a game at which fotherington-tomas can beat me, eh? i hav some pride.

Acktually fotherington-tomas is super at tenis, as he hav been coached by a pro at home i.e. he twiddle his raket and sa 'ruff or smooth?' and when he win he consider the direction of the wind, position of sun, met. forecast for next

It is strange wot a tenis raket can do.

twenty-four hours, trend on the stock xchange, his horo-scope for the week and sa finaly, 'i shall pla aganst the kool shade of the aple trees.' This mene that i am blinded by the sun and can only see fotherington-tomas crouched like a tiger on the other side of the net. Gosh, it take a bit for him to look like that it is strange wot a tenis raket can do. If i get a pill over at all he wam it back at 90 m.p.h. so there is not much of a game at all.

Gurls, of corse, pla a lot of tenis at skool so i expect this explane the matter.

You kno wot hapen at gurl's skools they always discover a gurl who is the uggly duckling who can get into the skool six when pritty antonia trumpington brake her leg. Need i add that the olde skool de mademoisells always win the match?

'*O, you juggins,*' *sa miss trent, the games mistress, crossly. Mavis bit her lip and faced the next ball with determination*

*written all over her freckled face. Miss trent's powerful serve
came into action agane but this time mavis faced it calmly and
swept the pill into the far corner. On the next serve it hapened
agane, then agane. 'Bravo, mavis,' cry miss trent. 'Well plaed,
sir!' ect.*

Personally i think in reel life miss trent would probably be
furious if any gurl swept her best serve into the far corner
but that do not seme to hapen in books. Insted, miss trent
put mavis in the tenis six and due to her briliant pla ect well,
you kno.

Now that they hav pro tenis, in fakt, it would be a joly
good wheeze if mavis and fotherington-tomas plaed a world
tenis circus. Everyone would be agog when the skore stood
at 499 matches each. Which will win the decider? Over to
humphrey, the wet, in the commentator's box.

*'mavis is serving. She hav thrown up the pill. It is still going
up, up, up. Now it is in orbit. No, it is coming down. Plunk!
Wot's this? O, ha-ha. v. funny i must sa. It landed on mavis
head. Thev're picking her up now. Second serve and the ball is
up. Lovely style, mavis has. Now it's coming down. Oh dear,
dear me, that is bad luck. It hav landed on mavis head agane.*

GAME TO FOTHERINGTON-TOMAS.

*fotherington-tomas to serve and he is standing on the tips of
his toes. He semes fascinated by clouds and sky. Bends to pick
un the ball. Goodness gracious, how unfortunate. He hav split
his trousis. He is covered in confusion and that is all. But who is
this uncooth skoolboy who is roaring with larfter at the poor
little chap's plight? Who can it be?*

i give you 1 guess it is me, molesworth, the goriller of
3 B, delited at the fate of ickle pritty fotherington-tomas. It is
a hard life to be a tenis star and, if mavis is an xample, you
need a thick head which make me wonder why i am no good
at the game. Oh well, back to the telly i must have mised 2
murders, 3 suicides and a few loonies. Still, we'll be getting
them tomorrow.

MIND MY BIKE!

Well i mean to sa gosh chiz wot next, eh? Wot next? Sitting in the old skool bibliotheque among the cobwebs and reading the newspaper as is my wont my eye leave the strip-cartoon and i see a headline. 'TESTS FOR CHILD CYCLISTS,' it sa.

'GAD!' i exclame, crumpling the paper into a ball and buzzing it at ye old mappe of the world which adorn the walls. 'GAD!'

Peason look up from the chair where he hav been drawing beetles on his knee.

'Don't you kno there is a Silence Rool in the lib, molesworth?'

'There is also a rool aganst chucking books, aganst building forts out of the colekted works of lord macaulay, aganst shooting peas at the bust of w. shakespeare. Probably there is a rool against drawing beetles on the knee also, thou weedy wet.'

'So wot, clot?' he retort, litely.

'Clearly you do not realise the importance of wot hav taken place. They are going to test child cyclists. They are going to give us weedy little badges if we pass and if we fale – you will never guess, peason. i canot bring myself to tell you.'

'Go on, molesworth, o you mite.'

'L-Plates,' i whisper.

Small wonder that peason grow pale benethe wot is his tan (i hope) Do not get me wrong, brothers and sisters, I am all for Road Safety ect becos it seme to me that the roads are v. dangerous places, especially when you see how GRIMES (headmaster) and SIGISMUND THE MAD MATHS MASTER drive their cranky old grids. But TESTS for veterans like me who have been awheel since my first fairy cycle at the age of 4! Curses! I know wot it will mean it will only be something more for me to fale becos the only thing i hav ever passed is molesworth 2 on his bike at mach. 1.

Wot with this and the 11 plus it seme that brave noble and fearless children are never going to be left alone until they become fearless metallurgists, clump press minders ect. You can imagine how it all hapened.

Time: 1839.

Scene: the headmaster's studdy at No. 10 *Downing Street. A kabinet meeting is in progress and GRIMES the prime minister is in the chair – altho i do not hardly think you could hav expekted him to be sitting on the floor.*

GRIMES: There's one more thing, gents, and strate i don't kno wot we're going to do about it. A scotish blacksmith called kirkpatrick macmillan hav invented a thing he call a bicycle.

THE MINISTER OF AGRICULTURE AND FISHERIES: Gosh!

GRIMES: Two wheels joined together with a bar and a saddle on top. Wheels within wheels ha-ha!

ALL: That's joly funny, sir. Ha-Ha!

GRIMES: Wheel, wheel, I'm glad you think so!

ALL: That's funy, too ha-ha-ha-ha-ha!

GRIMES: He must be a wheel proper inventer.

ALL: Stop it, sir, you're killing us!

GRIMES: All's wheel!

(*The Ministers disolve in fits of faned larffter. GRIMES strike the table with his kane.*)

GRIMES: That's enuff. It's not as funy as all that. The point is – wot are we going to do about it?

THE MINISTER OF TRANSPORT: We must hav action!

ALL (*thundering*): Action! Action!

GRIMES: Wot action are we to take?

THE MINISTER OF TRANSPORT: There's only one thing. We must set up a working party to report on the problem.

ALL: He's got it!

The P.M. get up, and shake him warmly by the hand: a decanter of port bursts like an H-Bomb, 6 topp hats sale into the air, the fr hav had it, the Gauls are at the gates of rome, wellington hav got his boots off, all's well with the world.

THE MINISTER OF AGRICULTURE AND FISHERIES:
(*chortling*): Wheel, wheel! That's really v. witty. Wheel, wheel!

We pass now from this unsavoury episode from the hist. books (and how many, let's face it, there are, how many) to the present day. This is the age of elektronick branes, of deisel-electrick locos, of atommick power stations ect, ect: all these added to the ink darts, kanes, lat. grammers, headmasters, boys and beasts which have been going for a long time. Wot hav been going on in the meantime? The working party is still on the job and the future of the BICYCLE is still at stake. Now, indeed, it is more at stake than ever for they have come to consider the report on st. custard's, my

The future of the BICYCLE is still at stake.

dere old skool hurrah hurrah hem-hem. Here is the report:

C/3342/MG/(357. st. custard's. Behaviour of skolars and tiny tots on bicycles.

Our spies hid in the bushes for weeks and were really upset by the spiders which did their best to hinder their observations. (We refer to the spies observations, not the spiders.) Wot our spies did observe was disstressing. i.e.

(a) One youth with pink bike, underslung handlebars, crash helmet, waterbotle, speedo, full tool kits detachable wheels ect ect. He appered to be known as grabber, head of the skool, wet, weed, sneke, monkey-face. owing to the strukture of his machine this youth rode with his nose near the ground and his hem-hem in conjunktion with the planet jupiter. He semed to hav contempt for those around him. We recomend L-Plates.

(b) A small boy of elfin appearance who employed a fairy cycle. His golden locks streamed in the breeze and he kept saing 'Hello clouds! Hullo, sky!' *L-Plate recommended.*

(c) molesworth 2 who zoom about on his bicycle with nose on the handlebars at 90 m.p.h. When questioned he repli that he is the last of the manned fighters and hav just brought down a guided missile.

(d) But who is this brave, staunch fellow who hav just finished oiling his machine? He mount, he ride steadily, he look left, right, left ect., he sound his bell, he is the pikture of quiet control. Who is it, eh? It is me, molesworth 1.

Well, there you are chiz. It isn't a state of affairs I am looking forward to but i supose if we had all ridden our bikes better in the past we shouldn't hav to go through all this now. If we all behave ourselves and do not zoom down hills they may set up another working party to consider whether fairy badges and L-Plates are not bosh and worth o. That at least is something to work for. Honk, honk, tinkle-tinkle and ho, for the wide open road. *WITH YORE EYES OPEN.*

Fr. and english are divided by more than the chanel.

FR. AND ENGLISH

You kno the trubble with paters and maters chiz, and particularly maters is that they are always trying to improve their dere little chicks. Hence the numerous corektions which we all kno at home i.e. you hav to hold yore knife properly, not make treakle pools in poridge, get clene hankerchiefs and take off yore hat to mrs jenkins ect. If you do all these things you will grow up to be as good a man as yore pater tho this statement makes your mater look a bit thortful.

Behold, then, the scene at ye olde molesworth brekfast table when there come the chereful rat-tat of the postman's knock.

'That's the postman,' sa the molesworths all together, for they are a brilliant family and full of branes hem-hem.

'Go and get the letters, nigel dere.'

'Wot me? Me? Why shouldn't molesworth 2 get them i got them the last time did didn't did ect.' (We don't kno why children go on like that but they do i am afrade.)

Eventually after this unsemely debate of which we ort to be thoroughly ashamed i do not think the letters arive at the table amongst the swete smell of korn flakes, marmalade ect.

'Ah!' sa yore mater. 'Here it is.'

She hold aloft a weedy letter written in purple ink with a fr. stamp which is not worth a d. as a swop.

'Armand is coming to sta with us in the hols,' she sa.

'Who, pray, is armand,' i repli, dealing a mitey blow to my hard-boiled egg. 'As far as i kno he is the weedy wet in the fr. book who sa the elephants are pigs.'

'He is a fr. boy who is coming to us to learn eng.,' sa mater with a swete patient smile. 'And you are to be v. nice to him as the pore boy will be far from home ect.'

Well, you can immagine wot any noble british boy would sa to that i.e. o *no*, mater, must we, gosh, wot a chiz ect. but it is no use. It is not any good pointing out that 'chez molesworth' he may learn a lot of things but one of them won't be eng. We kno when we are licked.

Interval of 3 weeks. Then A R M A N D arive you can well immagine him only he is worse than anything you can immagine.

Armand is 6 ft tall, wear short pants, and look upon molesworth 2 et moi as if we were a pare of shoppkeepers (c.f. napoleon in the hist. books). The trubble is he can speke eng.

'So ziz is yore owse?' he sa, glancing around with amusement.

'Oui, oui,' molesworth deux et moi.

'Eet eez so pretty.'

'Exquisitely so,' sa molesworth deux.

'My parents have a chateau, a flat in paris, a villa in the s. of fr. and a rolls-royce. Zizz is all you posess?'

'We have also a pen, a piece of india ruber, un morceau de papier, a cranky old car and a bag of bulls-eyes, my little cabage,' we repli. And with this riposte we zoom away into the bushes.

Things do not look good for the future chiz and mater is very cross with us ect. for our cruel and unfeeling behaviour but when she see wot armand eat she change her tune. Armand, in fakt, eat more than molesworth 2 and that is saing a v. grate deal: also we do not seme to like cotage pie, bread and butter pudding, spotted dick, corned beef and other kinds of homely food. He always zoom up to vilage shop on his bike and come back with pokets stuffed with food chiz which he eat all himself it nearly drive molesworth 2 mad.

'Last nite,' armand sa, 'i am having a beautiful dream.'

Wot can it be about? Hav he routed the beaks, stolen GRIMES the headmaster's kane, pinched ye old matrone's gin, placed a sukkessful booby trap on the door of the master's common room. No, it is none of these things which would delite the heart of the healthy english boy. Armand hav dreamed of fresh pineaple, lobsters, duck, sweet, cheese, fruit, cream, three wines and a brandy. Well, i mean to say, wot a thing to dreme about! Anyway, give me a good suck at a tin of condensed milk every time.

Anyway, he like GURLS aussi, so something must be wrong. Anyone who can get on his bike and ride 10 miles to meet angela winterbottom becos he kno she must pass along the lane on her pony must be bats. i supose i could manage lobsters but not angela winterbottom who giggle all the time and is uterly wet. It seme, konklude the grate sage molesworth, that fr. and english are divided by more than the chanel.

Guide to Grown-ups

Beware of addults, whether parents or beaks. They hav only one wish i.e. to make noble upright boys like them chiz. And look at them! Wot a lot, eh?

And here are the prizes for all the boys who hav not got prizes . . .

At least st. custard's turns out a finished product.

Mensam! . . . Yes, you've *got* it, Blatworthy!

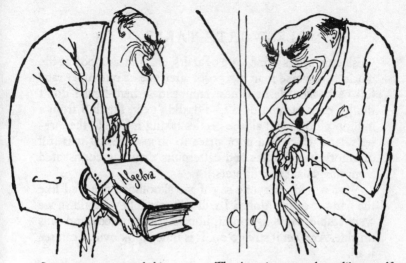

I want you to regard this as a chalenge, molesworth.

The Assyrian came down like a wolf on the fold, mogley-howard one.

Look, boys, here's Cecily come to tea.

I've no objection to him having a good hiding now and then.

MOLESWORTH TAKES OVER

Gosh chiz here's a fine state of afairs, eh? I mean, look at the world it is worse than big skool after one of our super rags full of broken desks (finest chippendale hem-hem i don't think), cries of 'you didn't,' did, didn't ect, the fluff from a million pillows and all the beetles taking refuge in the master's desk which is a poor place to choose, seeing it is full of empty beer bottles and catterpults they hav confiskated from the gallant boy fighters.

Wot would everyone say if we skoolboys behaved like the nations of the globe? I will tell you. They would sa we were stupid, crass, ignorant, hopeless, wet, weedy and sans un clue. And yet it still go on. It is time i took over. I can see it all.

Scene: A tent in Gaul, guarded with fossis and rampartibus maximus fortissimus. Labienus, Cotta, Balbus, Hanibul, Caesar, Hasdrubel and various other weeds are listening to the sweet voices of the gurls.

HANIBUL: (*at length*) gosh, wot a din it is somethink awful. How is the generalissimo toda?

CAESAR: In a filthy bate. He hav been ever since he turned good and gave up smoking. He is not the molesworth who put 99 consekutive subjects in the acc.

(*A flourish of trumpets. Enter Generalissimo molesworth with an old coal bucket on his tawny locks. His breath is coming in short ha-ha hee-hee you hav guessed it and he is dressed in the same.*)

ALL: (*acclaming*) Ave, dux!

GENERALISSIMO MOLESWORTH: And the best of luck. Wot is the situation? Does anybody kno? Put me in the piktchah. G.1?

G.1: i was hoping *you* would put *me* in the piktchah, sirra.

G. 2 to G 99: (*in sukcession*) same here, old top.

GENERALISSIMO MOLESWORTH: oh. Carry on, then.

BRITANNICUS, A DIRTY OLD SLAVE: If i may be permitted a word, sir, the situation is quite intolerable. Porridge Court hav cocked snooks at us, spoken foully of GRIMES, our revered headmaster, called us cowardly custardians and threaten our very existence by pinching our plaing fields. They hav also attacked the ditches with javelins and spears. It really is a tremendously bad show.

GENERALISSIMO MOLESWORTH: File a complante with uno as ushaual. Who's for conkers?

(*The sweet voices of the gurls brake out agane. The generalissimo starteth.*)

Gosh, blime, i can't stand this. We march aganst porridge court! Sound the trumpets, wake the horses, prang the airports, charge ta-ran-ta-rah.

That is the beginning. Despite cries and lamentations from fotherington-tomas st. custard's declare war on porridge court crying Pax. We must ensure there is Pax at all costs.

Scene: The same tent. Three months later.

GENERALISSIMO MOLESWORTH: Aren't we ready to move yet? Wot is the piktchah, G.1?

G.1: They are showing marylyn monro oh-ho over the naafi, sirra. Deffinitely worth a trip.

GENERALISSIMO MOLESWORTH: But didn't we declare bellum? Declare it agane.

ALL: Bellum, bellum, bellum, belli, bello, bello.

GENERALISSIMO MOLESWORTH: o.k. get cracking. Go in heah, heah and heah. Let me kno sometime how the battle goes.

G.1: O.k. sirra we will bring up the engines.

GENERALISSIMO MOLESWORTH: You don't need engines. You want catterpults. Engines pull tranes: they are 4–6–2 and 4–4–0 ect. Oh, i see. You are referring to ballista, like ensa, the siege engine? Why didn't you sa so?

(Silence except for the sweet voices of the gurls.)

And so the mitey forces of st. custard's move relentlessly in and occupy a small corner of the plaing fields. The lamentations of fotherington-tomas, who is a gurlie become louder and louder: then uno, the county council and the ratepayers association call for a cease fire. We obay.

Scene: A t.v. screen with the face of Generalissimo molesworth, blubbing.

G. MOLESWORTH: My frends, it is only in a case of national emergency that i would dare to interrupt robin hood. I come to explane the position we are in. It is grim. The skool playing field is vital to our existence. The plaing field must be free for us to come and go, freely. Where else could we be beaten 12 to nil by the village oiks, eh? Now we hav attained our objectives. The plaing fields hav been blown up by porridge court saing yar-boo and sucks. This will mean hardship. Skool sossages will be rationed, skool cheese cut by fifty per cent and lessons will continue all day. There will be less buble gum and if there ever had been any sugar that would hav been abolished too. However, it will be a mater for satisfacktion that the full supply of prunes will be maintaned. good evening.

And wot hapen then? uno, the county council and the ratepayers association anounce that they are making a police force. They sa they are giving themselves TEETH. This is a funny thing for any one to give himself but there it is.

And of wot is the police force composed? It is made up as folows:

>1 regiment of mice.
>fotherington-tomas.
>3 tree rats (with pea shooters).
>christopher robin.
>The 5th brigade of rabbits.
>andy-pandy.
>the skool dog.

Well, there you are. There hav to be a first time and this is the best they can do and, as for us wizard chaps, it prove something i.e. when we grow up we will be able to make even a bigger mess than this. So are we downharted? NO. We would not want to be anyone else. So boo to everybody and play up US!

THRO' HORRIDGES WITH GRAN

'I have been dealing here for 30 years,' sa gran to the assistant at horridges stores. 'Send for mr beckwith at once.'

Tremble, tremble quake quake how can she speke to an Assistant in the sossage dept. like that? i mean he is a perfect gent and wear striped trousis ect unlike headmaster GRIMES and other beaks we could mention and i would never dreme of ragging him. Wot will he do? To my surprise he bow low until his nose almost go wam on the sossage counter.

'Certainly, madam,' he sa.

End of part 1 now for the commercials, also query wot will happen when mr beckwith arive, eh? i am not a funk (cries of o, no, molesworth i do not think, may you be struck ded ect.) i am the goriller of 3 B yet i confess that i xperience a feeling of wishing to slink away and examine a nearby bakon machine. i have a feeling that mr beckwith if he arive at all will take out a gat and shoot gran to the ground. i begin to move when there is a stern cry i.e. nigel, stay where you are! There is no escape we will hav to shoot it out.

Perchance, molesworth, i sa to myself, mr beckwith will decide not to se gran? Perchance he will not obey this imperious summons?

Not a hope. mr beckwith arive who is a kindly old man with silver hair. He is just the sort of customer to whip out a Colt and go BANG! BANG! Got you! before the sherif of dodge city can inform him that killing is WRONG. But, surprise, he also bow low to gran who fix him with an eye of steel.

'mr beckwith,' sa gran, 'i have been dealing with horridges for 30 yrs. You are aware of that?'

'Yes, yes.'

'I have here my dere grandson, nigel, the pride and aple of my eye. He is a child of grate gifts, sensitive and inteligent, a fine young gentleman.

'Observe his noble brow, his blue eyes, the aristokratick maner in which he stands.'

i mene, i sa, this is a bit much. Enuff is as good as a feast the way gran go on I mite be fotherington tomas. It is about time that mr beckwith tell the truth and state that i hav a face like a squished tomato. But he bow even lower.

'Yes, yes,' he sa, agane.

gran draw herself up to her full height.

'MR BECKWITH, WHY ARE THERE NO SOPWITHS SOSSAGES FOR MY DERE GRANDSON?'

Mr beckwith turn pale and drop upon his knees for horridges are guilty of this hideous crime. He beg for mercy and sa that he will send out specially and deliver within the hour. He even pat me on the head chiz and sa i am a dere little chap. Gran look as if she will spurn him with her foot but sweep out of the sossage dept. instead.

'Come, nigel,' she sa.

Dashed embarassing, wot? i only relate this incident becos lots of grans behave like this in shops also they talk loudly in the bus they seme to hav no idea of the finer feelings of brave noble skoolboys. Also most grans are strikt. You may be a blue-eyed child in the sossage dept. of horridges but once grans get you home it is a v. diffrent story i.e.

WHEN I WAS A GURL little boys always stood UP when a lady come into the room. WHEN I WAS A GURL little boys always leave wun for mr manners. WHEN I WAS A GURL little boys did not put their feet on the cushions ect.

And so it go on. It seme a little impertinent posh prose to ask how long ago it was when gran was a gurl, i.e. about 1066 but i refrane. I am, in fakt, pritty GOOD when gran is around as i have found that crime do not pay chiz. On the other hand you get super meals and, if you are lucky you can read an old copy of chatterbox about wee tim who is a wet and a weed. On the whole, however, it is pritty much like prison or skool which parents should remember when they decide to go to the s. of france and leave their offspring with gran.

'We are too much of a handful for the older genneration,' I muse, absent-mindedly drawing beetles on the drawing room wall. 'We are —'

'NIGEL WOT ARE YOU DOING? GO TO BED AT ONCE WITHOUT ANY SUPPER.'

Well, you see wot i mean, eh?

3

N. MOLESWORTH
ACE REPORTER

AGGRICULTURE

CLANG-PIP, CLANG-PIP once agane it is the skool bell which sumon the fatheful of st custards also the louts oiks bullies cads wets and weeds who infest the place.

'oh well,' i sa litely just like bob cherry, harry wharton ect, 'old GRIMES, the head, hav caught molesworth 2 eating his mortar board and is going to give him the swish.'

'Cheese it, molesworth,' sa peason, 'that greyfriars stuff is out of date.'

i jab a compass into gillibrand. 'OW Yaroosh Garoo,' he splutter so it is not so out of date after all.

Wot hav this to do with traktors and aggriculture? Effort, old spud! Allow me to explane. When headmaster GRIMES come into big skool he hav a most unnatural smile upon his face which make it more dredful than before. Wot can be the meaning of this sinister event? Are we all to be kaned? i simply canot bear the thort, my dere, it is too much on a monday morning. i switch off and think of robin hood on t.v. ... *Sir guy of GRIMES is about to lash molesworth 2 whom he hav cobbed eating the king's deer when sudenly an arow WING out of the wood and split the kane in two. A figure in lincoln green emerge from Sherwood forest and vault litely over the skool roller. 'Ha, Sir guy,' sa robin moles ...*

The dreme fade. Not for the ushual reason, i.e. a stuning blow on the head. i am aware that the rest of the skool is cheering, desks are banged, fingers are flicked and fotherington-tomas hav fanted. One would judge them to be pleased. Wot can it be? A half-hol? i switch on agane.

'And the skool we shal visit,' sa Grimes, 'is a TRAK-TOR SKOOL.'

WIZZ-Oh! That is better than julius ceasar the silly old geezer ect. In fakt it is super and smashing. Wot can the day hold for us little chaps?

First we go to a traktor factory where all the men are puting the traktors together. SMASH, BIFF, BANG, WALLOP, A R-Um the noise is colossal just like st. custards on a wet saturday. Conveyor belts are zooming in all directions and there is an assembly line where chaps are bunging on wheels, engins, paint ect also whistling 'davy crocket' and working out football pools. A modern english faktory. It engage my interest and i step up to our guide with my reporter's notebook and fix him with a steely eye.

'How many parts are there in a traktor?' i rap.

'4672,*' he repli.

'Gosh!'

'And there are $11\frac{1}{2}$ miles of conveyor belts, we produce 230 traktors a day (approx) and a traktor come off the assembly line every 2 minits.'

'my dere, you simply stagger me.'

'Britain is the most heavily mechanised country in the world. It hav more traktors per acre than america or rusia.'

'Cheers cheers cheers hurrah for st. george and boo to everbody else . . .'

At this moment there is a suden cry. Where is molesworth 2? A hue and cry ensue. Where can he be? At last the truth is discovered he hav climbed on the conveyor belt and an absent-minded workman is bolting him on instead of a mudguard. molesworth 2 is rescued chiz more fritened than hurt (official communique) a lucky escape for a farmer who mite have got a traktor with 4673 parts one of which was molesworth 2 it would hav been a cranky old grid.

****** *All the fakts are CORECT for a change.*

He hav climbed on the conveyor belt and an absent-min

...kman is bolting him on instead of a mudguard.

Now to the TRAKTOR skool. Wot do we see? Wizard combine harvesters, traktors, sub-soilers, ploughs and fork-lifters. Everything for the young farmer in fakt. Agane my notebook come out.

'Why do you hav a skool for traktors?' i grit.

'A splendid wizard q.l!' exclame the guide. He turn to GRIMES.'Wot a brany, inteligent, outstanding pupil.'

'er . . . Yes,' sa GRIMES. (*thinks*: i hav always said molesworth would turn out well. A late-developer.)

'We hav a skool for traktors,' sa the guide, 'becos it is no use for a farmer having a traktor unless he kno how to use it and how to keep it in good repare. So we trane people from all over the world how to plow, ridge, avoid soil erosion and other worthy things. The result is more of everything – wheat, beet, turnips, cabage—'

CABAGE! At the mention of the word the whole skool think of cabage and give a groan. More skool CABAGE! And full of beetles and slugs even molesworth 2 will not eat slugs.

'CABAGE?' sa molesworth 1, the ace reporter. 'i supose we shall get more spinach as well?'

'Yes, yes.'

At the very thort the skool groan agane. Wot is the use of traktors if they get more CABAGE and spinach, eh? We shall get more skool sossages next. Our guide see that he hav made a bish. 'Who would like to drive a traktor now? Our traktor can be driven by a child of eight.'

A mighty cheer rend the air.

'Goody goody,' sa fotherington-tomas, jumping up and down. 'Hullo clouds, hullo sky here i come, trusty and true, a joly farmer who plow the good rich earth, who, simple soul that he be . . .'

WAM! 91 boyish hands are raised aganst him, but it is too late.

'You look a sturdy little chap,' sa the guide to fothering-ton-tomas. 'You shall drive the traktor and now i want a

volunteer from the masters to ride behind.' There is silence.
'How about you sir?' sa the guide to GRIMES.

'Me? Wot me?'

'Anybody else?'

With a cry like a hyena sigismund the mad maths master
spring upon the traktor and stand behind the saddle with
straws in his sparse hare. fotherington-tomas grasp the steer-
ing wheel zoom the throttle and away they go cheers cheers
cheers cheers. A RUM ARA ARUM mud fly in all directions and fotherington-tomas dash into a shed. Will he make
it? Out the other end, turn left, zoom through a hay stack
then round in a circle.

'Stop him stop him,' yell the guide.

fotherington-tomas turn three more circles and make for
the open country, then reverse back scattering all, heading
for the mane road. Wot will his fate be? But he hit another
haystack and stop chiz chiz chiz just when it was getting
interesting.

'Most stimulating,' sa sigismund the mad maths master.

'Goody goody,' sa fotherington-tomas. 'May I drive a
combine now?'

Well you kno a combine it is a mighty thing which harvest
the corn and put it into sacks you can imagine wot would
hapen we should all be harvested and put into sacks too. Anyway, the guide sa something but it is not 'yes' it sound quite
different. Conduct mark? 'Lack of control?' He seme quite
pleased that we canot stay any longer.

'Any free traktors?' sa headmaster GRIMES. 'i am very
poor the skool do not pay and business in jellied eels is friteful and wot with the cost of living going up—'

Agane the answer is 'no.' A pity. All the same the traktor
skool was wizard and a boy of 8 *can* drive one if he is
not utterly wet like fotherington-tomas. And don't forget
that traktors hav helped to double the harvest of wheat in
this country. Which is wizard if you like wheat. And i expect
it is the same for CABAGES too. *If* you like CABAGES.

CURRENT LIVING. That is wot it is called. It is better than lat. fr. algy. geom. ect., tho, and our next visit is to an AGGRICULTURAL SHOW.

Cheers cheers zoom out of the bus and dash into a large place with a lot of cattle, sheep, implements, BEER, ice creams, fleas, straw, beetles, bottles of pepsi-cola, fat ladies and FREE LEAFLETS. In fakt it is a shambles wot with all the cows mooing and the farmers jumping about becos somerset hav won victory in the killed meat competition.

st. custards descend upon the free leaflets it is every boy for himself. But molesworth 1 hav a sterner task i.e. to report the show without fear or favour. Wot do he see, eh? Look for a joly farmer going to raspberry fair ect. but only a lot of posh chaps smoking cigars. Then sudenly—
GRRHHMOOOOOOOOOOOOOOO

Gosh chiz! Jump six feet in the air and turn round to see an extraordinary sight. The objekt have a huge face, whiskers and long hare in fakt i mite be looking in a mirror and it is ME! We look at each other. Then i see a notice 'ABER-DEEN ANGUS FIRST PRIZE COW also mrs joyful prize for rafia work.' Promptly i grab my notebook and lick my h.b. pencil for the interview—

SOCIETY KOLUMN

ME: Yore hare look as if it hav had a shampoo and all the beetles washed out of it. Is that so?

COW: How nice of you but it look dreadful i can do nothing with it. i really must go to a new man.

ME: Yore cote is beautiful and glossy.

COW: It's simply in rags i would give my eyes for some of these farmers' wives minks they are wearing. If only my bull were not so mean.

ME: Any coment on somerset victory in home-killed meat?

COW: Poor Butercup! Such a sad end. I knew her well and such a good family. Now if you'll excuse me i simply must have my afternoon rest . . .

Of corse cows can't talk but it just show you should not believe everything you read in the papers. Heigh ho and back to the show where wizard shambles exists as fotherington-tomas hav been prodded by mechanical fork. Ho for sheep, traktors, meckanical milkers and the aggriculture of our land. If it had anything to worry about it hav much more now cheers cheers cheers, and rilly-me dilly-me.

Ho for sheep, traktors and
meckanical milkers.

THE FLYING MOLESMAN

'DAYVEE CROCKETT,
DAYVEE CROCKETT
KING OF THE WILD FRONTIER.'

Thus music pour from boyish throtes, golden locks stream in the air, and eager blue eyes are lifted to the skies.

'BE QUIET,' yell GRIMES, the headmaster. But no one hear him over the hideous din of this famous song which all boys love to sing. It is only when all boys are exorsted that GRIMES can make himself heard.

'Boys,' he sa, smiling cruelly, 'we are going to King's Cross station for a trip on ye olde trane, the "flying scotsman." You are to report on the journey.'

A hideous cheer rend the air. We may hav hoped to go on a space rocket but the 'flying scotsman' is better than weedy lessons, especially if you hav not done yore prep. And so to King's cross . . .

All are excited and fotherington-tomas skip up and down. 'Hullo steam! hullo smoke, hullo ralway station buffet!' he sa as the porter carry our bags. Then he lean towards me and whisper, 'did you kno that queen boadicea is suposed to be buried here, eh?' Quick as a flash i see a scoop! . . .

BOADICEA DONE. BURIED at king's cross.

Soon wires will be humming all over the world and ace newshawk molesworth will hav done it agane . . . but as this hav o to do with the 'Flying scotsman' i will desist. Nay, i must becos a loudspeaker in the roof boom:

'THE TRAYNE NOW STANDING AT NUMBER TWO PLATFORM IS THE 10 A.M. FOR EDINBURGH. GET CRACKING OR IT WILL GO WITHOUT YOU. I WILL NOW SING A VERY FAVOURITE TUNE'

'DAYVEE CROCKETT,
DAYVEE CROCKETT
KING OF THE WILD FRONTIER ECT.'

As the wild song continue and 100 voices take it up, the st. custard's cads go forward to the engine. For we are to ride on the footplate with the driver cheers cheers cheers. 'O goody! O cheers the engine is a streamlined Pacific Number O7666655438,' sa fotherington-tomas. 'Hullo coal, hullo spade, hullo tender.' Well, there will be plenty of chances to 'do' him on this trip that is one comfort. But now for some fakts. I butonhole joe binks the driver, alias 'mad jack.'

ME: Where does the 'Flying Scotsman' stop, eh?
BINKS: i think it's newcastle but i couldn't be sure. Where do we stop bill, did you read the notices?
ME: Never mind. How long has it been running?
BINKS: I simply haven't a clue.
ME: Did you always want to be an engine driver?
BINKS: Grate heavens no my dere. My parents forced me into it when i faled c.e.

Hem-hem this is wot is called 'colour' for no news stories are true. Aktually the 'Flying Scotsman' hav been running for eighty years: it stop once at newcastle and get to edinburgh in $7\frac{1}{2}$ hrs. which is not bad as it is 393 m.*
PEEP!
Gracious, gracious they are whistling us up, sa joe binks, and it is ten o'clock. Do be an angel and take the brake off!
WOMP! WOMP! WOMP! WOMP!
i do not kno if you hav ever been on the footplate of an express but when it start it is like a big gun going off. It is louder than big school on a wet saturday and even louder than when molesworth 2 pla fairy bells on the skool piano smoke is everywhere and all boys blub for mummy. The 'flying scotsman' is on its way and noone can hear themselves speak.
How to get my story? Luckily i remember the essay we are always set at the end of the summer hols e.g. a day at a railway station. It go as folows viz. '*Stations are niss nice. Tranes come to stasson stashion stasion and the pasengers get out, alternatively some of the pasengers get in. The sun is*

* *All fakts corect for a change.*

shining shinning shining. There is a statshion stashon stasson mast – there is a porter on the plaff—'

But wot is this? We are now at speed and approaching potters bar. and our coon skins are flying in the wind. On the slope beyond stevenage there was a world speed record for engines of 112 m.p.h. We are on our way north.

3.4. First stop newcastle.—

Chiz chiz the st. custard newshawks look as if it is the end of the first half v porridge court as they stager to the platform plafform plaform they hav had their chips. And wot is the first thing that comes to their deafened ears, eh? From the loudspeaker come

> *'DAYVEE CROCKETT,*
> *DAYVEE CROCKETT*
> *KING OF THE WILD FRONTIER ECT.'*

Now we leave joe binks and take our seats in a compartment and study a few more fakts e.g. the engine belong to the loco dept. and the rest belong to the traffick dept.

'No?' sa peason with brethless interest. 'that is the kind of thing which grip the reader. You are a born journalist, molesworth 1.'

'Do you reelly think so?'

'yes yes thou art also a measley worm and a wet but so are many born journalists. So they are reelly from 2 depts fasscinating but so wot so wot?'

'Supose,' i sa slowly, 'they forget to fix the engine to the trane? Supose the engine arive in edinburgh and the pasengers are still sitting in king's cross? Wot then, eh?'

This conversation is interupted by the dining car attendant who ask us to take our seats for tea. Zoom zoom there is a mad rush headed by molesworth 2 and we sit down to wizard toste, cakes buns ect. But i do not forget my assinement so i talk to the dining car attendant.

'No one seme to wonder how we manage in restaurant cars,' he sa, sadly. 'No one care how the food get here.'

fotherington-tomas burst out blubbing. 'i do i do' he sa.

'No no go on go on.'

'They don't mind that we hav to draw our food from the control dept in the cellars at king's cross. They are indifferent that we hav to turn up an hour and a half before the trane starts. They do not care all the cooking is done by electrissity in the kitchen.'

You could hardly expect it to be done in the guard's van ha-ha, i sa litely. The attendant look at me thortfully.

Who thinks of the cook when he go to the larder at king's cross? he asks. Now we are all blubbing and only molesworth 2 repli: i do, he sa, i am sorry i did not go with him.

Well you kno how many prunes, radiomalts, skool sossages he pinch all the time so i can see he is planing a new job when we get back. He is a weed.

Now the mity trane rumble over the royal border bridge and soon we are in scotland. we go back to our smoker and lite up our cigs.

Hav you ever considered, peason, i sa, that we hav been traveling north through country steeped in hist? That the trane folow the grate north road constructed by the romans and julius ceasar the silly old geyser?

'good heavens, you sla me, molesworth.'

... That at darlington station stands locomotion 1 the first to run on a public railway?

'No no go on go on.'

... That they sa queen boadicea is buried at king's cross station? But his eyes are closed and peason hav fallen asleep chiz chiz and so hav all the rest. All the same i let my mind pla upon dremes and fancies (posh prose) of the past.

caesar, livy, romulus and remus are sitting in a compartment.

CAESAR: We were ten minutes late at Eboricum and they call this a railway.

LIVY: Travelling on business i supose?

CAESAR: i am going up to attack the picts and scots. i hav finished with the gauls and hav attacked so many ramparts and ditches in Italy it will be a nice change.

ROMULUS: Scotios sunt weeds.

CAESAR: Be quiet, boy, and do not put yore nom in the acusative it's not grammer. Also stop sucking that pabulum. Did you kno that queen boadicea is buried at King's Cross station?

LIVY: No? How fasscinating!

(*He falls aslepe as j. caesar continue and do not wake until Romulus and Remus comence to sing an old roman ditty* e.g.

> '*DAYVEE CROCKETUS*
> *DAYVEE CROCKETUS*
> *REX OF THE WILD FRONTIER.*'

The dreme fade.

But wot is this? We are nearing our journey's end and steaming into edinburgh station. It is five heures et demie and the 'flying scotsman' is on time cheers cheers cheers. We hav traveled 393 miles in $7\frac{1}{2}$ heures. And wot is the first thing we hear as we get down on the platform plafform plaform? It is e.g.

> '*DAYVEE McCROCKET*
> *DAYVEE McCROCKET*
> *KING OF THE WILD FRONTIER.*'

And tomorrow we return to king's cross where, of corse, they sa queen boadicea is buried.

TAKING WINGS

It is a quiet day in the news room at st. custard's. 2 tipe-
writers are chatering, 16 boys are chatering harder, peason is
dreamily soaking ink from the well onto his blotch, gillibrand carve his initials on his desk, fotherington-tomas (our
litterrary critick) read t.s. eliot and the fearful News Editor
G R I M E S lounge at his desk chiz chiz chiz. Sudenly a well-
known figure enter, his hat is on the back of his head and a
cig droop from his lips. He slouch over and sit on G R I M E S
desk. It is ace-reporter nigel molesworth cheers cheers cheers
he fear nobody.

   'MOLESWORTH!' yell G R I M E S.
   'Y . . . Y . . . Y . . . Yep, Sir.'
   'Don't sa "Yep".'
   'N . . . N . . . N . . . Nope, sir.'
   'Or "Nope".'
   'Y . . . Y . . . Yep, sir.'
   This can go on for ever and G R I M E S kno that he canot
browbeat dauntless, questing newshawk ect. He canot . . .
W A M! the ruler come down on molesworth's fingers chiz
chiz chiz moan moan.

   'MOLESWORTH i hav a story for you. Get something on london airport. How it work, wot it do ect.'
   'Wot, sir, me, sir. Oh no, sir, i mean to sa, sir, that's a chiz,
sir.'
   'Get going, boy! Wot are you wating for? Do you want a
condukt mark? You are slack, idle, insubordinate, weedy
wet and a weed ect ect.'

·

ZOOOOOOOOOOM!

   Two hours after leaving london the car which cary the st.
custard's reporting team crawl past london airport, turn left,
through the tunel and with a screech of brakes pull up at the
door. 'Hullo planes, hullo passengers, hullo sky!' sa a gurly

voice so you can guess that fotherington-tomas is here also peason, grabber, gillibrand and molesworth 2 it is no wonder the porters think we are bound for belgrade and the guide who meet us make as if to run awa.

'Wot go on here?' i rap, licking my old h.b. 'Tell us the whole story and make it snappy.'

'You are "pasenger-processed".'

This sound v. much like wot go on behind the bushes at st. custard's when a new bug hav been cheeky you kno we give him the works. But at the airport they just pass you through a chanel as they call it and, by the end, this is very much the same thing.

'Imagine you are pasengers,' sa the guide. 'First you go up to this here desk (grammer) and hav tickets checked ect. Then yore baggage is put on a conveyor belt for the Customs, while you go up to the Concourse on a moving staircase to yore apropriate chanel. The grate thing about the system is that nothing can go wrong.'

O-ho O-ho i think you are uterly wet if you think nothing can go wrong with st. custard's about you wate. As usual i am rite all the reporters zoom up the moving staircase then charge ta-ran-ta-rah down the other it is beter than the pleasure gardens and it is FREE. It take the loudspeaker system to get them back.

'WILL ALL BOYS ATACHED TO ST. CUSTARD'S *KINDLY* COLECT THEIR MARBLES AND PEASHOOTERS. TAKE LEAVE OF THEIR FRINDS AND PROCEED TO CHANNEL 6?'

'Shan't,' sa molesworth 2.

'WOT'S THAT?' sa the loudspeaker, 'WILL ST. CUSTARD'S BOYS PROCEED TO CHANNEL 6 *IMMEDIATELY.*'

'Yar boo sucks.'

'LOOK 'ERE I DON'T WANT ANY MORE OF YORE LIP GET CRACKING OR ELSE.'

This, my dears, is language we can understand and it hav the desired effect. We asemble at the door where a beautiful AIRGURL is standing she is absolutely fizzing more lovely even than prudence entwistle the under matron. My eyes pop and mouth open but all i can say is 'g . . . g . . . gug.'

'London airport,' sa the guide, 'process over 2 million passengers every year, in fakt, to be acurate last year it was 2,683,605.'*

'g . . . g . . . gug.'

'It can handle 30 planes an hour at a peak period and over 119,000 each year. It is the busiest airport in the world in space. It hav 6 runways, the longest being number one which is 9,300 feet long.'

'g . . . g . . . gug.'

'*Are you listening, boy?*'

I come to with a start and take my eyes off the beautiful AIRGURL. She hav a smile on her face can it be for me? Now gosh she is bending towards me can it be true? But wot do she sa? Her words are torture, e.g. 'You seme unhapy, little fellow. Do not cry for mummy she would not like that. Let me take you by the handy-pandy.'

And she do chiz chiz chiz chiz while all st. custards cheer. Well anybody who take *me* by the handy-pandy are taking a risk, they are never savoury hem-hem but i supose AIR-GURLS hav to be tuough. And so, hand in hand, the little toddler by her side, she lead the way into the CUSTOMS. i shall never live this down.

CUSTOMS! brrh brrh it is like the cave in ali baba when the thieves come back quake quake wot will they do to you? And WOT is this? molesworth 2 hav come through on the moving belt with the bagage and they hav laid him on the counter. Well, if they make him declare wot is inside him i.e.

* *All the fakts are CORECT. They have been certified by the board of trade, ticked by Sigismund the Mad Maths Master and approved by the glassblowers union cheers.*

'Come on, cough it up. We can tell when you are lying.'

69 lickorice allsorts, 3 bubble gum, bits of bungy and 9 skool sossages they will get wot is coming to them. But i hav not time to concentrate becos i am standing in front of a man who look like capt. hook in weedy peter pan and rap the counter with his hook.

'Hav you read this? Anything to declare? Come on, cough it up. We can tell when you are lying. No compasses, watches, bungy, blotch, cigs, bikes, magic lanterns, brownie No o or other dutiable goods? No cribs, woollen pants, white mice, caterpillers or doodle bugs?'

He glare at me and I meet his eye quake quake i am about to confess when AIRGURL sa: 'This little boy is v. sad for his mummy.' Thwarted he scribble rude things hem-hem in red chalk. 'Take him to Immigration.' SAVED! but at wot cost! Immigration is O.K. they just check yore crimes and look at yore passport and then you are through and free to wing away into the blue ect.

Here i check my men. Of eight gallant souls only 2 hav got through. e.g. me and fotherington-tomas. Weep hem-hem for the rest who have perished on the miserable journey which is the worst in the world.

Hist! but now wot is this? Still grasping my handy-pandy the AIRGURL take me and fotherington-tomas to a door. She open it and take us through and wot grisly sight meet my tired eyes? It is a NURSERY chiz chiz chiz chiz full of rocking horses and ickel pritty babies. On all sides are teddy bears and sea-saws. 'O goody goody,' sa fotherington-tomas skipping weedily. 'Let us pla with the bears!' I turn to escape but the door hav closed. TRAPPED! Trapped with fother-ington-tomas, a Nurse, 16 babies, 90 coloured balls, 56 teddy bears and a pedal car it is an uggly predicament.

There is only one course i shall hav to fite my way out. 'Listen,' i drawl, drawing a gat, 'the first baby that draw a bead on me gets plugged, see? I'm kinda hostile to babies and my finger mite slip on the trigger.'

WAM! A mighty coloured ball which weigh 2 tons strike me on the nose and the party get ruough balls and teddy bears fly in all directions, a baby fly off the see-saw and strike his pritty locks on the ceiling and the NURSE fante. Paus-ing only to shoot out the lights i make good my escape. Out-side the guide is waiting.

'The London airport nursery service for children in transit is quite free. There children may be left in the care of a trained nurse and there are see-saws, shiny toys, teddy bears and baby's bottle can be quickly prepared.'

'G . . . g . . . gug.' I sa.

*

And so with this sobering thort we leave London Airport which is joly d. reely and may be completely finished one day and return to the gloom and beetles of our alma mater chiz.

4

I AM GOING TO BE GOOD

HERE WE GO AGANE!

O wild west wind thou breath of autumns being thou from whose unseen presence the leaves dead are driven like gostes from an enchanter fleeing. Posh, eh? i bet you 6d. it fooled you. 'molesworth at his rolling best. Sonorus and sublime' i expect you said. Aktually it is not me it is a weed called shelley and i copied it from the peotry book.

'Why?' sa molesworth 2 who zoom up like the wet he is. 'Why copy peotry when you mite be buzzing bricks, conking me on the napper or braking windows with yore air pistol go on tell me o you mite.'

'Becos,' i tell him, 'it autumn and the long hols are nearly over. Soon we shall be back at SKOOL.'

At these words he burst out blubbing and will not be comforted. I confess there hav been many times when the thort of GRIMES, the masters, the bullies cads, snekes wets and weeds would hav depressed me too. But not this time.

I AM GOING TO BE GOOD THIS TERM.

i will tell you how this hapened. The other day i am fed up with tuoughing up molesworth 2 and am stooging about saing wot shall i do mum wot shall i do eh?

To this she gives various replies i.e.

(a) *go for a walk.*
(b) *pla with your toys.*
(c) *watch t.v. childrens hour ect.*

none of these are acceptable to me so in the end she make a sugestion so rude hem-hem i canot print it here. It is thus i find myself locked in the atick until teatime chiz chiz chiz,

and find gran's old book called chaterbox 1896. There is o to
do so i turn its weedy pages and read the story of wee tim:

> *wee tim is riding in his grandpater's cariage as staunch
> and sturdy a litle felow as ever you would wish to see.
> Sudenly he see an old lady who is carying a heavy basket
> and he clutch his grandpater's knee.* '*Granpa granpa,' he sa,
> 'can we not let this pore old lady ride in our cariage, eh?
> She is so weak and frale.' Wot a good kind thort! His
> fierce grandpa sa 'O.K. tim even though i am an earl let
> us take her for a ride . . .'*

(molesworth thinks: this is where the story get craking.
Now wee tim will hit her with a COSH and pinch wot is in
the basket while boris the foul coachman look on with a
cruel grin. But no!)

> *'Will you ride with us, old lady?' sa tim and wot a
> pikture he looked with his long golden curls! 'Thank you
> young sir,' she sa. 'But i canot ride in the carriage of an
> earl.' 'He is a good earl,' sa tim, 'even though he look like
> that.' 'And i,' she sa, 'am really a rich old lady and becos
> you hav been good and gentle i will leave you my fortune
> when i die . . .'*

Coo ur gosh i mean to sa if that is wot you get for being
good it is worth it it is easier than the pools. I look back on
my condukt in the hols. Hav it been all it should be?

scene: the molesworth brekfast table.

ME: gosh chiz kippers again this is worse than skool.

FATHEFUL NAN: get on, nigel, you are ungrateful. The
pore boys would be glad to have nice kippers for brekfast.

MOLESWORTH 2: Yar boo and sucks molesworth 1 hav a
face like a flea.

ME: Et tu, weed, thrice over and no returns.

(*A kipper fly through the air*).

FATHEFUL NAN: No little gentleman thro kippers, nigel.

MOLESWORTH 1: Then i will thro korn flakes instead. Ha
ha ha witty boy ha ha ha ect. . . .

Aktually it is not me it is a weed called Shelley.

i blush with shame at the memory of this unsavoury incident and *let's face it, my dears*, it was only one of many. Would wee tim hav thrown a kipper at molesworth 2? Would he hav been cheeky to fatheful nan? I doubt it very much. He would hav given his kipper to the pore boys . . . O woe i am a weed chiz! Next term i will alter my ways. Already i can pikture the scene at st. custard's:

a thortful figure is walking among the dead beetles crushed biskuits and old buns which litter the skool passage. He is reading a peotry book.

MOLESWORTH 1: The asyrian came down like a wolf on the fold ect. . . . Wot a luvley poem! To think that even a term ago i drew tadpoles all over it and wrote 'turn to page 103 if my name ect!' How can i hav done such a thing? The asyrian came down . . .

At this moment a huge mob of cads, snekes, oiks, tuoughs, oafs and skool dogs charge ta-ran-ta-rah like the light brigade all covered with marmalade in my direction.

MOLESWORTH 1: Silence! (*There is a hush.*) Boys, this is foul condukt. You are ragging in the passage an offence under section 88888/b/107 of the skool rules. Go back to yore desks and be good in future. (*They slink awa with bowed heads.*)

GRIMES the headmaster hav been silently observing this good DEED and he pat me on the head make me head of the skool instead of grabber and give me mrs joyful prize for rafia work.

But, you kno, wot will really hapen? It will be quite different i am afraid and will go like this.

Scene: The klassroom. Enter master for lat. lesson. molesworth 1 hav all his books out, pencils sharp, AND BUNGY at the ready.

ME: Good morning, dere sir. i hope you slept well?

BEAK: (thinks) A trap! (He aim a vicious blow) Take that, you dolt. Do you think you can rag me, the scurge of the skool?

ME: i forgive you, sir. You look pale you hav drunk BEER last night. May i get you a pil?

BEAK: Stand on yore chair, molesworth. Any more and you will get 6!

ME: Do not open that desk, sir, it is full of old cucumbers put there by i kno not whom.

BEAK: Enuff! Wate for me outside.

(*A vale is drawn over the foul proceedings.*)

Am i rite in this foul proffecy? Shall it alter my determination to be like wee tim? Shall i shake in my resolution? onley time will revele all – wate fellow-weeds, with baited breath, and you mite catch a wopper, ha ha.

THE GRATE MASTER TRAP

Hay ho! Hullo birds! Hullo clouds! Hullo, skool dog! Hullo, sirup of figgs! Hullo, potts and pilcher fr. primer!

Who is this who skip weedily along the skool passage and out towards the den of ye olde skoole pigge? One would really hav thort it was fotherington-tomas so gay is he, so lite-harted. There, dere reader, you make a big mistake as c. dickens (auther of d. Coperfield the book of the film) would sa. No, dere, gentle reader who may chance to con these pages with so much sympathy ect, you make one helluva big mistake. You are way, way out, coyottes. It is i, n. molesworth, the ex-curse of st. custards, who skip weedily, who cry hay-ho, hay-ho ect. And wot hav i been doing, eh?

FLASHBACK! 2 minits ago.

N. MOLESWORTH: Matronne, i have brought you this pressed leaf. May i do yore flowers?

MATRONNE: (*reaching for her gat*) Scram, scruff! Or i will do you!

N. MOLESWORTH: i forgive you, matronne, for those uncouth words. A still tongue in a wise head.

MATRONNE: Git!

N. MOLESWORTH: i will, indeed. A rolling stone gathers no moss. Likewise, procrastination is the thief of time.

MATRONNE: *YAR!*

N. MOLESWORTH: As you plese. An empty barrel makes the most noise.

(*exit with a courteous bow.*)

It is a strange, lonely world when you are GOOD. Is it my fault that i hav been practising my handwriting in the copy books? Now i kno wot pore, pore basil fotherington-tomas, that wet and weed, hav gone through. People seme to avoid me – no friendly hale of darts and inkpots comes my way. Even molesworth 2 refuses my buble-gum and masters pat me on the head.

YET i MUST KEPE TO MY CHOSEN ROAD.

But, soft, wot is this? It is peason, my grate frend, who worketh upon some strange contraption near the pigge den. Wot mischief can he be up to?

'Hullo, peason,' i sa. 'The devil finds work for idle hands. Wot is that?'

'Nothing,' he repli.

'if't be nothing, yet 'tis something, for nothing is not but wot something semes (shakespere)' i riposte, litely. 'Yet if't be something—' He buzz a brick at me. No matter, i try agane.

'Go on, peason, you mite tell me go on, o you mite the same to you and no returns.'

'you would not be interested,' he grate, turning a nut with his spaner. 'Nowadays you are a weed, a wet and uterly wormlike. Gone are the days when we invented the moles-worth/peason lines machine together.'

'It hav a good streme-line effect and neat basket work. i like the way the electronick brane give easy control and at the same time there is wide vision and plenty of lugage space. Good points are—'

He buzz another brick and, sorowfully, i depart. Ah me, where is there to go? Who else luv me but my old frende the skool pigge, who hav never let me down? Hurrah, hurrah, he leap to greet me and place his piggy paws on the sty wall. He take my buble-gum graciously and lick my hand. i recite a poem i hav written e.g.

> *O pigge, you are so beautiful!*
> *I luv yore snouty nose!*
> *ect.*

n.b. pigs are the cleanest animals in the world, although i sometimes think there are exceptions.

And so, refreshed and strengthened, i return once agane into the wicked world of st. custard's where peason is still at work. Wot can it be?

It is a strange, lonely world
when you are GOOD.

Is it:
An atommic fast-bowling machine?
An automatick golekeeper?
A loudspeker for calling 'Fire!' in the middle of maths
lessons?
A measles-rash injector?
Curiosity overcome me and i return.
'No honestly, peason, word of honour cross my hart
fingers uncrossed and pax tell me, rat, wot it is or i will uterly
tuough you up.'
'That is better, clot. Now i will tell you – it is a MASTER
TRAP.'
Hurrah! Hurrah! A trap for beaks! Wot a wizard wheeze!
Gosh, absolutely super and smashing! Good show! Charge
ta-ran-ta-rah! Dozens of masters – lat. masters fr. geom.
algy. div masters all caught and eliminated. And it work for
mistresses, too! But chiz wot am i saing? For a moment i
thort the world mite be safe in future for children – i must be
careful.

'Kindly explane,' i sa, a triffel stiffly (but not enuff to make him withdraw into the silence usuhually so alien to him).

He tell me all. There is a bait of lat. books. Attracted iresistibly the beak creep stealthily in through the door and before he can get to ex.1. the trap hav closed. A see-saw tip him into a cold bath and an endless belt take him to a third chamber where he get six from the automatick caning machine.

'Yes, yes,' i sa, excitedly. 'Wot then! Wot devilish fate waits for them then?'

'They die sloly on a diet of skool food!'

'Gosh, yes! Or you mite hang a skool sossage eternally out of reach.'

'That would be no punishment, oaf. And you are lucky. i am going to make my first experiment with *YOU*!'

Too late i see the plot, chiz! A dozen hands with beetles and earwigs drawn on them scrag me. The leader is grabber, the tete de la skool. 'Make haste slowly,' i yell. 'Too many cooks spoil the broth; Help; Rescue.' But whereas in the old days fifty trusty boys would hav leaped from the thickets at the sound – today none come. None at all. And robin hood had better take note of it. i am pushed towards the infernal trap and my DOOM IS SEALED.

But wot is this? My trusty frende the skool pigge hav got there first. Before they can stop him he is inside: he eat the lat. books: enjoy the bath, the caning machine tickle him litely, he wolf the skool food and with one heave of his mitey flanks he knock the whole machine for SIX! Cheers, cheers, cheers i am saved. But wot a narow shave, eh? That nite i rite carefully in my dere copy book

Virtue is its own reward

'You're so right,' sa fotherington-tomas. 'So true, so true! Hullo, clouds! Hullo sky!'

This all needs a lot of thort.

'I hear you're rustlin' raffia work, pardner.

SO FAR SO GOOD

It is evening after prep at st. custard's. The curtanes hav been drawn, the gas lites are popping merrily and the crow hav long since gone to its nest, tho where else it could go to i do not kno. In every nook and crany, knee-deep in blotch pelets, bits of bungy, old lines and pages of deten the gay little chaps enjoy there freedom. Some toste sossages over the gas mantle, others, more adventurous, swing upside down on the chandeleres. The air echo with cries of *pax, unpax, fains, roter, shutup,* and *the same to you with no returns.* WOW-EEEEEE sa molesworth 2 zooming past as a jet bomber.

But who is this quiet student who reads The book of berds and there eggs, eh? It is me, molesworth 1 believe it or not, for i hav determined to be GOOD and it is easy pappy and absolutely o to it at all. E.g. soon i put down my book, mark the place with an old pressed leaf, put it in my tidy desk and make my way quietly to the study of GRIMES the headmaster. *Knock tap tap tap!*

Wot is it, molesworth? sa GRIMES, looking up from his pools.

i hav been reading a most interesting book, sir. It is called berds and there eggs. Take the jackdaw, sir. It frequents parks, old buildings and often perform aerial acrobaticks. It hav a propensity for hiding food and other objects. Eggs ushually 4 to 6.

yes, yes, molesworth, indeed? Thank you for the information. Now—

Sometimes, however, sir, only 2 eggs are to be found. The linet, on the other hand – shall i tell you about the linet?

Some other time, molesworth. i am very busy now. times are hard how about 5 bob till tuesday?

(*Thinks: it is worth a try. A mug is born every minit.*)

Here is a pound, sir, i sa, o forget yore gratitude it would be a pore hart who did not aid an old frend in distress. It is a gift. If you want any good deed done agane just let me kno.

(GRIMES thinks: stone the crows who would hav thort it? A hem-hem plaster saint. No need to take out the old whelk stall this week now.)

And so it go on. That is just one example. Another thing i hav become a swot and a brane. I am top in lat, hist, algy, geom, div. ect.

Brave, proud and fearless molesworth 1 can face the world safe in the knoledge that SWOTING ALWAYS PAYS.

Scene: a t.v. studio, poorly furnished, a table with three legs, lit by a candle in a botle. An interviewer in rags come forward.

INTERVIEWER: This is the 960 million quid programme. Who is the next contestant wot subjeckt do you choose?

ST. M. it is i. wigan, lancs. i certainly do. i would. me and the wife will certainly hope to. History.

INTERVIEWER: Half a mo. Wate for me to ask the q's. Who burned the cakes?

ST. M. Who pinched the cakes, you mean. molesworth 2, of corse.

INTERVIEWER: You hav won 6000 quid would you car to go for the jakpot? Go into the box can you hear me ect. Now for 960 quid wot berd frequents parks, does aerial acrobaticks, hides food and usually lay 4 to 6 eggs, eh?

ST. M. The – um – o gosh it's ur-er choke gosh garble.

INTERVIEWER: i'm sorry. i'm very sorry. i'm very sorry indeed. The answer was – A JACKDAW!

(Exit st. m. blubbing on the arm of a beautiful GURL.)

Well, there you are. Being GOOD is pappay. Try it. Try it toda. Try it brighter, try it whiter, try it with or without a hole in the family size. But wot is this? As i walk upon my pious way i come upon a MASTER who bendeth over. He is a sitting target. Wot a chance! With foot drawn back molesworth bare his fangs. Will he sukumb to temptation?

(see another daring, palpittating instalment in our next issue.)

THE KARACKTER KUP

'Boys,' sa GRIMES, the headmaster, smiling horibly, 'the time have come to present the scrimgeour kup for good karackter. This is never an easy kup to award' (of course not, it is ushually at the pornbrokers) becos there must be no doubt either in my mind or those of the staff' – he give an even more horible smile at the thugs seated around – 'that the winner is WORTHY of this supreme honor. The choice hav to be a most careful one ect.'

Aktually i do not see the dificulty. If you look at the 56 gallant little pupils of st. custards, each with his own peculiar ways, it is easy, pappy to devise a SYSTEM. You simply get rid of them in this way i.e. there are: 5 squits, 9 snekes, 19 cribbers, 2 maniaks, 3 bookmakers, 4 swots, 11 cig. smokers. Total 53.

Chiz this leaves only one pupil to whom the kup can possibly be awarded. Well, you kno, i mean to sa, i hav been joly GOOD lately and sucking up to the beaks. Obviously this fakt hav been noted. GRIMES continue:

'The boy who win this kup must be noble, upright, brave, fearless, intreppid and honnest. He must not have been afrade to stick up for wot he kno to be right. He must protekt the weak. He must luv the highest when he see it.'

Oh come on, gosh chiz this is going a bit far. i blush to the roots.

'Every boy at st custard's,' continue GRIMES, 'must search himself to see if he comes up to these high standards and if he do not the pot is not his. Hav he been a help to the masters?'

Well, that one is easy. Look wot hapened only yesterday.

Scene: Klassroom of 3B, early dawn. A pupil stands on guard with a sten gun, the rest snore at their desks. Outside a burd sings sweetly.

A beak drags himself in to his desk.
BEAK: Gosh blime, i feel terible.

MOLESWORTH: Pore sir, you have missed brekfast. Let me get you some skool fish or a nice runny egg.

(*Takt, but the beak do not seme to fancy my sugestion. He shudereth and groweth pale.*)

BEAK: Ugh. Wot lesson is it? I thort you was all due for woodwork in the carpentry shed. You can go along there if you like.

MOLESWORTH: Oh, no, sir. We prefer to stay with you and do our peotry.

BEAK: i was afraid of it. Gillibrand, say yore prep.

GILLIBRAND: Who, sir, wot me, sir.

BEAK: Wot was the name of the famous peom of which you were required to learn 24 lines?

The boy who win this kup
must be noble, upright, brave,
fearless, intreppid
and honnest.

GILLIBRAND: Search me, sir.

BEAK: (*some of his old fire reviving*) i do not wish to search you, gillibrand, i mite be appaled at wot i should find.

(*Ha-ha-ha-ha-ha-ha-ha-ha from all, gillibrand struggle to his feet, his mouth open like a fish, he stare, he stammer, he scratcheth his head and the ushual shower of beetles fall out.*)

You seme nonplussed, gillibrand. Can it be that you were drawing H-bombs during prep? TAKE A DETEN. Now which of you scum can sa the peom?

MOLESWORTH: (*flipping his fingers like bulet shots, dancing on the points of his tiny toes.*) Oh, gosh, sir. Please, sir. Gosh, sir, can i, sir?

BEAK: Ah, molesworth. i had not thort of you heretofor as one keen on the arts. Let us see. Sa prep.

(*molesworth stand to attention, fingers in line with the seam of his trousis, eyes straight ahead.*)

MOLESWORTH: 'THE SAND OF DEE BY C. KINGS-LEY.'

O Mary, go and call the catle home.
   And call the catle home.
   And call the catle home,
Across the sands o' dee.
The western wind was wild—

BEAK: (*hastily*) That's enuff, molesworth. v.g.v.g., indeed.

MOLESWORTH: – and dank wi fome,
And all alone went she.
The creeping tide came up along the sand,
and o'er and o'er—

BEAK: well done molesworth joly good ten out of ten you can stop now.

MOLESWORTH: – the sand,
And round and round the sand,
As far as eye could see:
The blinding mist came down and hid the land,
And never home came she.

(*fotherington-tomas burst out blubbing*)
O, is it weed, or fish, or floating hair?—
BEAK: Thank you, molesworth, thank you. excellent.

(*But nothing can stop me. i continue to the end of the peom despite a hale of ink darts. At the conclusion i bow low and strike my nose upon the desk. All look at me as if amazed.*)

Yes, i think i may sa i hav been a help to the masters the kup is as good as mine. Wot else? GRIMES looks around.

'Hav he been a help to the other members of the huge staff to whom i owe so much? (i.e. about 9 million quid back wages.) Hav he helped our very overworked skool gardener? And matron – how do he and she get on?'

All too well, old top, if you are thinking of PRUDENCE ENTWHISTLE, the glamorous under-matron. But it must be MATRON herself, who look like a gunman's moll in a gangster pikture. But even here my record is good—

Scene: Matronne's room, the doors of ye olde physick cupboard are open.
MOLESWORTH: i hav been reading of the labours of hercules, matronne, may i clean out yore cupboard? . . . Wot hav we here in the syrup of figgs bot? It smell like G-I-N . . . and wot can these BEER bottles be doing, as if hidden behind the radio-malt? . . . I will arrange them neatly in the front row . . . And wot is this which look like the skeleton of a boy chained to the wall . . . ect. O.K. there, you see. Now for the Kup.

'The winner must be of excellent repute, (o come, sire). Talented, (o fie!). Inspired.' (Enuff. You sla me.)

'And so,' sa Grimes smiling more horibly than ever, 'i hav no hesitation in awarding the kup to GRABBER.'

Well its the old story. A fat cheque and you can fix anything but right, i supose, will triumph in the end. In the meantime o mary go and call the catle home ect, or go and do something, i am fed up.

5

COO UR GOSH!

I LUV GURLS

Coo ur gosh i expect this is a bit of a shock especially for the gurls. As you kno it hav long been an open secret in 3b that i never intend to get maried. This hav been becos if you get maried it hav to be to a GURL chiz and hitherto my conviction hav been that GURLS are uterly wet and weedstruck. But this is Xmas the season of luv and goodwill cheers cheers crackers crak berds sing balloons pop and the fur from a milion davy crocket hats fly through the air.

AND SO as I sit here biting grate chunks from my old h.b. (n.b. why do not pencil makers produce a pencil out of buble gum, eh?) anyway as i sit here i write these fateful words which may cut me off for ever from my felow oiks, cads, bulies, and dirty roters – i am determined to LUV GURLS.

'Oh goody,' sa fotherington-tomas who see wot my bold hand hav written, 'I knew you would come round to my point of view, molesworth. Wot sort of gurls do you like?'

'All of them,' i repli. 'i shall spare myself nothing.'

'Even gurls who giggle?'

'Yes.'

'Even gurls who recite weedy rhymes i.e. *higldy piggledy i solicity umpa-la-ra-jig?*'

'Yes, yes.'

'Gurls with skipping ropes who sa "*Salt vinegar mustard peper* ect?"'

'Yes, but you are trying me hard, fotherington-tomas, very hard indeed.'

'Oh, goody. molesworth luvs gurls with skipping ropes.'

peason pass by with his face covered with ink splodges as per ushual. He faint dead awa and hav to be taken up to matron.

It is only now that i see wot this mean and i ponder on the nature of the feminine gender hem-hem. First of all, there seme to be as many kinds of gurls as there are licorice allsorts i.e.

GURLS WHO STARE. This is a very comon type. When a brave noble and fearless boy is engaged on some super project as it mite be making a stink bomb poo gosh or a man-trap for a master the GURL come up and look at him. She sa nothing. She just stand there looking soppy. The boy hope she will scram but she do not. The boy wishes to sa git and skit but maners prevent him and soon the master-hand which is engaged on the task grows nervous. He move off to another project. The gurl follow he canot get rid of her. Finally she speak. She sa 'One-two-three-four-five-six-sevving.' That is all. Is she bats or wot? i shal find it hard to luv these.

JOLLY HOCKEY GURLS. These gurls wear gym tunics and hav bulging muscles, they line the touchline and shout, 'Hurrah for Coll!' This is worse than at st. custard's where we sa 'go it grabber you'll never score. Wot a pass, man. buck up yore ideas.' Hockey gurls luv their school and if hermione misses a biff at gole in the cercle she hav let the whole place down. As it is falling down anyway this do not mater very much. On satterdays after a glorious victory over st. minniver's coll for ladies (without millicent at right half, too! Water on the knee the old trubble) they all sing the skool war cry:

> *HURRA for bat!*
> *Hurra for ball!*
> *Hurra for crosse and lax*
> *And all.*
> *Forty years on we'll still be chums.*
> *Ta-ran-ta-rah for st. etheldrums.*

(all copyright reserved by miss edwina prinknash, headmistress. Send stamped addressed envelope with P/O for 1/3.).

TOUGH GURLS. Believe it or not all gurls are not edducated at colls ect. Some there be (posh prose hem-hem) who hav not had the advantages of a pater on the verge of suicide trying to pay the fees. Such a one (it gets posher and posher, eh?) such a one is Ermintrude you kno the one who likes boiled sweets better if they hav been dropped on the carpet. ermintrude hav not washed for several years oh wot a thing wot a thing. Also she hang upside down on the railings and shout 'hi liberace' as you pass chiz chiz chiz. The only thing is to ignore gurls like these and when she buzz a conker at you pretend the incident hav not hapened. Still, this is dificult when she also refer to molesworth 2 as 'my bruther george.'

Such a one is Ermintrude.

Of corse i could go on becos there are many more types of gurls – fat gurls, gurls with dollies, bossy gurls and, on some occasions, gurls who are beter at lessons than you. ('Oh, nigel, don't you really know the ablative singular of armiger?' I don't supose you even kno what it *means*.')

But this thing must not go too far. Imagine wot would hapen at st. custard's if we were like gurls and got a CRUSH on somebody. e.g.

FOTHERINGTON-TOMAS: oh, nigel, may i take yore books to the fr. class this morning?

NIGEL: foolish little thing. Peason hav already offered.

FOTHERINGTON-TOMAS (*blubbing*): oh.

NIGEL: never mind. You may wash the tanks and tractors which i hav drawn off my bungy.

FOTHERINGTON-TOMAS: Oh, goody! And may I clean out yore locker for you?

NIGEL: at yore own risk.

And so it go on. ANYWAY, gurls are jolly d. They are pritty, super and smashing. Wot would we young chaps do without them at xmas parties, eh? Well, there'd be a lot more jelly and trifle to go round and, whether you like it or not, you hav to put up with them. So make the best of them.

n.b. any offers of mariage as the result of this will be considered in strikt rotation.

DANSEY DANSEY

The fell words are spoken chiz they fall upon my weedy shoulders like GRIMES lash, they strike a super shuder in my sole. Wot can these words be, eh? They are words which every brave, noble and fearless boy heard in his time i.e. when Mum sa swetely: 'It is time, nigel, you learned to dance.'

Any boy, except fotherington-tomas, hav the answer to this. 'No, mater, I won't, nothing will make me, i won't won't won't ect.' In the end, however, he always find himself in a weedy dancing klass sliding across the polished floor in shiny dancing pumps with darling bows on them chiz chiz chiz.

In fakt, come to think of it, there are not many times in his life when a weed is free from dancing klasses. It begin almost as soon as he can patter on his 2 tiny feet and his mum admire his long golden curls. There he is plaing with ratle and saing 'goo' over the top of his pla pen when his mum sneke up behind him and stick a gat in his ribs: 'o.k. blue eyes we're going to dancing klass. Get moving and no funny business.' The pore baby hav no answer to this and he hav to submit while he is dressed in a velvet suit chiz little todling shoes chiz chiz and look like little lord fauntleroy chiz chiz chiz. Then he is zoomed in a high-powered car to the klass.

Pikture the sordid scene with anxious mums, weedy little gurls with ribbons in their hair and 36 fauntleroys of whom YOU are one. Enter a huge woman flexing her muscles who beam britely and sa: 'Now we're all going to be little mice and little rats . . . no, let's change our mind . . . not little rats, let's be GRATE BIG RATS . . . Tippy-toes, nigel, tippy toes . . . *You* ort to kno how to be a grate big rat . . . in time to the musick . . . clap, clap, . . . now altogether jump into the air!'

Where else do she expect a tiny to jump, eh? Into the big drum? Though if he wear a fauntleroy suit it would be much beter if he did. But you see wot i mean, felow suferers? You're hardly born before you hav to dansey-dansey. The next attempt is made at a later age when yore mater try it on once agane to presuade yore stuborn boyish nature by swete reason.

Scene: The molesworth brekfast table. Pater and mater present : molesworth 2 eating the cereal with fine relish ha-ha. molesworth 1 sit corektly a smile flitting litely akross his finely moulded features.

MATER: But if you don't learn, nigel, how will you be able to dance with GURLS at parties?

ME: i shall manage to face that kalamity with composure, mummy.

MATER: (*to pater*) Ortn't he to learn to dance, my dere.

PATER: Eh?

MOLESWORTH 2: Pass the marmalade and buter. Make it snappy.

MATER: ORTN'T NIGEL TO LEARN DANC-ING? MY DERE?

PATER: How much do it cost?

MOLESWORTH 2: Toste and more tea.

ME: After all entertanement at parties you can't beat throwing the old pink blancmange, mims, my swete.

MATER: O.K., rat, you'll take dancing next term and like it.

That is the trubble with the youth of the world there is no justice, no court of appeal.

In the shabby finery of ye olde st. custard's dining room whose floor as usual is littered with old prune stones there were scenes of rolicking gaiety last nite. Undor the capable auspises of mrs maplebeck gay youngsters from the skool sported to the capable measures of miss pringle, the skool musick mistress.

'Take yore partners for the foxtrot!' yell mrs maplebeck.

Imagine with wot joy molesworth 1, the dasher of the palais, see that he is to dance with his best frend peason.

'May i hav the pleasure, o weedy worm?' he sa, bowing.

peason respor.i with a low curtsey.

'O.k., thou giant rat!' he sa, with a modest blush.

And so the dance begin and as the evening wear on the joy and xcitement mount to fever pitch as fotherington-tomas do a solo pas de deux with 90 m.p.h., 3000 c.c. jump which send him zooming into the honors board. Finally the skool piano blow up with mitey explosion sending up mushroom cloud of fluff, caterpillers, cig cards ect.

So you see. You may as well put up with it becos D A N C-I N G canot be avoided. Later on i am told you will grow to like it so perhaps at the moment we hav not enuff incentives. In the meantime H E I G H-H O for sir roger de coverly tipptoes and don't forget to make a luvly arch.

HEIGH-HO
for sir roger
de coverly

A FEW ROOLS FOR XMAS

Gosh super xmas is here agane cheers cheers. Every boy and weedy gurl must remember not only that this is a time of rejoicing but that they must BEHAVE. Here are a few of the molesworth-peason rools for xmas which we hope you will all obay:

ROOL 1
Claus, santa, rekognition of.

Everybode kno even tinies that santa claus is yore . . . well, hem-hem. It is a chiz for the pore old felow, however, if you let him kno you kno. When he entereth the bedchamber laden with presents, snore deeply: when he drop the lot, stir uneasily as if there were fairies about (see p. pan) Do *not* sit up in bed and sa: 'A masterly performance, yore timing is superb, even olivier ect could not hav done better.' If you do this yore pater . . . hem-hem will burst out larffing, molesworth 2 will fire a red moon space roket and you will do a handspring off the end of the bed. This may get yore mater in a bate, season of goodwill tho it be. Better far to lie quite still as she bends over the sleping cherubs and hear her doting words: 'If only he hadn't got your family's revolting nose he mite be quite good-looking.'

ROOL 2
Claus, Santa in shop and rekognition of.

Everyone kno this dodge it is only to attrakt trade. Tiny gurls and wee boys are led by the hand chiz and their mummies sa 'Look at santa claus.' (n.b. wot are they expected to do, kick him?) The effect of being told to look at santa differ widely among the younger genneration – some weep bitterly, some put their finger in their mouths, others run away screaming and there are some, like molesworth 2, who sa: 'O.k. santa. Wot you got for me?' For elder children the direct approche is required e.g. zoom out of the house of the elves and conduct an interview like a t.v. reporter.

'Is that beard real? Is it cotonwool?'

'Y . . . y . . . yes.'

'Is it true there's only sawdust in that sack?'

'No.'

'You're sticking to that?'

'Sawdust and wood shavings.'

'Would you or would not sa there is an element of deception tantamount to fraud in your conduct? Are you satisfied and do you contend that you came to this toy department in a reindeer sledge? Wot are you going to do about it?'

Father xmas ushually hav a simple answer to this. e.g. i'm going to chase you round the elves house, into the wonderful gardens, through aladin's cave and into the fairy grotto and if i get yer, mate, i'll do yer.' So beware.

ROOL 3
Dances, Fancy Dress, Corekt Deportment.

When told that dere mrs cracklby and dere lady fotheringay hav thort it a delicious idea to hav a fancy dress dance, most weedy gurls jump up and down in the air. 'Oh, mummy,' they sa, 'can i go as a pixie?' Boys are difrent. Being used to the horors of life at st. custards they take the dredful tidings with a stiff upper lip e.g. mater, nothing on earth will make me go. i uterly refuse. Comes the day, however, and there he is driven in the family tumbril, exposed to the jeers of the mob and why – he is dressed as a jester and smell of mothballs. Yore mater hav given you the famous words 'You will enjoy it once you get there' – and wot a mad delightful press of gay young people clad in multi-coloured costume greets the eye. Wate, however, until the eye getteth hit with a jelly bunged by little sally who hav come as tommy steel. WACKO! Lead me to the blancmange. Honor must be satisfied.

Gosh super xmas is here agane

ROOL 4
Wot to sa when another boy's present is nicer than yores.

Sa nothing. Just burst into tears and howl the place down.

ROOL 5
Parents, care and upkepe of, at xmas.

There would be no rcal xmas without parents. Therefore hem-hem it is as much their day as yores. There are several ways in which you can make it a true fragrant xmas for yore parents. Be sure to wake at 5.30 in the morning and trip down to their room to show yore presents. Paters get as much fun as the boys from tranes and cowboy pistols, altho the hour may be early. Then later do not forget to ask yore pater to mend the toys you hav broken and get him to share yore interests by making a vast dredger or cantilever bridge with yore bumpo construktion outfit. The really thortful will give him a nice elektric shok with their tiny toy crane. That will really make mums larff!

A Brite Future for Youth

DING-DONG-PIP-CLANG!
DING-DONG-PIP-CLANG!

Ye olde bells of ye olde church ring out merily – tower shake, rafters quake, death-watch beetles tremble in their shoes. Never hav there been such a din since molesworth 2 pla fairy bells on the olde organ

DING-DONG-PIP-CLANG!
DING-DONG-PIP-CLANG!

Ye olde bell-ringers drink more BEER and bells go
DONG-PIP-CLANG-DING!
PIP-PIP-PIP-PIP!

(n.b. wher hav DONG, CLANG and DING gone? They are lying flat on their backs like their extremely rude forefathers (peotry) and they will feel terible tomorrow.)

What is all this about? It is the NEW YEAR! Hooray, hooray, hooray! And the bells are ringing it in until the appeal for £1000 to save the church from destruction zoom from its perch and strike ye old vicar on his olde balde nut.

So once agane another year lie before us with all its brite promise. Everyone be he man woman or child (posh prose) will be wondering wot he can do to improve and, in some cases, it ought to take a whole year to find out. Take headmaster GRIMES for xsample. Pikture him if you can on jan 1 writing his resolutions in his study while the candle gutter fitfully in the botle. This is wot he write:

RESOLUTIONS

Less food and all tuck forbiden . . . more dissipline . . . buy 60 new kanes . . . put up skool fees . . . borow up to £100 from new master before others can tell him . . . more produktivity in lat. fr. algy, geom ect . . . tune skool piano . . . more water in ink . . . new chromium plated counter for whelk stall . . . buy super new car . . . molesworth?????????

398

So, pleased with his work, he larff fritefully and creep through the cobweb passages of empty st. custards to his iron bed.

But not all are like GRIMES most want to do GOOD in the new year tho there is not much chance of it. Youth is brave, noble, fearless ect and face the problems of the age with brite, clear-eyed confidence. Even weedy gurls make resolutions chiz which are absolutely wringing wet e.g. you can imagine wot ermintrude (you kno the one with an ickle-pritty bow who dance a fairy dance at parties) write in her little lavender book.

RESOLUTIONS

Take more cowslips to miss pringle . . . improve my salt, mustard, pepper at skipping until i am as good as basil fotherington-tomas . . . press more leaves . . . make a chum of gloria . . . take more and more cowslips to miss pringle . . . kepe my back so strate i fall over backwards . . . don't be nasty about jenifer's lipstick . . . kepe my desk tidy . . . take millions of cowslips to miss pringle.

And so it go on and even me, molesworth the goriller of 3B, am not unmoved by the sentiments of the season. Helping myself to 7 spoonfulls of sugar in my tea at brekfast i look pensive.

'Tell me, bro, wot are you thinking, o weedy wet?' sa molesworth 2, making a lake of treakle in his poridge.

i slosh him and return to my reverie.

Time 2000.

Scene: The laboratory of sir nigel molesworth, full of atommic instruments, retorts, bunsen burners ect. A copy of a horor comic lie on the table and, in the corner, a plektodotroscope revolve slowly, making calculations.

Enter molesworth 2, now grown more hideous than ever. He is an interviewer for t.v.

MOLESWORTH 2: Good evening, sir nigel. This place does not half ponk, if i may sa so.

'Ah yes, that removed the figgs from
syrup of figgs. A grate boon.'

SIR NIGEL: Even with the technical progress of the 20th century no one hav been able to elliminate ponks from labs. They used to be called 'stinks' you kno hee-hee-hee.

MOLESWORTH 2: now, sir nigel, one of your inventions was a cure for smoking, was it not, clot?

SIR NIGEL: Yes, yes, That was a simple matter. i made a cig that was so long no one could reach to the end to light it. A simple application of the laws of pythagoras hee-hee-hee.

MOLESWORTH 2: How weedy. But yore greatest invention, that by which you are world famous was the droposcope?

SIR NIGEL: Ah yes, that removed the figgs from syrup of figgs. A grate boon.

MOLESWORTH 2: No, clot, the droposcope.

SIR NIGEL: Ah yes, i'm sorry. A little hard of hearing. The droposcope. That was the first ballooon to go downwards: i'm afrade it made nonsense of sir isaac newton and, of corse, the rusians were grately discomfited.

MOLESWORTH 2: Was not a boy called peason, an old skool frend, associated with yore diskovery?

SIR NIGEL: Peason? Well, i did kno him and he did a little of the elementary alg . . . mind you, i don't want to sa a word against him . . . but you kno, on quite the wrong line . . . quite hee-hee-hee.

MOLESWORTH 2: Hav you anything else to sa, sir nigel, in the glory of your later years?

SIR NIGEL: Oui. Scram, you clot-faced worm, or i will utterly bash you up.

(*He seizeth the microphone and throweth it in the plektodotroscope. A bird sing. a worm turn ect.*)

And so it go on. But i do not think i will ever be the BRANE of BRITAIN as every other boy will be. Perhaps by that time there will be room in the world for a huge lout with o branes. In which case i mite still get a knighthood.

THE END